MARRIAGES
and DEATHS
of
Cumberland County
Pennsylvania

1821-1830

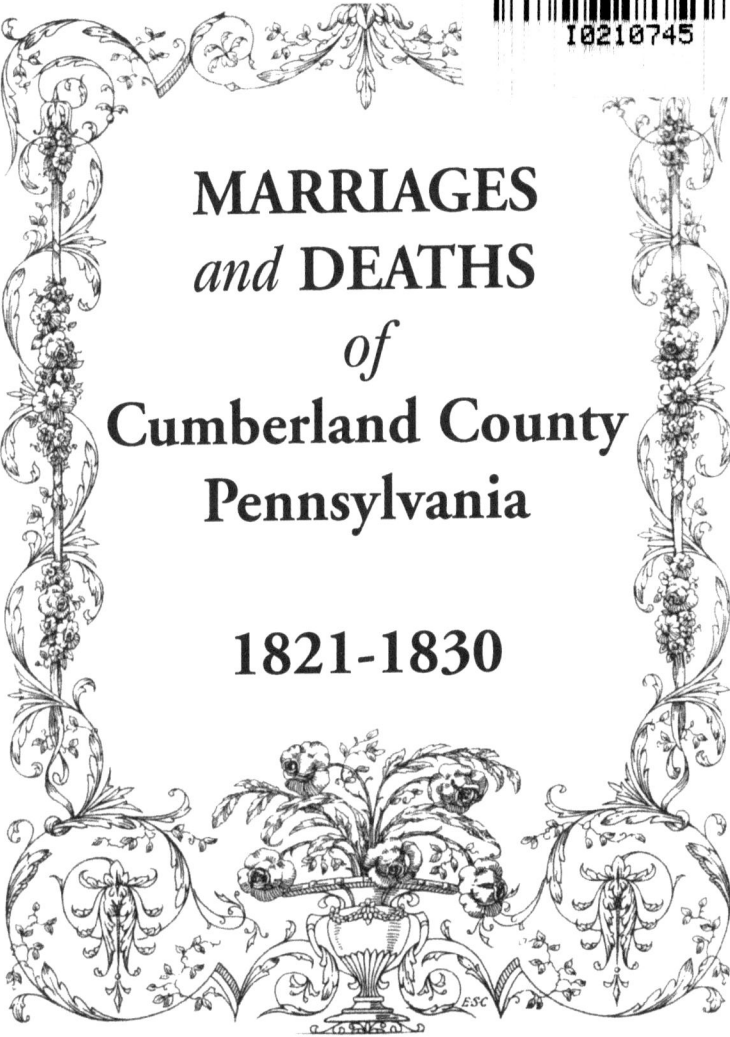

F. Edward Wright

HERITAGE BOOKS
2008

HERITAGE BOOKS

AN IMPRINT OF HERITAGE BOOKS, INC.

Books, CDs, and more—Worldwide

For our listing of thousands of titles see our website
at
www.HeritageBooks.com

Published 2008 by
HERITAGE BOOKS, INC.
Publishing Division
100 Railroad Ave. #104
Westminster, Maryland 21157

International Standard Book Numbers
Paperbound: 978-1-58549-186-5
Clothbound: 978-0-7884-7692-1

CONTENTS

INTRODUCTION

This book provides data on the marriages and deaths recorded in available records for the ten-year period, 1821-1830. It also allows a comparison of the information from various sources. In examining the newspaper announcements of marriages and deaths one becomes aware of the various errors and omissions. On numerous occasions I have commented on the differences [shown in brackets] in the announcements of the same event printed in different newspapers. Comparisons were not made with the church and cemetery records.

Newspapers and microfilm copies of newspapers were gleaned at the Library of Congress and at the Cumberland County Historical Society and the Hamilton Library Association in Carlisle. From the latter repository we gathered data from the church records, cemetery records and published church histories.

Prior to 1885 marriage licenses were relatively rare since notices through the publication of church banns precluded the need for licenses. Only for a brief period from 1852 to 1855 did the law require recording of marriages, births and deaths. This was done by the county Register of Wills.

The index refers to page number. The reader is cautioned that the name may appear on a page more than once. Included in the index are references to other states, showing some of the ties that Cumberland Countians had to other states, especially to Maryland, Ohio and Virginia.

Most of the abbreviations used are obvious. For those persons who have not examined early records let me point out that "inst" refers to the term "instant," used to indicate the current month and the term "ult" is our abbreviation for "ultimo," which refers to the previous month.

F. Edward Wright
Westminster, Maryland 1991

iii

AMERICAN VOLUNTEER (Issues held by Library of Congress)

1. Aug 2 1821 (Thursday)
Married Thurs 19th inst by Rev Dr. Helmuth, Rev George Schmucker, of York Pa, pres. of the German Lutheran Synod, to Mrs. Ann Weinert, of Phila.
Died in vicinity of this borough, Thurs last, after a lingering illness, Mrs. Catherine Dewing, eldest dau of Mr. G. Fahnestock.
- Same day of a cholick, Miss Catharine Snyder, dau of John Snyder, near Carlisle.
- On Sunday, Mrs. Greason, near Smoky town.

2. Aug 16 1821 (Thursday) - Died on 31 Aug inst, in Toboyne twp, Perry co, of a cholera morbus, in his 20th yr, Benjamin Taylor, son of Henry Taylor, leaving parents, brothers and sisters, after 8 days sickness.

3. Jan 10 1822 (Thursday) - Married Wed 24 inst at Harrisburg, John B. Galatian, of this place, to Miss Ann Shanklin, of Harrisburg.

4. Oct 16 1823 (Thursday)
Died Tues morning 30 Sep ult, in her 59th yr, after a lingering illness, Mrs. Margaret Davis, consort of Rev John Davis, of Shippensburg, member of Meth Episc Church for 33 yrs prev to her death [long obit.].
- At Harrisburg on 8th inst, Mrs. Mary S. Snyder, consort of late governor Synder, aged 55 yrs.
- On Mon morning 6th inst, Mrs. Sarah Lackey, wife of George Lackey, of Newville.
- On Thurs 7th inst, Philip Rhoads, of Newton twp.
- On Fri 3d inst, Mrs. Beatty, wife of James Beatty, of Newton twp.

5. Oct 23 1823 (Thursday)
Married 12th inst by Rev Dr. Lochman, Daniel Niedham, to Miss Catharine Eichelberger, both of this co.
- On 9th inst by Rev B. Keller, Andrew Heikes, to Miss Mary Crider.
- On 16th by same, John Wolff, to Miss Ann Hertsler, of South Middleton. On same day by same, Abraham Goodyear, to Miss Catharine Seip of South Middleton. On 19th by same, John Cook, to Miss Jane Crawford, both of this place.
Died Thurs evening Oct 2d in Carlisle, Mrs. Ann Mahon in her 47th yr. [Long obit.]
- Monday last, Mrs. Lee, dau of the above.
- At St. Augustine, E. Florida, Dr. Wm. M'Coskry, formerly of Carlisle, aged 23 yrs, wanting two days, attacked by the bilous fever, and was on the recovery, when a stoke of apoplexy deprived him of his life. He had succeeded to his brother's post as resident physician and had been appointed pres. of the Bd. of Health.
- Thurs 7th inst, Philip Rhoads, of Newton twp.
- On Sat 11th inst, William Kilgore, of Newton twp, at an

advanced age.
- On Mon 13th inst, General Thomas Buchanan of this co, an officer of the revolution.
- On Wed 15th inst, major James Woodburn, of Newville.
- On 16th inst, aged about 35 yrs, John Foose, constable of Tyrone twp, Perry co.
- Suddenly on Fri last, John Hendricks, of Mifflin twp.

6. Oct 30 1823 (Thursday)
Married last Thurs by Rev B. Keller, Dr. Julius Deppe, of this borough, to Miss Johanna Stewart, of Dickinson twp.
- On same day by same, Isaac Brandt, to Susannah Plylers, of Dickinson twp.
Died last week at his late residence in Adams co, Dr. William Crawford, formerly a member of the U. S. House of Rep, from this Congressional Dist.
- In Harisburg on Sat morning last, Miss Ellen B. M'Kinney, dau of M. M'Kinnney, Esq.
- On Thurs morning last, after a lingering illness, Rev Dr. John M'Night, in his 70th yr.   7.   Nov 6 1823 (Thursday)
Died Thurs last of a lingering illness, Mrs. Elizabeth M'Feely, consort of John M'Feely, of South Middleton twp.
- At Chambersburg on Sun last, after a short illness, in his 52d yr, Samuel Riddle, Esq., counsellor at law, of that borough.

8. Nov 20 1823 (Thursday)
Married Fri evening last, by Rev B. Keller, George Mathews, to Miss Ann Cairns, both of this borough.
Died Sat last, aged about 55 yrs, Mrs. Anne Moore, late widow of J. [James - Gazette] Moore, Esq. of Dickinson. For some time past she resided in this borough, where she died.
- Near Marietta, Ohio, Rufus Putnam, aged about 90, brigadier general by brevet at the close of the rev war, and afterwards a brigadier under Wayne, in the western army, formerly of Rutland, Massachussetts. The Marquis La Fayette is now the only surviving general of the American Revolutionary army.

9. Nov 27 1823 (Thursday) On Wed 19th inst, in Savill twp, Perry co, where William Irvine having been butchering, killed a steer; after which he went to his hog pen to shoot a hog, his second son was in front of him, when the gun went off, accidentally, and lodged the ball in his hip, which the surgeon could not discover to extract. The boy languished in great pain, until within a few days ago and expired. Mr. Irvine had but two children.
- A son of Mr. Cooper of Toboyne twp, was killed by a tree falling upon him on 1st inst. He was about 6 yrs old.
Married Thurs evening last, George Reisiner, of this borough, to Miss Mary Munholm, of Mechanicsburg.

10. Dec 11 1823 (Thursday)
Married 20th ult by Rev B. Keller, George Kolb, to Miss M'Alister, of North Middleton twp.
- On 29th ult by same, Alexander C. Wilson, to Miss Catharine

Stein, both of Harrisburg.
- On Thurs evening last by Rev Spencer, Thomas Lee, of Dickinson twp, to Miss Mary Noble, of Carlisle.

11. Dec 25 1823 (Thursday)
Married by Rev Benjamin Keller: - On 4th inst in East Pennsborough, Jacob Billman, to Miss Maria Weaber. - On 16th, Anthony Aker, to Miss Mary Warns, of Rye twp, Perry co. - On 18th, in East Pennsborough, Joseph Jacobs, to Miss Elizabeth Duey. - On same day, Abraham Mickey, to Miss Elizabeth Kelly, of North Middleton twp.
- On Thurs last, by Rev Dr. Lochman, Joseph Eberly, of Cumberland co, to Miss Maria Gram of York co.
Died on Wed last at his residence in Dauphin co, Gen. James Wallace, formerly a res in Congress.
- Suddenly on Thurs morning, 11th inst, Abraham Line, [aged 25 years - Gazette] of Dickinson twp.
- Same day in South Middleton, Mrs. Sarah Capperstein [Copperstone - Gazette].
- On Fri 12th inst, Mrs. Jane Hays, wife of John Hays, formerly of this borough.

12. Jan 8 1824 (Thursday)
Married 25th ult by Rev B. Keller, Joseph Kornbrobst, to Miss Sarah Cockley, both of North Middleton twp.
- On 1st inst by same, James Beaty, from Rye twp, Perry co, to Miss Elenor Brown, of North Middleton twp.
- On 25th ult by Rev Dr. Lochman, George Goodman, to Mrs. Catharine Romer, both of this co.

13. Jan 15 1824 (Thursday) - Married Thurs evening last, by Rev Winebrenner, Stewart Moore, to Miss Ann Dorshimer, both of Mechanicksburg.

14. Jan 22 1824 (Thursday) - Died suddenly in this borough, whither he had come to transact some business, on Sat evening last, Hugh Leviston, formerly of this borough, but late of Monaghon twp, York co; leaving wife and 6 or 7 children.

15. Jan 29 1824 (Thursday)
Married Tues evening last by Rev Joseph Spencer, Charles J. Jack, Esq. of the City of Phila, to Miss Leonorah, dau of Capt. Richard O'Brien, of this vicinity.
- On Thurs last by Rev George Duffield, William M. Henderson, esq. of north Middleton twp, to Miss Elizabeth Parker, of East Pensborough twp.

16. Feb 5 1824 (Thursday)
Married Tues 20th ult by Rev Moody, William Fleming of North Middleton twp, to Miss Rachael Moore, formerly of Franklin co.
- On same day by Rev John W. Hamm, Daniel Daelhousen, to Miss Barbara North, both of Mifflin twp.
- On same day by same, Thomas Hene [Heney - Gazette], to Miss Susanna Hendricks, both of Mifflin twp.

Died on 22d ult [27th - Gazette] at his residence in Millbaugh, Berks co, Henry Emanuel Shulze, brother of the governor, aged 52 yrs. James Dixon, esq. and general James Wallace, both soldiers of the revolution, died, lately, at their places of residence in Dauphin co.

17. Feb 12 1824 (Thursday)
Married on 15th ult by Rev B. Keller, Hosea Summers, to Miss Elizabeth Nagle.
- On 22d by same, Samuel Sowers, to Miss Sarah Spangler.
- Same day by same, Peter M'Cavitt, to Miss Sarah Sowers, all of Dickinson twp.
- On 5th inst by same, Samuel Hemminger, to Miss Elizabeth Spahr, of S. Middleton.
- On Wed last by Rev ---, David Sterm, to Miss Elizabeth Wolf, both of this borough.

18. Feb 19 1824 (Thursday) - Death of fellow citizen Capt. Richard O'Brien, of North Middleton twp at city of Washington, Sat night last at 11 o'clock, Consul General for the U.S. at Algiers.

19. Feb 26 1824 (Thursday)
Married 19th inst by Rev B. Keller, Wm. Gillilen, merchant, to Miss Catharine Cavanneugh, both of Dills-town.
Died Mon evening 23d inst, after a long illness, Mrs. Bridget Carney, wife of Mr. B. Carney of this place, leaving husband and and 4 young children.

20. March 11 1824 (Thursday)
Married 1st inst by Rev B. Keller, Azel Skinner, to Miss Margaret Pearson, of this place.
- On 2d inst by same, Andrew M. Smith, to Miss Susanna Emminger, dau of Andrew Emminger, both of East Pennsborough.

21. March 18 1824 (Thursday) - Married Thurs evening 4th inst by Rev Pearce, James M'Connel, to Miss Elizbeth Fenton, both of Shippensburg.

22. March 25 1824 (Thursday)
Married at Phila Tues evening 16th inst by Rev James P. Wilson, D.D., Charles B. Penrose, esq. of this borough, to Miss Valeria F. Biddle, dau of the late Wm. M. Biddle, esq. of the city of Phila.
- On 11th inst by Rev B. Keller, Jesse Hower [Bower - Gazette], to Miss Margaret Kiehl, of Frankford twp.
- On same day by same, Thomas Williamson Barber, to Miss Catharine Neigle, both of Allen twp. - On 16th inst by same, Jacob Henkle, to Miss Elizabeth Spidle, of Eastpennsborough twp.
- On Tues 16th inst by Rev Jacob Albert, Peter Whitmore, of South Middleton twp, to Mrs. Elizabeth Miller, of Adams co.
Died 16th inst, Mrs. Benjamin, widow of John Benjamin, late of Harrisburg, decd.

- On 12th inst, Mrs. Margaret Giffen, of North Middleton twp, in her 48th yr.
- Same day, John Huber, son of Jacob Huber, of this co.
- On 15th inst, Catharine Shireman, dau of Mr. Shireman of this co.
- At Easton Pa, on 1st inst, Henry August Hutter, one of the editors of the Easton Centinel [in the 24th year of his age - Gazette].

23. April 1 1824 (Thursday)
Died 25th inst of a lingering illness, Mrs. Mary Spangler of this borough, wife and mother. Remains were deposited in the Lutheran burying ground.
- Sat 13 March in North Middleton twp, Mrs. Martha Giffen, wife of James Giffen, esq. in her 48th year, for 12 months afflicted with a pulmonary complaint.
Married 25th inst by Rev B. Keller, Abraham Eckert, to Miss Mary Plyler, of Dickinson twp.
- On 28th, by same, Henry Boor, to Miss Sarah Mell, of East Pennsborough twp.

24. April 8 1824 (Thursday)
Married at Bellefonte, Pa, on 25 March by Rev Minshall, James M'Manus, to Miss Jane W. Armor, both of Carlisle.
- On evening of 30th ult by Rev Williams, William Duncan, to Miss Nancy Fulton.
Died after a very short illness, at his late residence in this borough on Monday morning last, general Henry Miller, an active officer of the revolution and late prothonotary of Perry co - in his 72 year. [of the inflamation of the bowels - Gazette]

25. April 15 1824 - Married 6th inst by Rev Dr. Lochman, Matthew Black of York co, to Miss Hannah Clark of this co.

26. April 22 1824
Died in Savannah Georgia, on 30th March last, Charles S. Walters, formerly of Lewistown, Pa. Persons are notified against crediting Mary Sanderson, otherwise called Mary Neithercoat, on my account ... alleges she is my wife, but the fact in truth is otherwise. At the time she alleges the marriage ceremony was performed, I was incapable of entering into such a contract, by reason of derangement of mind... Samuel Neithercoat, Shippensburg.

27. April 29 1824
Married Thurs last by Rev Professor Spencer, James M'Intire, to Miss Mary Davidson, both of West Pennsborough twp.
- On Tues last by Rev Dr. Lochman, William M'Cracken to Miss Ann Davidson, both of Cumberland co.
- On Tues 20th inst by same, David Brenizer of Cumberland co, to Ann Bauman of York Co.
- On Tues 13th inst by Rev Geo. Duffield, John Dunbar of Tyrone twp, Perry co, to Miss Ann Douglass, dau of Wm. Douglass of

Frankford twp, Cumberland co.
- On Tues last by Rev Williams, the Hon. Joseph M'Ewen, of Huntingdon co to Mrs. Mary Davidson of Dickinson twp, Cumberland co.
Died last week in South Middleton twp, Mrs. Rebecca Barber, wife of William Barber, paper maker, leaving husband and children. [died in her 47th year - Gazette].
Henry M. Campbell, esq. atty at law, formerly of this place, died lately in Easton, of an accidental wound in one of his legs, which terminated in a mortification.
Died - Judge Walker, late of Pittsburg.
- Molly Hardy known for many years as an inhabitant of this town and vicinity, on Sat last in this borough.
- On Sun night, 11th inst at his residence in Canton twp, James Johnson, formerly of Frankford twp, Cumberland co, Pa, aged about 74 years.

28. May 6 1824 (Thursday)
Married Thurs evening last by Rev R. S. Vinton, John Quigley, to Miss Ann C. Dipple, both of this place.
- In Cumberland co, on 26th ult by Rev Duffield, Alexander Simpson, Merchant of Cadiz, Ohio, to Miss Susan Williamson, dau of Thomas Williamson.
- On 15th ult by Rev B. Keller, Simon Eby to Miss Catharine Kerman, both of this co.
- On 22d by same, Samuel Minig, to Miss Catharine Kolb.
- On 29th by same, Adam Stucky, to Miss Maria Clouser.
- Same day by Rev Lochman, John Zimmerman, to Miss Eliza Miller, both of this co. Celebrated Ann Carson, of typhus fever, in Phila penitentiary, aged 38 years.
Pittsburg - On Monday night last, William M'Culley, a boatman and another person, returning by land from Brownsville to Pittsburg, stopped for the night at the house of widow M'Dermont, in Mifflin twp. M'Culley, who had liquor with him, refused to go to rest when the family retired at bed time, but remaining up, became noisy and abusive. James M'Dermot got out of bed and was met by M'Culley, who plunged a Spanish dirk knife up to the breast. James M'Dermot died. M'Culley has been captured.

29. May 13 1824 Thursday)
Married Thurs 6th inst in this borough, John Zinn, to Mrs. Susannah Stine, both of Harrisburg.
- On same evening by Rev Dwinn, Barney Carney, to Miss Catharine Livinger, both of this borough.
Died Fri morning last of the consumption in her 27th year, Miss Sarah Rudisell.
- On Sat afternoon 2d inst, Thomas Passmore, Esq., late Auctioneer, of the city of Phila.

30. May 20 (Thursday) - Died Tues last near this borough, Jacob Zug, at an advanced age.

31. May 27 1824 (Thursday)
Married 20th inst by Rev John S. Ebaugh, Jacob Wetzel, to Miss
    Catharine Walter.
- Same day by same, John Stevenson, to Miss Elizabeth Keller, dau
    of Henry Keller, all of the vicinity of Carlisle.
- On 23d inst by same, Jacob Greiner, to Miss Ann Anwerter, both
    of Lancaster co, Pa.
Died Fri morning last in his 46th year, of the dropsy, George
    Philips, proprietor and publisher of the Carlisle Herald,
    leaving widow and number of children.
- On 14th inst aged about 60 years, Mrs. Nancy Fritz, consort of
    Jacob Fritz, Esq. of Landisburg.
- On 19th inst, Miss Mary Searight, eldest dau of Francis
    Searight, esq. of South Middleton twp, in her 13th year.

32. June 3 1824 (Thursday)
Married Thurs evening last [2d - Gazette] by Rev Spencer, Robert
    C. Hall, esq. of Sunbury, Pa, to Miss Sarah Ann Watts, dau of
    the late David Watts, esq. of this borough.
- At Phila, on Thurs 27th of May by Rev Abercrombie, John
    M'Ginnis, jr., esq. of this borough, to Miss Charlotte
    O'Brien, dau of capt. Richard O'Brien, late of North Middleton
    twp, decd. Mifflintown, May 29 - Married Tues last, by Rev
    Hill, William Randolph, of Cumberland co, to Miss Margaret
    Fleming, of Armagh twp, Mifflin co.

33. June 10 1824 (Thursday) - Died Sat evening last, aged about
    36 years, James Huston, merchant, of Newville.

34. June 17 1824 - Married Thurs evening last by Rev Williams,
    James Shannon, esq. to Mrs. Martha Mathers, dau of Robt.
    Pebles [Peebles], esq., both of Newville.

35. July 1 1824 (Thursday)
Married Tues 15th ult by Rev Williams, Capt. William Ker, of
    Huntingdon co, to Miss Eliza Sterrett, of this co.
Died in this borough Sun last, Mrs. Johnston, wife of John
    Johnston.

36. July 8 1824 (Thursday)
Married Thurs evening last by Rev Vinton, John Flood, to Miss
    Jane Holmes, both of this borough.
Died yesterday morning of a lingering illness, in her 27th year,
    Mrs. Ann Biggs, eldest dau of Andrew Kerr, of this borough.
    [And adopted member of the Presbyterian Church - Gazette].
    Funeral from her father's house, corner of Louther and Bedford
    sts.
- On 29th ult of a consumption, Jacob Stayman, of East
    Pennsborough twp, aged 43 years.

37. July 22 1824 (Thursday)
Married Thurs morning last by Rev John M. Mason, Dr. Lewis L.
    Neare, of Pottsgrove, Montgomery co, to Miss Jane Ann Chambers
    of this borough.

Died suddenly Fri last, William Wheeler, of this borough,
formerly a clerk of the surveyor general's office of this
state.
- At Reading on 11th inst, in his 34th year, Rev George
Shenfelter, pastor of the Roman Catholic church of St. Peters,
in that borough.
- At Phila on 16 July inst, Tench Coxe, esq., aged 69 years.

38. July 29 1824 (Thursday)
Married Sun last (25th) by Rev Benjamin Keller, George Weibley,
to Miss Sarah Billow, both of North Middleton twp.
Died Thurs last at his late residence in South Middleton twp, of
a lingering illness [consumption - Gazette], Francis Searight,
esq in his 44th year.

39. Aug 5 1824 (Thursday)
Married Thurs evening last by Rev J. S. Ebaugh, John Collishaw,
to Mrs. Harriet Hutton, both of this borough.
- On Tues last (3 Aug) by same, William Wilcome, to Miss Leah
Greist, both of South Middleton twp.
- On Mon evening last by Rev Geo. Duffield, James Martin, to Miss
Eleanor Morrow, both of this borough.
Died at Pittsburg, 27 July, after a few days illness, Mrs. Nancy
Findlay, wife of William Findlay, esq. late governor of this
commonwealth, in her 61st year.
- On 27 July, Mrs. Catharine Rupp, wife of David Rupp, of East
Pennsborough twp.

40. Aug 19 1824 (Thursday) - Died Mon evening 16th inst, at his
residence in Lower Merion twp, Montgomery co, Pa., Charles
Thomson, in his 95th year, patriot of the Revolution.

41. Sep 2 1824
Married Thurs last by Rev Dr. Lochman, Peter Brenizer, to Miss
Susan Stauffer, both of this co.
- On same evening by Rev J. S. Ebaugh, Samuel Goudy, to Miss
Nancy Trough, of this borough.
Died at Shippensburg, on Mon last (30 Aug), William M'Elhare.
- On 14th ult at Canton, Ohio, of Cholera Morbus, William Smith,
formerly of this borough.
- John Sloan, editor of the Franklin Republican, attacked with
the fever on evening of 22d inst, died early yesterday
morning.
- At Shippensburg on Tues 24th Aug, after a short illness, Mrs.
Margaret Cochran, consort of Robert Cochran, dau of Daniel
Henderson, in her 20th year. She had been united to Mr.
Cochran 8 months.

42. Sep 9 1824
Died at Washington city on Tues 31st Aug ult, at the residence of
Samuel Hanson, of Thomas, Lieutenant John Smith of the army of
the U.S., in his 31st year - [youngest son of John Smith of
this borough - Gazette] formerly of the borough of Carlisle.
- Fri morning last, Mrs. Lacy M'Cord, wife of Robert M'Cord, of

this borough, leaving husband and three children [after a long
and severe illness - Gazette].

43. Sep 23 1824 (Thursday)
Died in the night of 15th inst at Landisburg, Robert Wilson,
    esq., atty at law, aged about 27 years.
- On 4th inst, Andrew M'Coskrey, farmer of Rye twp, Perry co, in
    his 48th year.
- In Green Castle on 13th inst, Rev John X. Clarke.

44. Sep 30 1824 (Thursday)
Married 21st inst by Rev B. Keller, John P. Lyne, to Miss Susan
    Wittich, both of this place.
- On 23d inst by same, Mr. Wunderlich, of South Middleton, to
    Mrs. Elizabeth Gramlich, of Eastpennsborough twp.
- On 9th inst by Rev Habliston, David K. Ebaugh, of Hopewell twp,
    to Miss Sarah Macdonald, of Shrewsbury twp, both of York co.
Died at Gettysburg, Sat evening last (25th), John M'Conaughy,
    esq. Counsellor at law, and pres. of the Gettysburg Bank.
- On 22d at Fredericktown, Md. Robert Ritchie, esq., editor of
    the Republican Gazette.
Gettysburg, Sept 29 - On Fri last, the dead body of a colored
    female who had resided with George Hersh, of this borough, was
    found in an old well, in West st. Coroner found that she
    drowned. This is extraordinary case: the water did not exceed
    three feet in depth in the middle (the sides were sloping) in
    which she lay with her face downwards. She was in an advanced
    state of pregnancy; murder is suspected.

45. Oct 7 1824 (Thursday)
Married 28th ult, by Rev B. Keller, Jacob Beltzhuber, to Miss
    Rebecca Leidig.
- On 30th ult by same, Archibald Gorrel, to Miss Nancy
    Sepplinger, all of Allen twp.
- On 5th inst by same, David Musselman, of York co, to Miss
    Sophia Feily, of Allen twp, Cumberland co.
Died yesterday morning, after a very short but severe attack of
    inflammatory fever, Matthew Miller, esq., of this borough, in
    his 65th year; to be interred in the family burying ground,
    about 4 miles from this place.
- On Wed evening, Sep 29th last, Mrs. Elizabeth Brown, of West
    Pennsboro' twp, in her 79th year.
- On 28 Aug last, aged 46 years, at Port Gibson, Mississippi,
    major William Carson, formerly in the U.S. service, and eldest
    son of the late judge Carson, of Franklin co.

46. Oct 14 1824 (Thursday)
Married 10 Aug last by P. Laverty, esq., John Knisely to
    Elizabeth Sulzberger, both of Allen twp.
- On 20th ult by same, Samuel Jones, to Barbara Spidle, both of
    East Pennsborough.

47. Oct 21 1824 (Thursday)
Married 7th inst by Rev B. Keller, John Harting, to Mrs.

Catharine Lebenstine, both of Eastpennsborough twp.
- On same day by same, George Weise, to Mrs. Eleanor Wunderlich, both of North Middleton twp.
Died Sat last (15th) at an advanced age, Mrs. Frances [Fanny - Gazette] Woods, wife of Samuel Woods, senr., of Dickinson twp.
- On Wed morning last in East Pennsborough twp, John Carothers, esq. formerly sheriff of this co.
- At the U. S. Cantonment, Belle Fontaine, Missouri, on 7th ult, Mrs. Elizabeth Littlejohn, late consort of Samuel H. Littlejohn of the U.S. army.
- On 9th ult in ascending the Missouri, after a short illness, Dr. Samuel H. Littlejohn of the U.S. army.

48. Oct 28 1824 (Thursday)
Died Mon 11th inst at his late residence in Greenwood twp, Perry co, capt. David Boal, zealous patriot in the revolutionary war, sorely wounded at Muncy, in an engagement with the savage allies of Great Britain.
- On 13th inst at the house of Joseph Clark, in Cumberland co, James M'Elravy of Landisburg, aged about 25 years. Fores.
- On Fri last, Mrs. Mary Carothers, relict of John Carothers, late of W. Pennsborough twp, was thrown from her horse about one mile west of this borough, and 4 miles from her home. She was put into a wagon but died before reaching home.

49. Nov 4 1824 (Thursday) - Married Thurs evening last (28 Oct) by Rev Dr. Lochman, John Weidman, of Cumberland co, to Mrs. Barbara Walker, of Dauphine.

50. Nov 11 1824 (Thursday)
Married Thurs last, by Rev Dr. Lochman, Philip Bovenmeyer, to Miss Hanna Coheen, both of this co.
- Same day by Rev John Winebrenner, Henry Ronenbaum to Miss Frances Carr, both of this co.

51. Nov 18 1824 (Thursday)
Married Thurs evening last by Rev G. Duffield, Andrew Carothers, esq. Counsellor at Law to Miss Isabella Alexander, both of this borough.
- Thurs last by Rev Dr. Lochman, Benjamin H. Mosser [Musser - Gazette], of York co, to Miss Elizabeth Rupley, dau of John Rupley, esq. of Cumberland co.

52. Nov 25 1824 (Thursday)
Married at Bedford, Thurs last (17 Nov) by Rev Henry Gerhart, Thomas B. Miller, late of Cumberland co, to Miss Charlotte M'Dowell, dau of Charles M'Dowell, esq. editor of the Bedford Gazette.
- On Tues evening, 16th inst, by Rev Patrick Dwin, James Johnston, of Lebanon co, to Miss Johana Beelen, dau of Francis Beelen, esq. of Perry co.
- At Washington City, by Rev E. Allen at the residence of com. Rodgers, capt. Alexander S. Wadsworth, of the U.S. Navy, to Miss Louisa J. Dennison, sister of Mrs. Rodgers.

Died Wed morning 17th inst, of consumption, Peter Wolf, wagon
maker, of this borough, aged 45 years.
- At New York on 19th inst, capt. Joseph Bainbridge, of the U.S.
navy.
- On the 16th inst in Millerstown, Perry co, Charlotte, infant
dau of Col. John Ramsey, of that place.

53. Dec 2 1824 (Thursday)
Married at Mercersburg, Franklin co, Wed evening, 24th inst, by
Rev David Elliott, John Findlay, Jr., Esq. to Miss Sarah, dau
of Robert Smith, Esq.
Died at New Orleans on 19 Oct last of the yellow fever, Joseph
Dipple, aged 18 years, only son of Michael Dipple of this
borough.
- At Little Rock, Arkansas Territory, 24th Sep, Capt. Grendville
Leftwich of the 7th Regt, U.S. Infantry, stationed at
Cantonment Gibson.

54. Dec 9 1824 (Thursday)
Married Wed evening 1st inst by Rev Professor Spencer, Tillotson
Friatt of Berkley co, Va, to Miss Ann Noble, dau of Capt.
James Noble, of this borough.
- On Thurs evening last by same, Charles Menich, Printer, of
Harrisburg, to Miss Grace Leyburn, dau of Robert Leyburn of
this borough.
- 25th ult by Rev b. Keller, William Allen, of Warren, Trumbull
co, Ohio, to Miss Catharine East, of Dickinson twp.
- On 28th ult by same, Henry Suesshoty, to Miss Lydia Billow,
both of North Middleton twp.
- On same day, John Ihrig, to Miss Elizabeth Lantz, both of
Frankford twp.
Died Mon evening last of billious cholic, John Galbraith, son of
Samuel Galbraith, of Dickinson twp.
- At Paoh, Illinois, 8th ult, Rev William Beauchamp, P.E. of the
Meth church, aged about 55 years.
- At Cincinnati, Ohio, on 16th ult, Rev Abdeel Coleman, of the
same church, in his 42d year.

55. Dec 16 1824 (Thursday)
Married Thurs last by Rev Francis Pringle, William Williamson, of
Carlisle, to Miss Mary Brown [dau of James Brown - Gazette],
of North Middleton.
- On 9th inst by Rev B. Keller, William Hannah, to Miss Sarah
Cole (Coler?), both of North Middleton twp.
Died Fri last, at Newville, Capt. Alexander Sharp, for some time
afflicted with the gravel, and underwent the operation of
extraction, some short time before by which was produced a
stone about the size of a nutmeg. He was far advanced in
life.
Married at Baltimore on 7th inst by Rev Dr. Jennings, Jacob
Squier, to Miss Dorothy Merrit.

56. Dec 23 1824 (Thursday) - Died Sat 11th inst at 6 o'clock in
the evening, Miss Margaret Henderson, dau of James Henderson,

of Hopewell twp, in her 24th year.

57. Dec 30 1824 (Thursday)
Married Thurs evening last by Rev B. Keller, Samuel Fetter, to
  Miss Mary Weise, both of this borough.
- Same day by same, William Sollenberger, to Miss Ann Baker, both
  of North Middleton twp.
Married on 19 Oct by Rev J. S. Ebaugh, John Smith, to Miss Mary
  Fisher.
- On 21st David Heppehamer to Miss Lidia Kurtz.
- Nov 25, John Baer to Miss Elizabeth Stohe.
- Dec 9, Peter Miller to Mrs. Jane A. Priester.
- Dec 16, Samuel Crall to Miss Mary Marks.
- Dec 23, Martin Frey to Miss Elizabeth Stevens
- all of the vicinity of Carlisle.
Died 4th inst, John Huggins, esq., proprietor of Liverpool, Perry
  co, in his 51st year.
- 20th inst, Benjamin Lease, esq., formerly Register and Recorder
  for Perry co.
- On 21st inst, Frederick William Hutter, one of the editors of
  the Easton Centinel, aged 24 years.

58. Jan 6 1825 (Thursday)
Married Fri 24th ult by Rev Duffield, Dr. Curtis, of New Holland,
  York co, to Miss Sarah Brown, of North Middleton twp,
  Cumberland co.
Died in the city of Lancaster, 22d ult, William Black, jr. aged
  23 years, 11 months and 7 days, son of William Black, late of
  this co, and now living near Middletown.
Married Tues last by Rev Geo. Duffield, William B. Sponsler, of
  this borough, to Miss Peelman [Beelman - Dem. Rep.], of Allen
  twp.

59. Jan 13 1825 (Thursday)
Died 5th inst in South Middleton twp, William Graham, in his 94th
  year, for many years an inhabitant of this co.
- On Mon evening last in this borough, at an advanced age, James
  Mitchell, soldier of the revolution; buried with military
  honors.
- At Fannettsburg, Franklin co, on 4th inst, William Maclay,
  esqr. in his 59th year.
- On 30th ult, James Sanderson, of Saville twp, Perry co, in his
  71st year.

60. Jan 20 1825 (Thursday)
Married 9 Dec last by Rev H. Habliston, Wm. Piper, to Miss
  Lucinda, dau of Col. Rippey, of Shippensburg.
- On 6th inst by Rev Ebaugh, Mr. G. Knob [Kolb - Dem. Rep.], to
  Miss Barbara Hoover.
- On 11th inst by same, Henry Jumper, to Miss Mary Henry.
- On 13th inst, Gotlieb Ostertag, to Miss Margaret M'Giery, all
  of the vicinity of Carlisle.
- On Thurs last, by Rev Dr. Lochman, Christian Martin, to Miss
  Mary Bruckhart, dau of Daniel Bruckhart, of York co.

61. Jan 27 1825 - Died Wed 12th inst of a paralytic affection, Thomas Henderson, son of James Henderson, of Hopewell twp, in his 30th year. Mr. Henderson arrived at home from city of Phila on evening of 11th, at 6 o'clock, in perfect health, took supper with the family, went to bed with his brother, and slept, awoke and asked his brother if the clothes were right upon them, went to sleep and a few minutes later awaked his brother by throwing his arms on him, and shortly thereafter expired.

62. Feb 3 1825 (Thursday)
Married at Harrisburg Thurs evening last by Rev Dewitt, major Willis Foulke, of South Middleton twp, to Miss Elizabeth Logan, of Frankford twp.
- At Newville, on same evening, by Rev Williams, William Barr, esq. to Miss Sarah Geddes, dau of Dr. Geddes, both of that place.
Died 26 Jan, after a short illness, John Wormley, esq. proprietor of Wormleysburg, of this co.

63. Feb 10 1825 (Thursday)
Married Tues 1st inst by Rev A. Sharp, Thomas Mathers, to Miss Polly Spear [Mary Spear - Dem. Rep.], both of the vicinity of Newville. [Note: Polly is a nickname for Mary.]
- On 7th inst by Rev J. Williams [Williamson - Dem. Rep.], John Bush, to Miss Rebecca Boilieu [Boylue - Dem. Rep.], both of Mechanicsburg.
- By Rev J. S. Ebaugh, on 20th Jan last, Peter Leib, to Miss Mary Machamer, both of Carlisle.
- On 26th ult, Jacob Hehl, to Miss Catharine Tobias.
- On 27th ult, William Sanderson, to Miss Hannah Wolf.
- On Thurs last, Stephen Skegs [Skeys - Dem. Rep.], to Miss Eliza Fisher, all of the vicinity of Carlisle.
Died in this borough on Fri last, of a consumption, captain Joseph Somerville, aged about 49 years of age.
- At his late residence in Milford, Pike co, Pa, Dan Dimmick, esq. aged 50 years, formerly a member of the legislature of this state.

64. Feb 24 1825 (Thursday) - Married Tues 15th inst by Rev Dr. Lochman, John Hiestand, of Lancaster co, to Miss Maria Wormley, of Wormleysburg, Cumberland co.

65. March 3 1825 (Thursday)
Married 24 Feb by Rev B. Keller, Philip Baker to Miss Catharine Hetich.
- On same day by same, Joseph Wolf, of Allen to Miss Esther Frees, of South Middleton twp.
- On same day by same, Adam Peffer, of Dickinson twp, to Miss Mary Kerr, of this borough.
- On 17 Feb by same, Henry Martin to Miss F. Horst.
- On 20 Feb by same, John Sugar to Miss Fanny Steigelman.
Married on Tues 22d ult by rev. F. Pringle, Henry Logan, jr. to

Miss Martha Ohail, both of Monaghan twp, York co.
- On Thurs last by Rev Dr. Lochman, John George Keller to Miss Catharine Brownawell, both of this co.
- On 9th ult, by Rev Smith, William Neilson of Tyrone twp, to Miss Rebecca Bull, dau of William Bull, of Juniata twp, Perry co.
- On 10th ult by Rev J. Winebrenner, Andrew Castle to Miss Jane Ackeson, both of Lisburn.
- At Baltimore, Thurs evening last, James D. Nicholson, to Miss Angeline M'Ilwain, both of that city.
Died at Shippensburg, Mon 21st ult of a lingering illness, Rev William Brandeberry, of the Meth connection.
- On Sat last [suddenly - Dem. Rep.], Jacob Hunker, [whose occupation was baker - Dem. Rep.] of this borough.

66. March 10 1825 (Thursday)
Married 4 March inst by Rev J. S. Ebaugh, John Paul to Sarah Roads; John Hoppel to Lydia Miller; and John Zimmerman to Mary Strack, all of Cumberland co.
- On 3d inst by Rev Moeller, Isaac Swartzwelder, merchant of Hagerstown, to Miss Sarah Rothbaust, of Chambersburg.
Died Sat last, Andrew Brown, son of James Brown, of Allen twp. -
On Mon [Mon morning, aged about 53 years - Dem. Rep.] last, in South Middleton twp, major James Moreland.

67. March 17 1825 (Thursday) - Died Thurs last, while at a vendue in Franklin co, John Heckman of Shippensburg.

68. March 24 1825 (Thursday)
Married Wed evening March 16, by Rev J. S. Ebaugh, Wm. Shaeffer, of Sunbury, Pa, to Miss Rachel Weise, of this borough.
- On Tues last by Rev George Duffield, Samuel Davidson, to Miss Mary Gray, of this borough.
Died Fri morning last in his 73d year, Simon Lamberton, of North Middleton twp.

69. March 31 1825 (Thursday)
Married 22d inst by Rev B. Keller, John Zeigler, to Miss Mary Weise, of North Middleton.
- On 24th, Michael Coons, to Miss Mary Hager, of East Pennsborough twp.
- On same day, George Sudbury, to Miss Ann Sowers, of Dickinson twp.
- By Rev J. Williams, Mr. Harper, to Miss Isabella Huston of Newton twp.
- By same, Samuel M'Cormick, to Miss Susan, dau of Major Alter, of West Pennsborough twp, Cumberland co.
Died Sun evening 20th inst in 78th year, at his seat near Germantown, Col. Thomas Forrest, revolutionary officer, and not long since a member of Congress.
- On Sun evening 20th inst, Daniel Bloom, esq., old inhabitant of Toboyne twp, Perry co.

70. April 7 1825 (Thursday)
Married 31 March ult by Rev B. Keller, Andrew Dickson, to Mrs.
Margaret Graham, of this place.
- On Wed evening last by James Sturges, Esq., Lemuel G. Davis, to
Miss Catharine Reynolds, both of Shippensburg, Pa.
Died Mon 28th ult of consumption, Miss Ann Glenn, in her 19th
year, dau of Wm. Glenn, esq. of this co. Daniel Knisely,
Samuel Knisely, John Knisely and Joseph Stayman, owners of the
real estate of George Knisely, late of Cumberland co, seek to
show satisfaction on a mortgage to Daniel Smith.

71. April 14 1825 (Thursday) - Died Sun [Sun morning - Dem.
Rep.] last after a long and severe illness, Mrs. V. Smith
[Violet Smith - Dem. Rep.], wife of Peter B. Smith, Esq. of
this borough.
72. April 21 1825 (Thursday) - Died at Harrisburg Tues 12th
inst, of a nervous fever, Englehard Reehm, cabinet maker in
his 50th year, formerly of Carlisle.

73. April 28 1825 (Thursday)
Married Thurs 14th inst by Rev Williamson, Dr. Joseph Junkin, to
Miss Adeline Crain, dau of Richard M. Crain, esq. of this co.
[all of Esatpennsborough twp - Dem. Rep.]
- On Thurs evening by Rev Dr. Lochman, captain John Armor, of
Bellefonte, formerly of Carlisle, to Miss Magdalena Rahm, of
Harrisburg.
- In Phila, on evening of 6th inst by Rev Dr. Wilson, Douglass W.
Hyde, esq. editor of the Chronicle of the Times, to Miss Mary
Shenfelter, both of Reading, Pa.

74. May 5 1825 (Thursday)
Married at Woodland, Cumberland co, Pa, Thurs evening 28th inst,
by Rev J. Williamson, Theodore Myers, M. D. formerly of
Baltimore, to Sarah Ann eldest dau of Matthew Irwin, Esq.
- Last evening by Rev Geo. Duffield, Benjamin M'Intire, esq to
Miss Ann Thomson, dau of James Thomson, esq. of this borough.
[Her surname is spelled "Thompson" in the Dem. Rep.]
- On 21 April by Rev J. Shull, John Titler of this co, to Miss
Magdalena Harman, of Toboyne twp, Perry co.
- On 28th ult, by Rev B. Keller, David Arris of Monrow twp, to
Miss Susanna Eigleberger, of Silver's-spring twp, also Daniel
Gebman [Gehman - Dem. Rep.] to Miss Margaret Souder, both of
Frankford twp.
- On Tues last by Rev Williams, James Kennedy, to Maria Barr,
both of Newville.
Died Sat evening last of a pulmonary complaint, Mrs. Nancy Doyle,
wife of Elisha Doyle, esq. of this borough. [Ann Doyle - Dem.
Rep. [Nancy is a nickname for Ann.].
- On 23d ult, John Kinch, of Buffalo twp, Perry co. On Monday
last during the military parade at Shippensburg, a young man
named Robert Bretton was shot in the arm by the accidental
discharge of a gun; the wound, we have heard, is likely to
prove mortal.

75. May 12 1825 (Thursday)
Married Thurs last by Rev G. Duffield, Mr. J. Wallace, silver
  plater, of Harrisburg, to Miss Nancy Culbertson of this
  borough.
- In Fannettsburg, Franklin co, on Wed 27th ult by Rev A. A.
  M'Ginley, Dr. John P. Gettys, of Newville, to Miss Catharine
  J. Maclay, dau of hon. Wm. Maclay, late of Franklin co, decd.
- Tues last by Rev B. Keller, Joseph Frost, to Miss Rachel Ann
  Baxter, both of Silver's-spring twp.
Died Thurs morning last, Mrs. Esther Steel, aged 72 years, widow
  of Ephraim Steel, esq. late of this borough, decd.

76. May 19 1825 (Thursday)
Married Thurs last in this borough, by Rev B. Keller, William
  Scott, to Miss Sarah Wenrick [Wenrich - Dem. Rep.], both of
  Harrisburg.
Died Tues 10th inst at Kelso's Ferry in this co, William Kelso,
  aged about 30 years, of a lingering consumption.
- On Thurs last at the residence of his father, in Monroe twp, of
  billious cholic, aged about 23 years, William Crockett, son of
  Geo. Crockett, senr.
- Dem. Rep.], of North Middleton twp.
- On Sat last, Mrs. Wibley [Mrs. Weibly, aged 99 years
- On same day at an advanced age, Mrs. Catharine Sterrett, of
  this borough.

77. May 26 1825 (Thursday)
Married 19th inst by Rev B. Keller, John Pickart, to Miss Marian
  [Mary Ann - Dem. Rep.] Scholly of South Middleton twp.
- Same day by same, Stephen Losh of this place, to Miss Catharine
  Ann Cockley, of the neighborhood of Lisburn.
Died Wed evening 18 May, inst, John Stockdale, of this borough,
  aged about 40 years [native of Ireland - Dem. Rep.].
- In this borough Sat last, capt. Henry Shell, patriot and
  soldier of the rev war, in his 80th year.

78. June 9 1825 (Thursday) - Died at Sunbury, Pa, 5th inst, of a
  billious cholic, in his 23d year [aged 23 years - Dem. Rep.],
  William Shaeffer [Scheaffer - Dem. Rep.], formerly of this
  place.

79. June 23 1825 (Thursday) Elisha Sharp, of Sussex co, Del,
  murdered his wife and her young child, in a fit of jealousy,
  on the first of this month.
Married at Wilmington, Del, Thurs evening, 9th inst, [by Rev E.
  W. Gelbert - Dem. Rep.] Henry W. Peterson, printer, formerly
  of Carlisle, to Miss Hannah Ann Jones, of the former place.
Died Thurs 16th inst, John French, of Frankfort twp. [of
  consumption - Dem. Rep.]
- On Thurs night last, Mrs. Anna Maria Bowermaster, of this
  borough, in her 74th year.
- On 16th inst, Thadeus Province, grandson of Mrs. Mary Ramsey,
  of this borough, aged about 11 years. [aged about 10 years, of
  consumption - Dem. Rep.]

- At New Orleans 5 May, colonel James Sterrett, naval officer of the port, formerly of this co.

80.   June 30 1825 (Thursday)
Died at Phila on 17th inst [15th inst - Dem. Rep.], of a consumption, in her 20th year, Miss Ann Smith, dau of Patrick Smith, formerly of Carlisle.
- At Reading on 11th inst, Mrs. Elizabeth Hiester, wife of gen. Joseph Hiester, late governor of this state.

81.   July 7 1825 (Thursday)
Married Tues 21 June by Rev Henry Habliston, Jacob Kauffman, to Miss Jane Hutchins, both of Shippensburg.
- On 23d June by same, Joseph Dornbaugh, of Southampton, to Miss Susannah Cobaugh, of Shippensburg.
- On same day by same, James M'Curdy, to Miss Catharine Hertzell, dau of Peter Hertzell, of Shippensburg. Killed by the discharge of an old iron cannon following 4th of July celebration, a young man named William Bell, and mortally wounded, Dr. John S. Givin, who survived but a very short time. His body was interred at Presbyterian graveyard. A number of other persons were wounded but none seriously. Dr. Given was in his 28th year, son of James Givin [merchant - Dem. Rep.] of this borough.

82.   July 14 1825 (Thursday) At Charlestown, Md. on the 4th of July, John Clarke was killed by the explosion of a cannon used in firing a salute in honor of the day.
Died Sat 9th inst in this borough, Christian Leonard, aged 74 years, officer in the American Rev. Phila, July 8, death of rev soldier and patriot, Thomas Leiper, of this city, in his 80th year.

83.   July 21 1825 (Thursday) - Died Tues morning last in the prime of life, Robert S. Miller, of Mount Rock.

84.   July 28 1825 (Thursday)
Died Sat last, major John Miller, of Mount Rock, brother of Robert S. Miller, whose death was announced last week.
- Sun last, Mrs. Margaret Rine, widow of John Rine, late of this borough, decd.
- Tues last, David Sterrett, of Mifflin twp.
- At Butler, Pa, 8th inst, Mrs. Jane Bredin, aged 65 years, mother of James Bredin of this borough.
- Fri 15th inst, at his residence in Toboyne twp, Col. John Maxwell, one of the board of Commissioners for Perry co, aged about 50 years.
- On Mon evening, 18th inst, aged 75 years, Josiah Roddy, old resident of Tyrone twp, Perry co. James Orr of Shippensburg was drowned, in a mill-dam near that place, a few days since. He went into the dam with another person, for the purpose of learning to swim but getting into deep water he sank, and remained so long at the bottom, that when taken out he was past recovery.

85. Aug 4 1825 (Thursday) - Died in Mechanicksburg Fri week,
John Gosweiler, Jr. of that place.

86. Aug 11 1825 (Thursday)
Married Mon evening last by Rev Griffith, Martin Lutz, printer,
to Mrs. Mary Harry, both of this borough.
Died 29 July at the house of David Quail, esq. (his son-in-law)
in Strabane twp, Washington co, Pa, John Walker, esq. in his
75th year, for many years a resident of Cumberland co.

87. Aug 18 1825 (Thursday)
Married Sun 7th inst by Rev Dr. Lochman, Jacob Rupley, son of
John Rupley, esq. to Miss Catharine Swartz, all of this co.
Died after a few days illness Sat evening last, at Big Spring,
James M'Culloch, in his 63d year [of Newton twp, Auditor of
Cumberland co - Dem. Rep.].
- Yesterday morning in his 28th year, Josiah Barclay, Esq.,
treasurer and deputy attorny general of this co.
On Sat evening last as John Welsh of Perry co was returning home
with wagon and horses, from this side of the mountain, it is
supposed that he fell from the saddle horse, and was so much
injured by either the wagon or horses, that he died about 8
o'clock on Sunday morning.
On Mon afternoon the corpse of a Mr. Eckart was brought to this
town from or near the Bedford Springs, whither he had lately,
with some friends, travelled for his health; and where he
died. We understand he was a resident of Berks co, to which
place his remains (covered with ice and salt) were carried,
for interment.

88. Aug 25 1825 (Thursday)
Married at Martinsburg, Va, on 17th inst, by Rev Reily, William
Main, jr. of this borough, to Miss Catharine D. Gorgas, dau of
Samuel Gorgas, formerly of this place. [of the former place -
Dem. Rep.]
- At Clark's Ferry, by R. Clark, esq. on Mon evening 15th inst,
Alexander Watson, to Miss Priscilla M'Coy, both of Rye twp,
Perry co.
- On Thurs last by Rev Dr. Lochman, Jacob Miller, jr. to Miss
Sophia Mann, both of Cumberland co.
Died at Mechanicsburg Thurs morning last, Mrs. Ann Ford, wife of
Henry Ford, esq., one of the Commissioners of this co, aged 55
years.
- On Mon last in this borough, Mrs. Hunter [Ann Hunter, aged 78
years - Dem. Rep.], widow of John Hunter, decd, formerly a
schoolmaster of this borough.
- Suddenly in this borough yesterday morning, Mrs. Wrenshall
[Nancy Wrenshall, wife of John R. Wrenshall - Dem. Rep.], of
Pittsburg; she was the dau of Dr. George Stevenson, formerly
of this place. She had laboured under a pulmonary affection,
and with her husband and brother, was on a journey to her
father's residence in Delaware.

89. Sep 1 1825 (Thursday)
Married at Harrisburg Thurs last by Rev John Winebrenner, Henry
   Critzman, formerly of this borough, to Miss Margaret Zeigler,
   dau of Jacob Zeigler, of Harrisburg.
- On Tues evening last by Rev Williamson, William Mateer of Allen
   twp, to Miss Mary Ann Porter, of East Pennsborough twp.
- Yesterday morning by Rev B. Keller, Adam Wert, of Mifflin, Pa,
   to Miss Sarah Ulerich, of this borough. [dau of Nicholas
   Ulerich - Dem. Rep.]
Died at Wilkesbarre, Mon 15th ult, Samuel Maffit, esq. aged 38
   years, and for 15 years editor of the Susquehanna Democrat.

90. Sep 8 1825 (Thursday)
Died at Huntingdon, Pa, at a very advanced age, Tues 23d ult, Rev
   Thomas Smith, pastor of the Associate Congregation of
   Huntingdon and Shaverscreek.
On Tues last, during public worship at the Camp Meeting south of
   this borough, an interesting child of Captain William Myers,
   of Mechanicsburg, was drowned in the Yellow Breeches, whither
   it had been taken by its nurse, a black boy of 14 or 15 years
   of age.

91. Sep 15 1825 (Thursday)
Married Thurs last by Rev Augustus H. Lockman, Joseph Wolf, to
   Miss Elizabeth Boyers, both of Cumberland co.
Died Thurs night last, aged 42 years and 1 day, David Smith,
   esq., one of the Commissioners of Cumberland co.

92. Sep 22 1825 (Thursday)
Married Tues morning last [Thurs - Dem. Rep] at the residence of
   captain Jesse Elliot in this borough, by Rev Geo. Duffield,
   Dr. Martin, to Miss Rebecca Hughes, both of Hagerstown, Md.
- On Tues evening last by Rev Griffith, James Postlethwaite, to
   Miss Catharine Mell, both of this borough.
- At Mechanicsburg, by Rev Augustus H. Lochman, Jonathan
   Ensminger, to Mrs. Mary Forney.

93. Sep 29 1825 (Thursday)
Died at his residence in Toboyne twp, Perry co, of a bilious
   fever, on the night of 20th inst, Samuel M'Cord, in his 55th
   year, leaving widow and 7 children.
Chambersburg, Sep 27 - Died Wed morning last, William M.
   M'Dowell, Esq., atty and Counsellor at Law, of this place, in
   his 32d year.

94. Oct 6 1825 (Thursday) - Died Wed last in his 54th year,
   James Wood, Esq. of Green-Castle. About a week before his
   death, he received a severe contusion in the head, and was
   otherwise much injured by being thrown out of a dearborn, his
   horse having run off. At an early period of life he entered
   the military service of his country and was in the memorable
   battle in which Gen. Wayne defeated the Indians in 1794.
   During the late war he marched as Major of a battalion of

volunteers and militia, ordered from this county into Canada and was in the battles of Chippewa and Bridgewater, in the latter of which he received a severe wound; later commissioned as Justice of the Peace.

95. Oct 20 1825 (Thursday)
Married at Chambersburg Tues evening last, by Rev Rauhouser, Joseph Pritt, to Mrs. Nancy Sloan, proprietress of the Franklin Republican.
Died on 14th inst, captain Joseph Halberrt, of this borough [parent and husband, of a pulmonary illness - Dem. Rep.].

96. Aug 30, 1827 (Thursday)
Married Thurs last in Carlisle, by Rev Ebaugh, William Wiley, of Mechanicsburg, to Miss Harriot Negly, of Silver Spring twp.
Died suddenly Tues evening last, David Culins [Culings - Dem. Rep.], of this borough.

97. Sep 6 1827 (Thursday)
Married Tues 28th ult, by Rev J. Shull, Adam Wampold, of Juniata twp, Perry co, to Mrs. Jane Wheeler, of Landisburg, widow of late William Wheeler, esq. of Carlisle. Death of John Underwood, in his 79th year, father of the editors. He lingered for some time in a state of debility and at half past ten o'clock, Sat night last died. He was a native of the county Antrim, Ireland; came to this country at the dawn of the Am. Rev., took an active part in the war. [He entered as an Ensign in 1775; after the war he located himself in this county. - Dem. Rep.]
Died Fri evening last, after a short and painful illness, Mrs. Charlotte R. consort of John M'Ginnis, esq., and dau of late Captain Richard O'Brien, decd, in her 27th year.
- On 24th ult of typhus fever, Philip Peffer, aged about 19 years, son of Henry Peffer, of Dickinson twp.
- Suddenly, on 27th ult, Nicholas Hartman of North Middleton twp, aged about 65 years.

98. Sep 20 1827 (Thursday) - Died at Fort St. Philip, near New Orleans, 14 Aug last, Barnabas Hagen, carpenter, formerly of Carlisle.

99. Sep 27 1827 (Thursday) - Died Thurs evening last, after an illness of a few days aged about 36 years, John Collishaw, of this borough [chairmaker of this place - Dem. Rep.].

100. Oct 4 1827 (Thursday) - Married Wed 26th ult by Rev Dr. John M. Mason, Rev Erskine Mason, pastor of the First Presbyterian Church in Schenectady, N.Y. to Mary, dau of the late Dr. Samuel A. M'Coskry, of this place.

101. Oct 11 1827 (Thursday)
Married Tues last, by Rev B. Keller, Rev Nicholas Sharretts [N. G. Sharretts of Indiana, Pa. - Dem. Rep.], to Miss Louisa, dau of Capt. Lindsey Spottswood, of this borough.

Died Mon 10th Sep last, Andrew Irwin, Jr., merchant, of Dayton, Ohio, formerly of Shippensburg, Pa, aged about 32 years.

102. Oct 18 1827 (Thursday)
Married Thurs Oct 4, in Newton twp, by Rev Williams, George Logue, of this borough, to Miss Ann M. Houston, of Newton twp.
Died morning of the first inst, of consumption, in her 25th year, Mrs. Maria M'Candish, merchant, of Newville, and dau of James M'Cormick, esq., late of Carlisle, decd.
- In Clarksburg, Montgomery co, Md., Sun 7th inst, Rev Caleb Reynolds in his 44th year, Meth Episc preacher.

103. Oct 25 1827 (Thursday)
On Sat 28th inst, a man name Wm. Hogan, laborer on the canal at the Kiskiminetas river, was beat so severely by Bartholomew M'Carty, that he died on the following Tuesday. The body was secretly buried in the night, but suspicion being excited, it was disinterred and an inquest held. No one knows where Hogan was from. Kittaning Gazette.
Married in this borough Tues evening last by Rev W. R. Dewitt, William M'Clure, Esq. atty at law, to Miss Ellen D. Campbell, both of Harrisburg.
Died 16th inst, hon. Jacob Bucher, one of the assoc. judges of Dauphin co, aged 63 years, 4 months. Whereas my wife Sarah on the 17th Sep last, left my bed and board, I forewarn persons that I am determined to pay no debts of her contracting. John Wolf, Silver Spring twp.

104. Nov 1 1827 (Thursday) - Died Sun morning 21st ult in her 23d year, Mrs. Catharine Musselman, wife of William Musselman, of Westpennsborough twp, and dau of Joseph Showalter.

105. Nov 8 1827 (Thursday) - Died 29th ult, col. James Quigley, of this co. [of East Pennsborough, aged about 60 years. - Dem. Rep.]

106. Nov 15 1827 (Thursday)
Married 1st inst, by Rev Alexander Sharp, Andrew Coil, of Perry co, to Miss Eliza M'Cullough, of Newton twp, Cumberland twp.
- Thurs last by Rev Benjamin Keller, John Cocklin [Cockley - Dem. Rep.], to Miss Susan Snyder, both of Allen twp.
Died in Harrisburg Wed 31st ult, William White, printer, aged about 45 years.

107. Nov 22 1827 (Thursday)
Married Thurs morning 15th inst by Rev Henry Habliston, Adam Cobaugh, to Miss Catharine Ann, dau of George Croft, all of Southampton twp.
Died at Lancaster Fri last, hon. Thomas Duncan, one of the Judges of the Supreme Court of Pa. His remains were brought to this borough on Sat and interred on Sun at the family cemetery at Carlisle.

108. Nov 29 1827 (Thursday)
Died at Petersburg, Adams co, Thurs last, Thompson T. Bonner,
    esq. one of the members of Assembly elect, of Adams co.
- Suddenly Sun morning last, of effusion of the chest, Samuel
    Weakley, 3d son of William Craighead,. sr. of South Middleton,
    aged 7 years.

109. Dec 13 1827 (Thursday)
Died Sat 1st inst at residence of col. R. M. Crain, of a
    lingering disease, Dr. Joseph Junkin, lately of Mechanicsburg,
    in his 26th year.
- Same day at an advanced age, Mrs. J'y Rowan, consort of David
    Rowan, of this borough.

110. Dec 20 1827 (Thursday)
Died Thurs evening 13th inst in her 6th year, Ann Hays, dau of
    John S. Hays, of this borough.
- In this borough Sat last, Mrs. Elizabeth Leyburn, wife of
    Robert Leyburn.

111. Dec 27 1827 (Thursday)
Married Thurs 6th inst by Rev Alexander Sharp, William Brown, to
    Miss Hannah, [last name not given] both of Mifflin twp.
- On Tues 18th inst by Rev Francis Pringle, Adam Reath, to Miss
    Margaret Campbell, both of Frankford twp.
Died Tues last, Michael F. Natcher, [merchant - Dem. Rep.] of
    this borough, in his 29th year.
- On Tues evening, 11th inst, in Lewistown, Miffin co, after a
    short illness, Robert Patton, formerly of Cumberland co, aged
    65 years.

112. Jan 3 1828 (Thursday)
Married Thurs morning, 27th Dec, by Rev G. Duffield, William
    Alexander to Miss Mary Aughinbaugh, dau of B. Aughinbaugh,
    esq., all of this borough.
- On Mon, 24 Dec, by Rev Stroh, James Elliott, to Miss Elizabeth
    Askew, both of Dickinson twp.
- On 26th ult at Baltimore, by Rev Stansbury, Elisha Doyle, esq.
    of this borough, to Miss Sarah Ann Feaster, of Baltimore
    [Sarah Ann Fister dau of John Fister - Dem. Rep.].
- Last evening, by Rev Joshua Williams, lieut. William Woodburn,
    to Miss Margaret Gettys, both of Newville.

113. Jan 17 1828 (Thursday)
Married Tues 1st inst by Rev John Niblock, John H. Thompson, esq.
    to Miss Rebecca Steel, both of Buffalo twp, Perry co.
Died at Middlesex, Mon evening last at an advanced age, Mrs.
    Sarah Irvine, widow of the late John Irvine.
- On Tues evening last, Mrs. Sarah Keith, consort of William
    Keith, of Carlisle.

114. Jan 24 1828 (Thursday)
Married in this place, 16th inst by Rev B. Keller, Rev Nicholas
    Stroh, to Miss Eliza Givler, both of the vicinity of Newville.

- At New York, on 3d inst, by Rev Berrien, Gabriel A. O'Brien, esq. of the U.S. navy, to Miss Elizabeth Watkinson, dau of Henry Watkinson, esq. of that city.
- On Thurs last by Rev John S. Ebaugh, James M'Haffy, to Miss Eliza Wareheim; also on Tues last by same, Francis S. Hutchison to Mrs. Magdalane Galbreath, all of the vicinity of Carlisle.
Died Thurs morning last, Ann Mary Holtzapple, of West-Pennsborough twp.
- Same day, Susan Alsbaugh, of this borough.
- On Wednesday 16th inst, Martin Frey, senr. of West-Pennsborough twp.
- On 13th inst, Mrs. Catharine Hikes, wife of John Hikes, of West Pennsboro' twp.
- In Carlisle Sun morning last, James Irvine [Irvin - Dem. Rep.], native of Ireland, aged about 45 years, employed as a stage driver for a long time; buried in Presbyterian grave yard.

115. Feb 7 1828 (Thursday)
Mouth of Conodoguinnet, Jan 31, 1828 - Died, Samuel Wilkinson Gregg, aged 11 years, 9 months, son of Richard Gregg.
From Lewistown Gazette, Jan 31 - Richard Barry and Edmond O'Reglan found guilty of murdering John Gallaher, Barry of murder in the 2nd degree; O'Reglan of manslaughter.

116. Feb 14 1828 (Thursday) - Married Thurs last by Rev J. B. Clemson, Jacob Stroop, esq. of Landisburg, to Mrs. Isabella Littlejohn of Hoguestown.

117. March 13 1828 (Thursday)
Married 28th ult by Rev Alexander Sharp, James Fulton to Miss Grissella Blean, of Newton twp.
Died in the prime of life on Tues last, of a pulmonary affection, John Guthrie, eldest son of Robert D. Guthrie, esq. of this borough.

118. March 20 1828 (Thursday)
Married Tues morning last by Rev M'Clelland, William A. Irvine, to Miss Ann Junkin, both of this borough.
- By Rev John S. Ebaugh, on 28 Feb, Isaac Venasdlen, to Miss Sarah Belshoover [Beltshoover - Dem. Rep.]. March 4, Christian Lehman to Miss Elizabeth Buckwalter [Burkwalter - Dem. Rep.]. Same day William Ferguson, to Miss Margaret Roads. March 6, William Moudy, to Miss Nancy White. March 13, Samuel Dierdorff to Miss Elizabeth Howenstein. Same day, Jacob Baker, to Miss Margaret Cornman - all of Carlisle and its vicinity.
From the York Gazette, March 13. Supposed murder. George Aubel of Windsor twp, in this co, aged about 60 years, has been missing since Thurs 6th inst. He was last seen near Creutz Creek bridge; he was on his way home from Columbia.
The Lancaster Journal of Fri last states that on Sun evening last, William M'Cullough, Esq. received a wound from a butcher

knife in the hands of a negro named Joshua Bacon, which proved
mortal on Wednesday. Bacon has fled. [apprehended later]

119. April 3 1828 (Thursday)
Married at Munster Mills, Chester co, Tues evening, 18 March, by
Rev George Duffield, of Carlisle, Amos Alexander, to Miss
Amanda Duffield, both of Chester co.
- At the same place,, by same, Tues evening, 25 March, Mark
Alexander Hodgson, to Miss Sophia Duffield, both of Chester
Co.
Died at Isabella Furnace, Va, Sat 15th ult, William P. Leeper,
son-in-law of Benjamin Blackford, esq. in his 40th year.

120. April 10 1828 (Thursday)
Married Thurs evening last by Rev Ebaugh, John Spottswood, to
Miss Margaretta R. Cart, dau of Jacob Cart, all of this place.
- On 3d inst by same, John Spahr, to Miss Elizabeth Stum.
Died Thurs last in his 14th year, John Matthews, son of Michael
Matthews of this place. He received a stab in ths side with a
knife in a quarrel with one of his school mates a few weeks
ago, from which he died.

121. April 24 1828 (Thursday)
Died at Shippensburg Tues, 8th inst, Samuel M'Clure, aged about
60 years. About 10 o'clock in the morning he was suddenly
attacked with a paralytic affection and fainted away, but
recovered - then died that evening about 11 O'clock.
- Wed night last, aged about 24 years, Mrs. Isabella Spangler,
wife of Michael Spangler, and dau of Andrew Kerr, of Carlisle.
- In York, Pa, on 16th inst, Jacob Barnitz, Esq. for many years
Register and Recorder of that co, aged about 70 years; officer
in the Rev War, and suffered many privations, in consequence
of a wound received in that memorable struggle.
From the Perry Forester, of April 17 - Matthew Brannan, John
Murphy, Edward Fox, and Michael Carrell, charged with the
murder of John O'Regan, and the beating of others, were
brought to trial. [Apparently they were laborers on the
canal, came to the house of a Mr. Dolton, who keeps tavern at
Montgomery's Ferry on a drunken frolic.]

122. May 1 1828 (Thursday)
Married by Rev John S. Ebaugh 26 March, William Henwood, to Miss
Catharine Reifschneider.
- March 27, John Duey, to Miss Margret Nellow [Margaretta Nellaw
- Dem. Rep].
- Same day, George Wetzell, to Miss Barbara Stoufer.
Died Thurs last, [Wed evening past - Dem. Rep.] Walter Bell, of
this borough.

123. May 8 1828 (Thursday)
Married 1st inst by Rev John Davis, Christian Stayman, to Miss
Eliza Coffman, both of East Pennsborough twp, Cumberland co.
Died Tues evening last, in this borough, Dr. James Armstrong, in
his 81st year, for several years an Assoc Judge for Cumberland

co; he died in the same house and room where he was born.
- Tues last, George Myers, farmer of North Middleton twp.

124. May 22 1828 (Thursday)
Died Sun last of consumption, Miss Sarah Smith, of this borough,
   aged about 23 years.
Died in Perry co, Mon 12th May inst, Daniel Smith, printer.
Married Thurs morning last, by Rev A. Griffith, Mr. W. Irwin, of
   Newville, to Mrs. A. Fowler, of this borough.

125. June 5 1828 (Thursday) - Married Wed 28 May by Rev Boyer,
   William D. Ramsey, esq. to Miss Charlotte Arnold, both of
   Adams co.

126. June 12 1828 (Thursday) - Married Tues last, by Rev J. F.
   Moeller, Philip Aughinbaugh, of Waynesburg, to Miss Ann
   Catharine Raum Hubley, of Shippensburg.

127. June 19 1828 (Thursday)
Married Tues week at Harrisburg, by Rev De Witt, Stephen Duncan,
   Esq. to Miss Louisa Pollard.
- Thurs week by Rev J. Shull, John Waggoner, to Miss Elizabeth
   Topley, all of Landisburg, Perry co.
- On 29th ult by Rev E. Keller, John Ockerman, of Perry co, to
   Miss Elizabeth Pickard, of E. Pennsbro' twp, Cumberland co.
Died Sun morning, 15th inst at Phila, of small pox, John
   Vanderbelt, cabinet maker, in his 23d year.

128. June 26 1828 (Thursday)
Married Thurs evening, 12th inst, by Rev A. Griffith, Joseph
   Gant, of Perry co, to Miss Mary M'Gowan, of this borough.
- On Thursday evening last, by Rev Ch: A. Davis, Samuel Crop,
   jun., of South Middleton, to Miss Mary Matthews [Mathewson -
   Dem. Rep.], of this borough.
- On Wed 18th inst, in Chambersburg, Elijah Zinn, to Miss Hannah
   Lamb, both of this co.

129. July 3 1828 (Thursday)
Died Fri morning last, after a short illness in his 26th year
   [27th year - Dem. Rep.], John C. Baehr, apothecary and
   druggist, of this place. - On Mon night last, after a
   lingering consumption, aged about 57 years, John Spottswood of
   this place. - On Wed 25th ult, at the city of Washington,
   Richard W. Meade, esq.
- In New York, recently, John A. Black, printer, formerly of this
   place.

130. July 10 1828 (Thursday)
Married at Chambersburg on 3d inst, by Rev Ferdinand M'Cosker,
   John Dwen, of Virginia, to Miss Eliza Josephina Hagan, of
   Carlisle, Pa.
- At Chambersburg, Thurs last, by Rev Prettyman, Thomas J.
   Wright, to Miss Elizabeth, dau of Conrad Brown, all of that
   place.

- On Tues last at Carlisle, by Rev John S. Ebaugh, Mr. J.
  Stevenson, to Miss Leah Shriner, both of Wormleysburg.
Died Sat last, aged about 34 years, John Crockett, of Monroe twp.
- On Fri, [Thurs night - Dem. Rep.] Mrs. Hemminger, consort of
  Samuel Hemminger, of the vicinity.
- On Thurs, Miss Bryan [Jane Brien - Dem. Rep.], of this borough,
  aged about 19 years.

131. July 17 1828 (Thursday)
Married 8th inst by Rev John S. Ebaugh, David Stevenson, to Miss
  Leah Schreiner
- On Tues evening, 8th inst by Rev Henry R. Wilson, James Willis,
  to Miss Elizabeth Moore, both of Southampton twp.
- On Thurs evening last, by Rev A. Griffith, John Strawhower, to
  Miss Frances Smith, of this borough.
- Tues evening by Rev Dwen, James Kiernan, of Franklin co
  [Chambersburg - Dem. Rep.], to Miss Anistatia Dwen, of this
  borough.
- Same evening in this place by Rev Davis, Henry Sweitzer, to
  Miss Maria Beeghler, both of Harrisburg.
Died at Oley Furnace, Berks co, on 14th inst, Daniel Udrie, esq.
  aged 76 years, 11 mos, 10 days.

132. July 31 1828 (Thursday)
Married Tues evening 22d inst by Rev C. A. Davis, Moses M'Coy to
  Mrs. Mary A. Feris, both of this borough.
- On Tues evening, 22d inst by Rev Jacob R. Shepherd, James S.
  Brandeberry, to Miss Issabella Donavin, both of the borough of
  Shippensburg.
Died Tues night last, John Wilson, merchant of this borough.
- At Baltimore on night of 17th inst, John Montgomery esq,
  formerly mayor of that city, and a native of Carlisle - of
  apoplexy.

133. Aug 7 1828 (Thursday)
Married Tues 5th inst by Rev F. Heyer, Jacob Fanwell, to Miss Ann
  Elizabeth Shawley, both of North Middleton.
- On same day by same Jacob Uhler, to Miss Mary Wright, both of
  this Borough.

134. Aug 21 1828 (Thursday)
Married in Centre co [Belfonte - Dem. Rep.], Pa, on 10th inst by
  John Thompson, esq., James Armor, formerly of Carlisle, to
  Miss Ruth Benner, dau of Gen. Philip Benner [of Centre Co. -
  Dem. Rep.].
Died in Shippensburg, on Thurs last, aged about 24 years, John
  Wolf, leaving a wife, joined in wedlock but a few months.
- On Thurs morning last, George Pattison, Esq. aged about 60
  years, of this borough.
- On Thurs morning last, after a short illness, in her 66th year,
  Mrs. Sabina Barbara Huber of this borough.

135. Aug 28 1828 (Thursday) - Married Thurs last at Pittsburg,
  by Rev Taylor, John Hoffer, formerly of this borough, to Miss

Mary Myers, of Pittsburg.

136. Sep 4 1828 (Thursday) - Died at Pittsburg, Wed 20th ult,
James Scanlan, aged 57 years.

137. Sep 11 1828 (Thursday)
Married Tues morning last by Rev George Duffield, Robert
Snodgrass, merchant, to Miss Margaret Noble, dau of Capt.
James Noble, all of this borough.
Died at Clark's Ferry, Perry co, Fri last, after a short illness,
Mrs. Jane Boden, wife of John Boden, Esq., formerly of this
borough.
- In Staunton, Va., on 23d ult, Rev Enoch George, one of the
Bishops of the Meth Episc Church, aged about 60 years.

138. Oct 2 1828 (Thursday) - Married at Pittsburg Thurs morning
18th inst, by Rev Hopkins, Hugh Denming, to Mrs. Catharine
M'Farland, widow of Jno. M'Farland, decd, printer, formerly of
this borough.

139. Oct 9 1828 (Thursday)
Died Sun morning 28th ult, Mrs. Maria MCartney [consort of John
M'Cartney, aged 32(?) years - Dem. Rep.], of this borough.
- On Sun last, captain John Sailor, of Monroe twp [aged about 60
years - Dem. Rep.].
- On Tues last at the residence of Thomas Urie, esq., Mrs.
Rebecca Gustine, widow of Dr. Lemuel Gustine, late of
Carlisle, decd.

140. Oct 23 1828 (Thursday)
Married 9th inst by Rev John S. Ebaugh, William Brown, to Miss
Elizabeth Nickey, of Frankford twp.
- On 14th inst by same, Rev John G. Fritchey, to Miss Mary A. E.
Hendel, of Carlisle.
- On 18th by same, Daniel Meyers to Miss Margaret Schwonger.
- On same day by same, John Richards, to Miss Mary Miller, of
Monroe twp.
- On 2d inst by same, Jos. Lightcap, of Gettysburg, to Miss
Elizabeth Foster, of Cumberland co [Dickinson twp - Dem.
Rep.].
- On Tues evening 14th inst by Rev Pringle, Charles Savage, to
Miss Martha Glen, both of South Middleton twp.
- On Thurs 16th inst by Rev Henry Wilson, William Carothers, of
West Pennsborough twp, to Miss Ann Line, of Dickinson twp.
- On Mon 20th inst by Rev Griffith, Daniel Armstrong, of
Hagerstown, Md., to Miss Eleanor Noble, dau of John Noble,
sen., decd, late of this borough.

141. Oct 30 1828 (Thursday)
Married Mon morning last, at Roxbury, Franklin co, A. Smith
M'Kinney, esq. of Hopewell twp, Cumberland co, to Miss
Margaret Reynolds, of the former place.
Died Sat last of palsy, at his residence in South Middleton twp,
Barclay Donahoe, native of Ireland, leaving wife and large

family of children who depended almost entirely on his
exertions for their support. Remains deposited in Catholic
church yard of this borough. [died at Spring Forge, Barkley
Dunahu - Dem. Rep.]
- Same day, John Hannah, of North Middleton twp.

142. Nov 6 1828 (Thursday)
Died Sat 9th inst, Ann Call, in her 70th year.
- On 25th ult, James Logan, citizen of Frankford twp, in this co.

143. Nov 13 1828 (Thursday)
Married evening of 15th ult by Rev J. M. Olmstead, Samuel Bell,
of Landisburg, Perry co, to Miss Nancy Lightner, of Cumberland
co.
Died Thurs 30th ult, aged about 53 years, Archibald Gribble, of
Mifflin twp.
- Suddenly of appoplexy, Tues last, Jacob Kreider, of Silver
Spring twp, aged between 50 and 60 years.
- On 5th inst, at Stoughstown, Cumberland co, Pa, after a short
illness, John Ford, a stranger, travelling Eastward, who
stated that he was 38 years of age and by profession a miller,
and that his relations live in Chester co, Pa, near the Paoli.
- On Fri evening last, a poor man aged about 45 years, deranged,
unknown, who took lodging at a public house; buried in burial
ground adjoining this borough.

144. Nov 27 1828 (Thursday)
Married Tues 18th inst, by Rev A. Griffith, George Stauter, of
Adams co, to Miss Christiana Myers, dau of late Rev Abraham
Myers of West Pennsborough twp, Cumberland co.
- In Bucks co, Jacob Lukens, aged 81 years, to Miss Rachel
Childs, aged 25. She is a niece to her husband, an aunt to
her mother, and a mother to her grandmother! Whereas Erasmus
Holsapple, my husband, has absconded from my bed and board,
all persons are cautioned against purchasing any goods or
property, from said Erasmus Holsapple. Elizabeth Holsapple.

145. Dec 11 1828 (Thursday)
Married Tues week by Rev Williamson, Dr. A. T. Dean, to Mrs.
Adeline C. Junkin, dau of R. M. Crain, esq. of this co.
- By Rev De Witt on 27th ult, Levi Markle, to Miss Susanna
Martin, both of Allen twp, Cumberland co.

146. Dec 25 1828 (Thursday)
Married Tues 10th inst [16th inst - Dem. Rep.] by Rev Williamson,
Leopold N. Wikoff, of Blockley, Phila co, to Miss Elizabeth,
dau of Richard M. Crain, esq. of this co.
Died 10th inst, consort of Joseph Shrom, junr. of this borough,
leaving huband and children.

147. Jan 1 1829 (Thursday)
Married at Mechanicsburg, Thurs last, 25th inst by Rev Keller,
Dr. Ira Day, to Miss Elizabeth Forry, both of Cumberland co.

- On Thurs 18th inst by Rev Heyer, Isaac Shafer, to Miss
  Henrietta Sanno, both of this place.
- On same day by Rev Williamson, Dr. David S. Hays, to Miss Mary
  Ann Coover, both of Dickinson twp.
Died Thurs morning last, Col. Ringwalt, old inhabitant of North
  Middleton twp [formerly of Lancaster co, Pa. - Dem. Rep.]
- In Attleborough, Deacon Elkanah Wilmarth, aged 100.

148. Jan 8 1829 (Thursday)
Died in Perry co, Mon last, of a pulmonary complaint, Holmes A.
  Pattison, lately of this borough.
- Yesterday morning Jan 2d, [in Washington City, formerly of this
  place - Dem Rep.] James Alexander, printer, of Carlisle, aged
  about 46 years.

149. Jan 22 1829 (Thursday)
Died Wed evening 14th inst, aged 77 years [in his 77th year -
  Dem. Rep.], Thomas Foster, of this borough. Shortly before
  his decease, he was afflicted with paralysis.
- On 26 Oct last in Sangamo co, Il, Dr. Thompson M. Glenn, late
  of this co, by a stroke of a board, inflicted by a man with
  whom he had altercation.

150. Jan 29 1829 (Thursday) - Married in this borough Tues last,
  by Rev J. S. Ebaugh, Michael Wise, to Miss Catharine Williams,
  both of North Middleton twp.

151. Feb 12 1829 (Thursday)
Married 1st inst by Rev F. M'Cosker, Christian Dish, of
  Cumberland co, to Miss Mary O'Donnel, of Shippensburg.
Died on Fri 30th ult, at Lisburn, Cumberland co, Mrs. Isabella
  Creigh, relict of the late Judge Creigh, decd, in her 58th
  year, of a pulmonary disease.

152. Feb 19 1829 (Thursday)
Married in this borough on 10th inst by Rev George Duffield,
  Thomas Chambers, esq., [Chambersburg - Dem. Rep.] of Franklin
  co, to Miss Catharine Duncan, dau of Hon. Thomas Duncan,
  formerly of this borough, decd.
- Same day by Rev Heyer, Martin Horst, to Miss Elizabeth
  Hundsberger, all of this co.
Died morning of 6th inst, Gen. John Rea, after a very short
  illness, aged 74 years. He went to Chambersburg with some of
  his neighbours on Wed and while preparing to return home in
  the evening, he suddenly became ill and died in less than a
  day and a half. He was a rev soldier, and for 8 successive
  years, a member of Congress from Franklin co.
- On 10th night of this month, Mrs. Ann Barber, aged 39 years [in
  39th year - Dem. Rep.], wife of David Barber, of this borough.
- On 10th inst in Dickinson twp, aged nearly 80 years, Samuel
  Weakley, esq. one of the first settlers in this co.
- On Thurs last in this borough, Mrs. [Mrs. Jane Godfrey - Dem.
  Rep.] Godfrey, at an advanced age, after a lingering illness.
- On Mon last in the prime of life [in his 25th year - Dem. Rep.]

in the bloom of apparent health, but a few weeks ago, William
Cart, step-son to Robert M'Clan, esq. of this borough.

153. Feb 26 1829 (Thursday)
Married by Rev John S. Ebaugh, on 12th inst, David Irvine, to
Miss Rosanna Kirk. Peter Kissinger, to Miss Mary Pechert on
17th, Samuel Hahn, to Miss Harriet Kreitzer, all of the
vicinity of Carlisle.
- By Rev Henry R. Wilson on 19th, William M. Grier, esq. [Atty.
at Law - Dem. Rep.] to Miss Sarah Mahon, all of Shippensburg.
Died at Dillsburg, York co, Thurs last, William Chambers,
formerly of Cumberland co.

154. March 5 1829 (Thursday)
Died in this borough, Sat morning last of dropsy in the chest,
Daniel Weakley, leaving wife and 5 small children.
On Sun night the 18th ult, the dwelling house of Jacob Harris, of
Pike twp, Perry co, Ohio, took fire in the absence of himself
and wife. Five children were asleep in the house, the eldest
a boy of 12 years of age. One of the younger children died.

155. March 19 1829 (Thursday)
Married Thurs 5th inst by Rev Albert Helfenstine, Jacob Baughman,
to Mrs. Isabella Firman, both of Cumberland co.
Died at Harrisburg, Mon, 9th inst, John De Pui, Clerk of the
Senate of Pa.

156. April 2 1829 (Thursday)
Married Tues evening 17th ult, by Rev John S. Ebaugh, Peter
[Peter B. Lechler - Dem. Rep.] Lechler, of this borough, to
Miss Catharine Rupert, of North Middleton twp.
- On Thurs evening, 19th ult by same, David Shenk, to Miss Maria
Hauenstein.
- Same evening by Rev Heyer, James Crawford, to Miss Maria
Spottswood, of this place.
- On Mon 16th ult by Rev Williamson, Andrew Roberts, to Miss
Catharine Krotzer, both of Newville.
Died Mon last of consumption, Michael Spangler, of this borough.
- On Sat last at Harrisburg, E. S. Kelley, esq. a member of the
Senate of Pa, from the 24th senatorial dist.
- On Sun evening last, at Harrisburg, William Lehman, esq. a
member of the House of Rep of Pa, from the city of Phila.
- On Thurs last in his 61st year, Jacob Dechert, Postmaster of
Chambersburg.
- On Thurs evening last, the wife of Henry Lauch, near Kreider's
mill, in this co, was shot in the abdomen, by a lad 10 or 12
years of age, and died in excruciating pain, about 5 hours
after. It appeared to be an accident. There were two
families living in the house, one above the other. From the
family above, some man who had been gunning, borrowed a
saddle, and was carrying it down stairs, with his gun, which
he gave to the boy to hold, while he saddled his horse - Mrs.
Lauch and her daughter were standing in the door when the gun
went off.

157. April 9 1829 (Thursday)
Married Thurs evening last by Rev Charles A. Davis, Jacob Hoffer,
to Miss Mary Ann, dau of Abraham Mayer, esq. [of this borough
- Dem. Rep.]
- On Tues evening last by same, Professor [Jacob F. Huber - Dem.
Rep.] Huber, to Miss Mary Ann, dau of Robert Smith, all of
this borough.
Died on 26th ult near Oyster's Point, William Carothers, in his
59th year.
- On Sat morning last, of a pulmonary affection, in her 14th
year, Maria Neill, dau of Rev William Neill, Pres of Dickinson
College, Carlisle.
- The same day, in the prime of life, Amelia [Emily - Dem. Rep.]
Buchanan, dau of Arthur Buchanan, of this borough. For the
last year she was conscious of her rapidly approaching
dissolution - leaving aged parents.
- On Sun last, Francis Brumbaugh, at an advanced age, of this
borough.
- Same day, after 3-4 days illness, in Perry co, John Carothers,
aged about 33 years [aged about 30 years - Dem. Rep.], son of
John Carothers, esq. [late sheriff, Silver Spring twp] late of
this co. His remains were deposited in the burial ground at
Silver's Spring.

158. April 16 1829 (Thursday) - Married Thurs inst at
Harrisburg, by Rev J. ...[torn], John Moltze to Miss
Gep...[torn], of Cumberland co.

159. April 23 1829 (Thursday) - Married Thurs morning last by
Rev Duffield, Doctor Henry Smyser of Gettysburg, to Miss Mary
B. Fahnestock, of Carlisle. [dau of Dr. John Fahnestock, late
of this borough, decd - Dem. Rep.]

160. April 30 1829 (Thursday)
Married Thurs evening last by Rev Geo. Duffield, Rev George A.
Lyon, to Miss Elizabeth Sterrett, both of this borough.
- By Rev John S. Ebaugh, on 17 March, Peter Lechler to Miss
Catharine Rupert. On 19th David Shenk, to Miss Maria
Hauenstein. On 26th Philip Bachman, to Miss Mary Wetzell. On
9th of April, Jacob Wolf, to Miss Magdalene Haverstock. On
16th, Daniel Humer, to Miss Margaret M'Clure. On 24th, John
Minnich [of Gettysburg - Dem. Rep.], to Miss Elizabeth Stoner
[of Newville - Dem. Rep.]. John Westheffer, to Miss Margaret
Shuh [16th]. And Jacob Leidig, to Miss Catharine Ritner
[16th] - all of Cumberland co.
Died Sat last at a very advanced age [in her 80th year - Dem.
Rep.], Mrs. Phoebe Armor, one of the oldest inhabitants of the
borough.
- On 18th inst of a consumption, Thomas Jones, of this borough.

161. May 7 1829 (Thursday)
Married Thurs evening last by Rev Charles Davis, Andrew Keiser
[John Kiser - Dem. Rep.], esq. of Lewistown, to Miss Mary

Butler, of this place.
- On 24th ult by Rev J. S. Ebaugh, John Menich, of Adams co, to
  Miss Elizabeth Stoner, of Newville, Cumberland co.
Died Sat lat, near Dillsburg, York co, Lieut. Wm. Laird, formerly
  of Letart. His remains were deposited with military honours,
  in the grave-yard adjoining this borough [aged about 45 years,
  formerly of this co. - Dem. Rep.]
- At Mount Pleasant, Westmoreland co, Sun 26th ult, Rev Wm.
  Speer, aged 65 years, graduate of Dickinson College, commenced
  the study of divinity under Dr. Charles Nesbitt, Carlisle, was
  licensed to preach in 1791, ordained in 1793. He preached
  first at Chambersburg; afterwards at Chillicothe, Ohio; and
  closed his useful life, after labouring 27 years in the
  Congregations of Unity and Greensburg.

162. May 21 1829 (Thursday)
Married 5th inst by Rev Charles A. Davis, John Sadler, to Miss
  Rachel Deitrick, both of Adams co. On Mon, 18th inst John
  Earnest, to Miss Margaret Bradley, both of Carlisle.
- On 12th inst, near Mercersburg, by Rev Elliott, Francis Wyeth,
  editor of the Argus, to Miss Susan H., dau of William Maxwell,
  of Franklin co.

163. May 28 1829 (Thursday)
Died at Wilmington, Del, Fri evening, Doctor George Stevenson, in
  his 71st year, an officer in the rev war, member of the
  society of the Cincinnati, formerly of this town, then of
  Pittsburg, and latterly of Wilmington.
- Suddenly on Sat last, of an appoplectic fit, Jacob Krider, jr.
  of this borough. He attended market in the morning, and
  before evening he was a corpse. [Jacob Crider, aged about 45
  years, his body was interred with military honors. - Dem.
  Rep.]
- On Sat May 16, in Toboyne twp, Perry co, Ross Hackett, in his
  34th year.
- On 18th inst, Eli Miller, innkeeper at Rider's Ferry, Perry co,
  aged about 27 years.
Married Thurs evening last by Rev George Duffield, Rev John W.
  M'Culloch, to Miss Mary Louisa Duncan, of this place.

164. June 4 1829 (Thursday)
Married Thurs morning last by Rev George Duffield, George W.
  Shaeffer, merchant, to Miss Eliza, dau of Barnet Aughinbaugh,
  esq., all of this borough.
- Last month, by Rev A. Griffith, Thomas Milligan, of Allegheny
  co, to Miss Mary Ann Shortess, of Perry co.
Died Thurs morning last, David Parker, of this borough, aged 38
  years [formerly of Frankford twp.- Dem. Rep.].
- On Fri last, Daniel Ruff, of this borough, aged about 50 years.
- At Harrisburg, Sat last, James Maginness, Esq. in his 54th
  year, of consumption.

165. June 11 1829 (Thursday)
Married 6th inst by Rev Dwen, Dennis Harkens, to Miss Allison

Brady, both of Perry co.
Died Mon last week at the house of Thomas Craighead, Oyster's
   Point, Cumberland, Truston Jackson, formerly of Delaware co,
   near Phila.
- On 28th ult at his residence in Ohio, [near Hamilton, Ohio -
   Dem. Rep.] Capt. John Cleves Symmes.

166. June 18 1829 (Thursday)
Married Thurs morning last by Rev George Duffield, James Rea, of
   Newville, to Miss Adeline Weaver, recently of this borough.
- On Fri 15th ult at Newark, N.J., Rev John Holmes Agnew, to Miss
   Sarah Eveline Taylor, of that place.
Died in Frankford twp [June 11th, aged 40 years, of consumtion. -
   Dem. Rep.], John M'Dowell, esq. He had been in a delicate
   state of health for some time.
- Same day [Wed evening last, of consumption, aged 28 years, wife
   of Rudisell Natcher - Dem. Rep.] in this borough, Mrs. Hannah
   Natcher, wife of Mr. R. Natcher.
- On Fri last of consumption, Dr. John Elliott, of this borough,
   son of John Elliott, esq. aged about 32 years [aged 33 years -
   Dem. Rep.].

167. June 25 1829 (Thursday) - Married Thurs morning last by Rev
   George Duffield, Rev Daniel Zacharias [of York, Pa - Dem.
   Rep.], to Miss Jane Hays, dau of Joseph Hays, of this borough.

168. July 2 1829 (Thursday)
Married Mon evening last by Rev George Duffield, Jason W. Eby, to
   Miss Ann Margret Scobey, both of this borough.
- On Thurs last by same, Paul Randolph, to Miss Ann Nesbitt, both
   of North Middleton twp.
Died Thurs last, aged 48 years, Mrs. Sarah Williams of this
   borough.
- Last week of tetanus, occasioned by breaking his thumb, Joseph
   Alexander, of South Middleton twp.

169. July 16 1829 (Thursday)
Married Thurs last by Rev C. A. Davis, William Keith, to Mrs.
   Margaret Eckert, both of this borough.
Died in this borough on Sat last, Mr. Vance.
- On Monday of a lingering complaint, aged about 70 years, Jacob
   Kreider, a soldier of ther revolution; his remains were
   interred with military honors.

170. July 23 1829 (Thursday)
Married 11th ult by Rev Heyer, Samuel Goudy, to Miss Eliza Savage
   [dau of Archibald Savage - Dem. Rep.], of South Middleton.
- On Thurs last, Mr. J. Swischer [John Swisher - Dem. Rep.], to
   Miss Maria King, dau of George King, of Carlisle.
Died at Gettysburg, Adams co, Sun last, John Galloway, esq., aged
   58 years.

171. July 30 1829 - Married Tues evening last by Rev Dr. Neill,
   Doctor David N. Mahon, to Miss Elizabeth, dau of Rev Dr.

Neill, Pres. of Dickinson College, all of this borough.

172. Aug 6 1829 - Married Tues 21st ult, John Bredin, Esq.,
    editor of the Butler Repository, to Miss Nancy M'Clelland, of
    Franklin, Venango co.

173. Aug 13 1829 (Thursday)
Died Thurs last in East-Pennsborough twp, Mrs. May, wife of
    Frederick May.
- In South Middleton on Thurs last, Mrs. Elizabeth Eby,, aged
    about 59 years, wife of David Eby.

174. Aug 20 1829 (Thursday)
Married Thurs evening last by Rev Helfenstein, Frederick B.
    Phillips, printer, of Carlisle, to Miss Eliza Leonard, of Penn
    twp, Phila co.
- On 21st ult by P. Laverty, esq., Benjamin Dickover, to Miss
    Elizabeth Books, both of East Pennsborough twp.
Died Thurs last, after a severe attack of pleurisy, George Park,
    aged 18 years, 9 months, 13 days, son of John Park of this
    borough.
- On Sun last of dropsy, James Edmiston, for some years an
    inhabitant of this borough. [On Sat last of chronic
    inflamation of the digestive organs, James Edmunson, of this
    borough, aged about 27 years. - Dem. Rep.]
- On Mon last in this borough, where he arrived a short time
    since, James Orr, native of Scotland, aged about 34 years. A
    wife and 3 children remain at Hudson, N.Y. [For some years he
    was a resident of Hudson, N.Y. - Dem. Rep.]
- Suddenly Tues morning last, John, infant son of James Bredin,
    aged 8 months, 19 days [3 months, 19 days - Dem. Rep.].
- On 11th inst, at Martinsburg, Va, Samuel Gorgas, for a number
    of years an inhabitant of this town.
- Lately on the Eastern Shore of Maryland, Mrs. Spencer, the
    mother, and Ellen, the dau of Rev Joseph Spencer, of this
    borough.
- On Fri morning last, of a short but severe illness, Mrs.
    Elizabeth Stroop, in her 24th year, consort of George Stroop,
    Esq. of Bloomfield, Perry Co.
- Near Harrisburg, on Thurs week, Jacob Bomberger, at the age of
    85; interred in Shearer's burial ground. Known as old
    Bomberger - native of Lancaster co.

175. Aug 27 1829 (Thursday) - Died Tues last in this borough,
    Miss Elizabeth Miller at an advanced age, sister of Matthew
    Miller, esq., late of this borough, decd.

176. Sep 3 1829 (Thursday)
Died Thurs last [Fri morning last - Dem. Rep.], after a short but
    severe illness, [at an advanced age - Dem. Rep.], Mrs.
    Officer, wife of John Officer, of this borough.
- On Mon last [Sun last, Marks Brindle - Dem. Rep.] in South
    Middleton twp, Marks Brindel, aged 74 years, 7 months, 14
    days, soldier of the revolution.

- Mon night John Rankin, of this borough [of a lingering illness in his 66th year, native of Ireland, and for many years a resident of this borough. - Dem. Rep.]
- Same night, [On Sun evening last, aged about 36 years - Dem. Rep.] captain Samuel Bosler, of this borough.
- Mon, Dr. John Trough, son of Mr. J. Trough, of this borough. [of consumption, aged about 19 years, son of John Trough. - Dem. Rep.]
- Tues morning, John P. Forbes, of West Pennsborough twp [of Frankford twp. - Dem. Rep.].
From the Kittanning [Pa] Columbian - Died in this borough Mon night 16th Aug inst, Thomas Hamilton, esq.,, native of Belfast, Ireland, and for many years a citizen of Kittanning, aged about 62 years. He received his education at Belfast, emigrated to the U.S. in 1785. He resided for some time with his late brother, James Hamilton, esq. in Carlisle, Pa. In 1788 he took up residence in Greensburg, Pa, and in 1793, was appointed Prothonotary, &c. of Westmoreland co and continued in that office until 1809 when he removed to Kittanning, where he continued to reside until his death.

177. Sep 10 1829 (Thursday)
Married Tues morning last, by Rev Joseph S. Spencer, Edmund M'Ginnis, of the city of Phila, to Miss Amelia [Emely - Dem. Rep.] M'Ginnis, dau of Col. John M'ginnis, of this borough.
- On 6th ult [5th ult - Dem. Rep.] by Rev J. S. Ebaugh, John Heffelfinger, to Miss Elizabeth George.
- On 18th ult by same, Thomas M'Glauchlin, to Miss Elizabeth Iherer [Sherer - Dem. Rep.].
- On 3d by same, Christian Mayer, to Miss Elizabeth Dalhouser [Dalhousen, all of this co - Dem. Rep.].
- On 3d inst, by Patrick Laverty, esq., Joseph Fisher, to Mary Sheely, both of East-Pennsborough twp.
Died 2d inst, after a lingering complaint, Mrs. Agness M'Kean [widow of Robert M'Kean, formerly of South Middleton twp, decd] of this borough.

178. Sep 17 1829 (Thursday)
Died Thurs last, William Main, junr. of this borough, aged 27 years.
- On Fri last, at an advanced age, Mr. Richeson, of this borough.
- Fri last, Mrs. Mary Black, wife of Anthony Black, of Dickinson twp, aged 36 years.
- At Waynesburg, Greene co, on 27th Aug, Robert Whithill, Esq., res of that place, and formerly of East Pennsboro', Cumberland co.

179. Sep 24 1829 (Thursday)
Married Thurs evening last, by Rev Charles A. Davis, Jefferson Worthington, to Miss Ann Kernan, dau of Thomas Kernan, of this borough.
- Fri, 11th inst, by Rev Shull, Rev David Hassinger, of Newville, Cumberland co, to Miss Catharine D. Gibson, dau of Francis Gibson, esq. of Tyrone twp, Perry co.

Died Fri last, Louis Degal, of this borough.

180. Oct 1 1829 (Thursday)
Married Thurs week, by Rev John Herbest, General Samuel White, of
   Petersburgh (York Springs), to Miss Margaret Armstrong, of
   Franklin co.
Died Wed 23d ult, in his 75th year, Mathias Clay, resident of
   Frankford twp.
- On Tues morning last, at an advanced age, Mathias Brownawell,
   inhabitant of North Middleton twp.
- Thurs 17 Sep, ult, [Mon 21 Sep, in her 35th year - Dem. Rep.]
   Mrs. Margaret Sweigert, wife of Geo. Sweigert, of North
   Middleton twp, and dau of Andrew Zeigler. -
Died Wed morning, 23d ult at Fredericktown, Md., Rev Jonathan
   Helfenstein, late pastor of the German Reformed congregation
   of that place, in his 46th year.

181. Oct 8 1829 (Thursday)
Married Thurs evening last, in this borough, by Rev A. Griffith,
   John Peterman, to Miss Catharine Oldwine, both of Hagerstown,
   Md.
- In Bellefonte, Thurs 22d ult by Rev James Linn, Alfred
   Armstrong, formerly of this borough, to Miss Mary, dau of John
   Rankin, esq. of the former place.
- In Phila, on 13th Sep, by Rev Dunohoo, James Hogan, to Miss
   Sarah, dau of Edward Pendergrass, of this borough.

182. Oct 15 1829 (Thursday)
Married Wed evening 7th inst at Newville, by Rev Joshua Williams,
   Joseph Arthur Ege, son of Peter Ege, of Pine Grove, Dickinson
   twp, to Miss Jane Elmira Woodburn, dau of col. James Woodburn,
   late of the former place, decd.
- On Fri 2d inst by Rudolph Krysher, esq., Michael Nagle, of
   Southampton twp, to Sarah Bruner, of Monroe twp.
Died Mon morning last, Mrs. Jane Smith, wife of Mrs. Robert
   Smith, of this borough.
- On Sat last, at Green Spring, in this co, Mrs. Mary L.
   Speakman, wife of William Speakman, and dau of Henry
   Burkholder, of South Middleton twp, aged 26 years.
- Suddenly, yesterday morning, Dr. John V. Johnson, of this
   borough - formerly of Dauphin co.

183. Oct 22 1829 (Thursday)
Died Thurs last, Ralph Hurst, of this place, native of Ireland.
- On Tues 13th inst, Dennis Brady, of Harrisburg.
- On Sat night last, I. F. Muhlenburg, infant son of John
   Rudisill, of this borough, aged 14 months.
- At his residence in Prince George's Co, Md., in his 75th year,
   Col. William Dent Beall, Officer of the Rev Army.

184. Oct 29 1829 (Thursday)
Married Tues evening, 20th inst, by Rev David Crall, Thomas
   Devor, of the borough of Shippensburg, to Miss Jane Patterson,
   of Toboyne twp, Perry co.

Died Mon morning, 19th inst, John Nevin, vicinity of Shippensburg, in this co. John Herr and his wife, of Perry twp, Wayne
co, Ohio, were both instantaneously killed on 29th ult, on the
road between Canton and New Lisbon, by a tree falling on them.
They were travelling in a carryall, and the tree fell
diagonally across the carryall, broke it down, and the horse
was standing when they were discovered, quietly in the shafts
unhurt, and not a particle of the gears unloosened! (Some of
our citizns believe that Mr. Herr was formerly an inhabitant
of Carlisle.)

185. Nov 5 1829 (Thursday)
Married 23d ult by Rev Geo. Duffield, John M'Kehan, [M'Keehan -
Dem. Rep.] esq. of West-Pennsborough twp, Cumberland co, to
Miss Elenor Cissna, of Perry co.
- On 29th ult, by Rev Shull, Josiah Roddy, of Bloomfield, to Miss
Nancy Lightner, dau of Henry Lightner, of Tyrone twp, Perry
co.
Died at Meadville, on 14th ult, Mrs. Melinda B. Power, consort of
Charles B. Power, esq., of Bloomfield, Perry co.

186. Nov 19 1829 (Thursday)
Married by Rev John S. Ebaugh, on 3d Sep, 1829, Christian Mayer,
to Miss Elizabeth Dalhouser.
- By same, Sep 10, John Wirt, to Miss Mary Kiehl.
- By same on 24 Sep, Samuel Miller, to Miss Hannah Phillips.
- By same on 1 Oct, Baltzer Beistlein, to Miss Ann Maria Smith.
- By same on 8th, James Davis, to Miss Elizabeth Sponsler.
- By same on 15th, Peter Schwanger, to Miss Maria Donahu.
- By same, same day, Joseph Heffelfinger, to Miss Barbara Brim.
- By same, on 5 Nov, Samuel Cook, to Miss Jane Duey, both of
South Middleton twp. - Dem. Rep.].
- By same, on 12th, George Baish, to Miss Elizabeth Greybill -
all of the vicinity of Carlisle.

187. Dec 3 1829 (Thursday) On Mon evening last, in the vicinity
of this borough, George Swords, of S. Middleton twp, was
stabbed with a pitchfork, one prong of which entered his right
eye and penetrated his brain; he died shortly thereafter.
John M'Laughlin, a labourer of Mr. Swords has been charged
with the act and lodged in the gaol to await his trial.
Married by Rev A. Griffith, Thurs 12th ult, Benjamin Myers, to
Miss Mary Carothers; both of Westpennsborough twp.
Died Sat last, in Dickinson twp, Mrs. Houk [Salome Houk - Dem.
Rep.], wife of Adam Houk, senr.
- On Sun morning last in this borough, of a dropsical affection,
William M'Cord, well advanced in years.

188. Dec 10 1829 (Thursday) Reading, Dec 1 - On Sun 22d ult, Dr.
August Klein was mortally wounded by Adolph Hatzfield, Esq.,
receiving several stabs in various parts of the body, with a
sword cane, of which wounds he expired in great agony, on Fri
evening last. Klein left a widow whom he married from a
highly respectable family of Montgomery co, about 18 months

since; and Hatzfield has a distressed wife. At one time they
had been intimate friends, both residing under the same roof,
for many years, until "the green-eyed monster" stole into the
bosom of Hatzfield.
Married Wed 2d Dec inst, by Rudolph Krysher, esq., Abraham
Henneman, of Monroe twp, Cumberland co, to Miss Mary
Drawrbach, of Fairview twp, York co.
Died in Fredericktown, Md, on 2d inst, Col. John M'Pherson, in
his 69th year, after an illness of a few days. He was a
native of Pennsylvania, came to Frederick in 1781, when he had
just attained the period of manhood. Not long before the
conclusion of the Rev war, he received a Lieutenant's
commisson in the service of his native state, after which he
was appointed agent for the supply of prisoners, quartered in
Frederick. Two years afterwards, he contracted marriage,
which confirmed his residence in Frederick. He was rep in the
State Legislature, and later assoc. judge of Frederick co.

189. Dec 17 1829 (Thursday)
Died Fri last, John D. Wunderlich, of North Middleton twp, aged
72 years, 1 mo.
- On Fri last, Mrs. Brown, wife of Samuel Brown, of North
Middleton twp. - On Mon last, Mrs. Main, wife of William Main,
senr. of this borough.

190. Dec 24 1829 (Thursday) Married Thurs evening last by Rev
Davis, Jacob Pretz, of Gettysburg, to Miss Mary Dipple, dau of
Michael Dipple, of this borough.
- Tues evening last, by Rev Hyer, William Bair, to Miss Elizabeth
Wunderlich, dau of Mr. S. Wunderlich - all of this borough.
- On Tues last in this borough, by Rev Charles A. Davis, John
Reed, to Miss Mary Manley, both of Mechanicsburg. Died Wed
morning, 16th inst, in his 89th year, Andrew Gray, father of
John Gray, of this borough.
- In Shippensburg, on Fri 11th inst, after a long and tedious
illness, aged about 34 years, Samuel Westley Brandebery,
Printer.
191. Jan 7 1830 (Thursday) Married at Phila on Tues 29th ult by
Rev Livingston, Gad Day, of Carlisle, to Miss Ann De Pui, of
the former place.
- Thurs last by Rev Lochman, of Harrisburg, William Windle, to
Miss Ann Stakemiller, of East-Pennsborough twp, Cumberland co.

- Thurs evening last by Rev John S. Ebaugh, Charles Fleeger, to
Miss Mary Wetzel, both of this borough.
- By same in this borough on Tues last, Christopher Leas, to Miss
Julia Ann Brandt, both of Monroe twp.
- At Phila, on Thurs last by Rev E. Stiles, Wm. B. Hendel,
printer, formerly of Carlisle, to Mrs. Ann Maria Kyle, of
Phila.

192. Jan 21 1830 (Thursday) - Married 13th inst by John S.
Ebaugh, V. D. M., John Burns, to Miss Anna Maria Wunders. Same
day by same, Jacob Wisler, to Miss Elizabeth Black. - all of

Cumberland co.

193. Jan 28 1830 (Thursday) - Married in this borough on Tues
last, by Rev J. S. Ebaugh, Christopher Hursh, of Allen twp,
Cumberland co, to Miss Catharine Sparr, of Monaghon twp, York
co.

194. Feb 11 1830 (Thursday) Married by Rev John S. Ebaugh: 21st,
George Rouse, to Miss Catharine Peffer. 26th, Christian Kost,
to Miss Catharine Spahr. Feb 2d, Samuel Wetzel, to Miss
Rebecca Pekin. 4th, Joseph Ingrane, to Miss Mary Ann Black -
all of Cumberland co.
Married Thurs by Rev John Bryson, John C. Montgomery, Esq. of
Danville, to Miss Debra Kerr, youngest dau of Jacob Kerr, of
Turbut twp, Northumberland co. The day after the marriage
they started in a sleigh from her father's residence, and
proceeded but a short distance when the horses took fright and
upset the sleigh, by which she was thrown against a fence and
killed!

195. Feb 18 1830 (Thursday) Married Tues 2d Feb inst by Rev
Sharp, James Dunlap, of West Pennsborough twp, to Miss
Catharine Kyle, dau of Matthew Kyle, of Dickinson twp.
- On Thurs last by same, James Gillaspie, of West Pennsborough
twp, to Miss Catharine Watson, of Newton twp.
- On Thurs last by Rev Geo. Duffield, Thomas Loudon, of Buffaloe
twp, Perry co, to Miss Sarah Irvine, dau of late John Irvine
of Middlesex, Cumberland co.
- On 28th ult by Rev John Niblock, Isaac Lemons, of Silver
Spring, Cumberland co, to Miss Nancy Eckles, of Shearman's
creek, Perry co.
Died on Fri last, Michael Hoover, sr., of Monroe twp, aged 75
years, 11 mos, 21 days.
- At Natchez, Mississippi, his late residence, on 17 Jan, 1830,
Samuel Duncan, M. D., native of Carlisle. Pa.
- On Sun morning last, William Shannon, Sergeant at Arms of the
Senate of Pa.

196. Feb 25 1830 (Thursday) Married Tues morning 23d inst by Rev
F. Heyer, William M. Leaman, to Miss Catharine, dau of Abraham
Mayer - all of this borough.
Married Sun last, at Clermont Farm, near Carlisle, by I. Todd,
esq., John Carty, of East Pennsborough twp, Mrs. Laughlin,
widow of James Laughlin, formerly of this borough.

197. March 4 1830 (Thursday) - Died Thurs evening last, Mrs.
Zollinger, relict of the late Jacob Zollinger, of this
borough, afflicted with cancer.

198. March 11 1830 (Thursday)
Died Mon last, Mrs. Margaret Noble, aged relict of John Noble,
formerly of this borugh, decd. She has nearly attained her
80th year.
- On Thurs, Col. Geo. R. Horter, transcribing clerk of the

senate.
- At York, Sat morning, very suddenly, Frederick M. Wadsworth,
  Esq., Counsellor at law, and formerly a rep in the state
  legislature, from Perry co.

199. March 18 1830 (Thursday)
Married by Rev F. Heyer, Thurs March 4, John Lutz to Miss
  Catharine Miller. On Tues March 9, by same, William K. Tritt,
  to Miss Catharine Black. On Thurs, March 11, by same, Thomas
  Paxton, to Miss Maria, dau of Samuel Galbraith. - All of this
  co.
Died Sat last, Mrs. Hannah Beetem, in her 29th year, wife of
  George Beetem, of this borough, and dau of Captain John Zinn,
  of this co.

200. March 25 1830 (Thursday)
Died 17th inst in this borough, Mrs. Mary Ann Irvine, in her 90th
  year.
- On Sun last in her 70th year, Mrs. Mary Frank, relict of Jacob
  Frank, decd, of this borough.

201. April 1 1830 (Thursday)
Married Tues evening, March 23, by Rev A. Jones, John B. Nicklin,
  of this borough, to Miss Catherine T., dau of Benjamin
  Pendleton, at Locust Grove, near Charlestown, Jefferson co,
  Va.
- On 23d ult by Rev F. Heyer, Edward Davis, to Miss Jane, dau of
  James Spottswood, sr. of this borough.
Died in Bedford on Sat morning, 27th inst, Hon. John Todd, one of
  the assoc judges of the Supreme court of Pa.

202. April 8 1830 (Thursday)
Married by Rev John S. Ebaugh, 25 March, John Clay to Miss
  Catharine Waggoner; also George Wetzel to Miss Madalen Clauser
  - all of Carlisle and its vicinity.
Married 25 March by Rev J. Shull, Frazier Funk to Miss Elizabeth
  Clay, both of Rye twp, Perry co.
Died Thurs morning, Apr 1, 1830, Mrs. Catharine Traugh, dau of
  late John Roudrock, of Bucks co, Pa, and consort of John
  Traugh, innkeeper, of Carlisle, in her 48th year.
- Sat last in Perry co, Mrs. Catharine Shull, wife of Rev J.
  Shull, and dau of Leonard Keller, of this borough.
- At Phila on 29th ult, Joseph Watson O'Brien, in his 19th year,
  youngest son of the late capt. Richard O'Brien, of the
  vicinity of this place.
- On Sat night, March 27, Joseph Diven, of Tyrone twp, Perry co,
  aged about 40 years.
Sunbury, Apr 3 - Died Sun last in this borough, in his 14th year,
  Jeremiah Snyder, said to have died in consequence of eating
  apple butter that had been put up in earthen crocks which had
  imbibed the glazing, made of red lead. Mr. Snyder, his wife,
  and three others of the family, also used the butter, and
  became very sick.

203. April 15 1830 (Thursday)
Married Thurs last, 8th inst by Rev George Duffield, Abraham
   Lamberton to Miss Margaret E. Clark, both of North-Middleton.
- In the borough of Newville, Thurs, 8th inst by Rev J. Williams,
   Jacob Kinsley, to Miss Charlotte, dau of capt. John Roberts,
   decd.
Died Thurs morning last, Miss Ann Baughman, of this borough, in
   her 23d year.
- 3d inst, at Lancaster, Pa, Samuel Slaymaker, sen., esq. in his
   56th year.
- Sun last, Conrad Kuntz, of N. Middleton twp, in his 73d year.
- At Hamburg, Berks co, on 7th inst, Samuel D. Franks, esq.,
   formerly Pres Judge of the 12th Judicial Dist.

204. April 22 1830 (Thursday)
Married in this borough on Fri last by William Irvine, esq.,
   James Caldwell, of Harrison co, Ohio, to Mrs. Elenor Johnston,
   of Lancaster co, Pa.
Died Sun last, Conrad Hoffman, of this place, occasioned by the
   rupture of a blood vessel, leaving large family.
- On Mon last of the measles, Stephen, son of Edward J.Stiles,
   Esq. of this place, aged about 4 years.
- In South Middleton, Sun last, Samuel Goudy.
- In Berlin, Adams co, on 9 April, Jefferson Stevens, in his 27th
   year.
A letter dated Washington City, Sat night, April 17 ... death of
   Hon. Alexander Smyth, of Virginia, 20 minutes past 12 today,
   at his residence in Washington... from a fever originating in
   a slight cold.

205. April 29 1830 (Thursday)
Married Thurs evening last by Rev Geo. Duffield, David Denwiddie,
   of Taney town, Md., to Miss Sarah Bolander, of Carlisle.
- In this borough, Thurs last by Rev Hyer, John Shanklin, to Miss
   Elizabeth Shofner, both of Harrisburg.
- By same Tues last, Philip W. Seibert, of Chambersburg, to Miss
   Catharine Humell, of Harrisburg.
Died Thurs last, in Monroe twp, Joseph Fleming, old inhabitant of
   Cumberland co.
- On Fri morning, of paralysis, Louis Larsillier, native of
   France, aged about 47 years, for several years a citizen of
   this borough.
- On Tues 20th inst, near Bloom, Richard Smith, aged about 21
   years, son of William Smith, formerly of Carlisle.

206. May 6 1830 (Thursday)
Died Fri last in North Middleton twp, Samuel Fisher, lately of
   this borough.
- Same day, Robert Taylor, son of capt. Robert Taylor, late of
   this borough, decd - aged about 22 years.
Joseph Fleming died Wed, 21 April, in his 72d year. [Long obit.]

207. May 13 1830 (Thursday)
Married Thurs evening last by Rev George Duffield, Dr. Charles R.

Cooper, to Miss Mary, dau of Joseph Hays, all of this borough.
Died 3d inst, of pulmonary affection, aged 21 years, Edward J.
Lowry, of Bellefonte. He graduated at Dickinson College in
1828; entered law, but those habits which he had formed with a
view to usefulness, both to himself and the community,
terminated his earthly career.

208. May 20 1830 (Thursday)
Married 13th inst by Rev Augustus H. Lochman, Benjamin Weiser, to
Miss Maria, dau of Michael Hebeisen, esq. both of this co.
- Same day by same, Alexander Dickerson, son of Joshua Dickerson,
late Secretary of the Land Office, to Miss Catharine, dau of
John Bigler, of Harrisburg.
Died Thurs morning last, in this borough, John W. Salter, musical
instrument maker, of Germantown, Pa., leaving, we are
informed, a widow and 6 children. His remains were deposited
in the public burial ground.

209. May 27 1830 (Thursday)
Married Tues morning, May 4, by Rev F. Heyer, William Yeager, to
Miss Mary Haviser, of this co. On Thurs evening, May 20, by
same, William R. Gregg, to Miss Eliza Bradley, both of this
borough.
- On Tues morning last, by Rev George E. Hare, James Noble,
junr., to Miss Cynthia B. Johnson, both of this borough.
- On Thurs last in this borough, by Rev George E. Hare, Henry
Quigley, to Miss Elizabeth Ann Nabb, both of Harrisburg.
- On Tues evening last, by John Phillips, esq., Thomas M'Dannel,
to Miss Juliann Smith, both of North Middleton twp.
- On 18th inst by Rev Moody, David Witherspoon of Frankin co, to
Miss Massian Carothers, of Cumberland co.
- On 22d ult at Marietta, by S. Cook, esq, Charles Samuel
Swartwout Barton, of Belmont co, Ohio, to Miss Mary Wilhelmine
Fustin Caroline Louis Fredericke Zeigler, of Marietta.
Died Thurs last, Mrs. Sarah Neidich, wife of Samuel Neidich, of
this borough.
- On Thurs last in Newton twp, George Grayson, formerly of this
borough.
- On Sun last, at an advanced age, Mrs. Johnston, of this
borough.

210. June 3 1830 (Thursday)
Married Thurs last by Rev Williamson, William Kline, formerly of
this borough, to Miss Abigail Wyeth, of Harrisburg.
- On Wed, 19 May, ult by Rev A. Sharp, Moses Kirkpatrick, of
Franklin co, to Miss Margaret M'Cune, of Newton twp,
Cumberland co.
- On Mon evening last by Rev Samuel Brison, James Spottswood, to
Miss Margaret Kants, of this borough.
- On Mon evening last by Rev Wm. R. De Witt, James M'Cormick,
esq., to Miss Eliza Buehler, both of Harrisburg.
- On Tues, May 25, by Rev Zacharias, Frederick May, to Mrs.
Christina Yaengst, both of Cumberland co.
Died Sun last, John Gordon, of this borough. Greensburg Gazette

- At Robstown, in this co, on Fri last, an affray took place
  between William Nash and Robert Fleming, both of that place,
  which resulted in the death of the former. Fleming was
  immediately arrested.

211. June 10 1830 (Thursday)
Married Tues morning last by Rev P. Dwen, John Faller, to Miss
  Maria Snyder, both of this borough.
- On Sun 30th ult by George Monroe, esq. Charles Orwan, to Miss
  Mary E. M'Dowell, both of Juniata twp, Perry co.

212. June 17 1830 (Thursday)
Died Sun evening, 6th inst, Mrs. Nancy Piper, consort of Andrew
  Piper, of Springfield, leaving an infant of two week, and
  husband.
- Recently at his residence in Greene co, at an advanced age,
  Isaac Weaver, Esq., formerly speaker of the House of Rep of
  this state, from Nov. 1800 to Feb 1803, when he was appointed
  State Treasurer, in the room of Jacob Carpenter, decd.

213. June 24 1830 (Thursday)
Died Tues 15th inst, Col. Thomas Sharp, of Newton twp, aged about
  28 years.
- On Sat last at Landisburg, Perry co, A. Fulweiler, esq. Being
  heated, he drank copiously of cold water, which, it is
  supposed, caused a spasmodic affection of the stomach, which
  terminated his existence. At Norfolk, Sun morning, 13th inst,
  Lieut. Col. William Anderson, of the U.S. Marine Corps, after
  a short but violent attack of the putrid sore throat. A dau
  of Col. Anderson died the next morning about 2 o'clock. This
  is the second dau buried within 7-8 days, being attacked with
  the same disease. Henry Prizer, tailor of Millerstown, Perry
  co, aged about 40 years, drowned Mon last in the old lock at
  North's Island, whilst engaged in fishing with a hook and
  line. He left a wife and several small children. Perry
  Forester.

214. July 1 1830 (Thursday)
Married Tues June 22, at St. John's Chapel, New York, by Rev Dr.
  Berrian, Rev George Emlen Hare, pastor of the Protestant
  Episcopal Church of Carlisle, to Miss Elizabeth Catharine, dau
  of Right Rev. Bishop Hobart.
Died Thurs last, Mary, infant dau of Peter B. Smith, esq. of this
  borough.

215. July 15 1830 (Thursday) - Died Mon 5th inst at Lewistown,
  Mrs. Jane Thomson, formerly of South Middleton twp, Cumberland
  co, in her 86th year.

216. July 22 1830 (Thursday) York Gazette - Died yesterday in
  this place, Capt. Tillotson, who had been for some time
  engaged in instructing young men of the science of
  self-protection against any antagonist in the shape of man.
  He was found about 3 miles from town in state of derangement.

He was conveyed to the poorhouse, where he died.   Interred in
the Episc graveyard. Another Revolutionary Patriot gone.
Died at the residence of his son, near Newville, Thurs 15th inst,
Philip Duck, in his 84th year.

217.   July 29 1830 (Thursday)
Died Sat last, after a lingering illness, Mrs. Mary M'Pherson, in
her 39th year, wife of Robert M'Pherson of this borough. On
Sun an inquest was held on the body of Benjamin Job, who was
found dead, near the turnpike about 2 miles west of this
borough.   It is supposed that he must have died a day or two
previously. He had been to town for medicine, which was in
his pocket, and was within a few miles of his home, when he
died.   He was buried the same evening in the public grave yard
of this borough.

218.   Aug 5 1830 (Thursday)
Married evening of 22d ult by Rev D. Steele, Wm. Curriden, of
   Chambersburg, to Miss Elizabeth Deal, of Shippensburg.
- On 29th July by Rev John S. Ebaugh, George Kennedy, to Mrs.
   Jane Smith.   John Wickert to Mrs. Elizabeth M'Cord. And on
   Tues last, Elias Smith to Miss Eveline Stoke - all of the
   vicinity of Carlisle.
Married by P. Laverty, esq. Elijah Rice, to Miss Margaret
   M'Coskry - all of Allen twp.
- On 29th ult by Rev A. H. Lochman, Henry Kilheffer, to Mis Sally
   Shitz; both of Cumberland co.
Died at Harrisburg Wed July 29, after a short illness, Dr. Samuel
   C. Wiestling, aged about 38 years.
- On Thurs last, at Harrisburg, Michael M. M'Kinley, printer, in
   his 28th year.
- In Phila, a few days ago, Stephen Cullen Carpenter, aged 78
   years, well known many years ago, in Charleston, District of
   Columbia, and elsewhere, as a writer for the newspapers, and
   as author of some political works of a more formidable
   character.
- Mon morning last, at Hoguestown, George W. Ewing, formerly a
   resident of this borough.

219.   Aug 19 1830 (Thursday) - Died at Bloomfield, Perry co, on
11th inst, Rev John Niblock, pastor of the several
Presbyterian congregations in the vicinity of that place, aged
about 32 years.

220.   Aug 26 1830 (Thursday)
Married by Rev John S. Ebaugh, Aug 3d, Elias Smith, to Miss
   Ebeline Stohe.   Aug 19th, Jacob Vanasdlen, to Miss Catharine
   Wolf.   Same day, Henry Sides, to Miss Susan Fordrey. Aug 23d,
   Jacob Maxwell, to Miss Elizabeth Ruf. - Tues evening last by
   Rev A. Griffith, James Spottswood, of Newville, to Miss Mary
   House, of the same place.

221.   Sep 2 1830 (Thursday)
Married 31st ult by Rev John S. Ebaugh, Samuel Miller to Miss

Jane Worts.ac.er(?).
Died Thurs morning 26 Aug, after a short but severe illness,
Mary, dau of Mr. B. Kennedy, of North Middleton twp, aged 10
years, 8 mos, 22 days. On the morning of 23 Aug she
discovered symptoms of indisposition, an intermitting bilious
fever.
- Sun 22d ult, In Silver-spring twp, Jacob Kast, in his 68th
year.
- On 19th ult, Mrs. Mary M'Murray, aged about 58 years, wife of
Thomas M'Murray, innkeeper, of this borough.
- At Fort Armstrong, Rock Island (Upper Mississippi) on 27 July,
ult, Dr. John Gale, Surgeon, U.S. Army, aged 35 years.
- Sun last, James Shannon, Esq., of Mifflin twp.

222. Sep 9 1830 (Thursday)
Married by Rev John S. Ebaugh, on 2d Sep, John Hoover, to Mrs.
Mary Martin, both of Mechanicsburg. Jacob Shriver, to Miss
Susan Stout. Peter Minich, to Miss Elizabeth Wolf. John
Ebright to Miss Catharine Kiehl.
Died at Middlesex, North Middleton twp, Mon morning last, Mrs.
Rachael Bell, widow of Robert Bell, decd, aged about 67 years.
- Tues 31st Aug last at his farm near Butler, Pa, James Bredin,
senr., (father of James Bredin, merchant of Carlisle), aged
about 87 years.

223. Sep 16 1830 (Thursday) - Died Sun evening last, Henry
Cornman, blacksmith, aged 54 years, 5 days, of North Middleton
twp.

224. Sep 30 1830 (Thursday) - Died at the Poor House in this co,
21 Sep inst, Mrs. Hester Baker, native of New Jersey, aged 109
years.

225. Oct 7 1830 (Thursday)
Died at Pittsburg, 21st ult, aged 55 years, Mrs. Mary Kennedy,
consort of John Kennedy, Esq. and dau of Hon. John Creigh,
late of this borough, decd.
- On Sun last in this borough, Mrs. Hall,of a few days' illness,
aged about 58 years.
- Near Mount Rock, on 1st inst, Miss Mary Stewart, aged 31 years.

226. Oct 14 1830 (Thursday)
Married Thurs 7th inst by Rev Duffield, Rev John M. Krebs, to
Miss Sarah Holmes, dau of Andrew Holmes of this borough.
- At the city of Lancaster, Tues morning last by Rev Richards, of
New Holland, the Hon. William Line of Cottage Mill Farm, to
Mrs. Catharine King, of Harrisburg.
Died Thurs morning last, David Rowan, of this borough, aged about
86 years; among the first residents of this place.
- At his late residence in Dickinson twp, Fri evening, 8th inst,
James Stuart, esq. in his 53d year, kind brother, just
magistrate, professor of religion.
- At Reading, Tues Oct 5, Hon. Frederick Smith, one of the Judges
of the Supreme Court.

227. Oct 28 1830 (Thursday)
Died 17th inst at his residence in Potter twp, Centre co, Samuel
Armor, formerly of this borough, in his 44th year.
- On 17th inst, in Dickinson twp, Mrs. Peffer, aged 77 years, and
the next morning, her husband, Philip Peffer, aged 83 years.
- On Fri night last, Mrs. Ann Catharine Keller, aged 70 years, 6
months, 22 days, wife of Leonard Keller, of this borough. For
a long time she lingered under disease.

228. Nov 4 1830 (Thursday)
Died Sun morning Oct 24, in this town, aged 43 years, Mrs. Nancy
Roddy, consort of Josiah Roddy, Esq., Sheriff of Perry Co.
- Recently, at Landisburg, at an advanced age, Mrs. West, relict
of Edward West, formerly of that place. Perry Forester.
Orphan's Court notice to all heirs and legal representatives of
Henry Holler, late of Mifflin twp, Cumberland co: widow
Holler; Sarah, who married Christian Zollinberger; Henry
Holler; John Holler; Susan who married John Kuntz; Jeremiah
Holler; Catharine who married Joseph Henly; Elizabeth Holler
and Lavinia Holler, who have Samuel Westheffer as their
guardian.

229. Nov 18 1830 (Thursday)
Married by Rev John S. Ebaugh: - On 9 Sep, Jacob Sheely, to Miss
Elizabeth Eberly, near Mechanicsburg.
- On 14th, Thomas Kincaid, to Mrs. Susan Noel, of the vicinity of
Carlisle.
- On 16th, John Main, to Miss Elizabeth Reehm, of Carlisle.
- On 21st, George Thornburger, to Miss Sophia Oldwein, of
Hagerstown, Md.
- On 7 Oct, Andrew Holmes, to Miss Nancy Low, of Carlisle.
- On 12th, William Zeigler, to Miss Susan Rhodes, of Newville.
- On 19th, John Palm to Miss Susanna Klink, of Stoughstown.
- On 28th ult at Lewis town, by Rev J. Bennet, Rev Samuel Bryson,
of Carlisle, to Mrs. Mary Patterson, of Lewistown.
Died Fri last, aged upwards of 92 years, Martin Kitch, of North
Middleton twp.
- On Sun morning last, Jacob Wise, of South Middleton twp, aged
85 years, 9 mos, 5 days. He was in usual health the day
before, intending to attend the funeral of an old friend, Mr.
Kitch.
- On Mon last, Adam Cornman, of North Middleton twp.

230. Nov 25 1830 (Thursday)
Married by Rev John S. Ebaugh, on 28th ult, Philip Wareheim to
Miss Ra'l Duey. - On 11th inst John Slonecker to Miss
Elizabeth Phillips. - On 18th John Barenbaugh to Miss
Elizabeth Brandt. - On same day, Thomas Harris to Miss
Elizabeth Secil - all of this co.
Died Tues morning last, John Ramsey, aged about 35 years, son of
Archibald Ramsey, Esq. of this borough.

231. Dec 2 1830 (Thursday)
Married Thurs 1st by Rev A. Griffith, William Delap to Miss
   Susanna Doll, of Adams co.
- On Tues evening last, by Rev R. Bryson, Jonathan Bierbower, to
   Miss Lucetta Carey, both of this borough.
Died Sun morning last in this borough, John Clark, native of
   Ireland; remains deposited in the Catholic Church yard.
- Same morning, John Hackett, innkeeper, of this borough, leaving
   wife and several children.

232. Dec 23 1830 (Thursday)
Married Thurs 9th inst, in this borough, by Rev A. Griffith, John
   Spangler, to Miss Ann Delap, both of Adams co.
- On 7th inst, by Rev John S. Ebaugh, Solomon Smires(?) to Miss
   Rachel Shur.
- On 16th inst by same, Thomas Humes, to Miss Leah Wortz, of
   Carlisle.
- On Tues last by Rev Shaeffer, Frederick Williams, to Miss Susan
   Rheem, both of North Middleton twp.

233. Dec 30 1830 (Thursday) - Another Rev. Patriot Gone - Died
   Sun 19th inst at his residence in Mifflin twp, William
   Denning, in his 94th year. He was an artificer in the army of
   the Rev. He made the only successful attempt ever made in the
   world to manufacture wrought iron cannon, two of which he
   completed at Middlesex in this county and commenced another
   and larger one at Mount Holly, but could get no one to assist
   him who could stand the heat, which is said to have been so
   great as to melt the lead buttons on his clothes. This
   unfinished piece, it is said, lies as he left it, at either
   Holly Forge or the Carlisle Barracks. One of those completed
   was taken by the British at the battle of Brandywine and is
   now in the Tower of London. He was able to walk to the
   village of Newville, 2 miles from his residence, until 6
   months ago.

- - - - -

DEMOCRATIC REPUBLICAN

Democratic Republican, and Farmer's Museum (Published at
Carlisle). The name of the newspaper was changed to Democratic
Republican and Agricultural Register with the Jan 21 1825 issue
(volume 1, No. 1)

Issues held by the Library of Congress

234. Jan 14 1825 (Friday) - Married Thurs evening 7th inst by
   Rev S. R. Vinton, Samuel Clark, to Miss Nancy Kid, all of
   this place.

235. Jan 21 1825 (Friday) - Married on Sat 8th inst, by Rev D.
Lochman, Jacob Harman to Miss Margaret Stener, both of this co.

236. Feb 2 1825 (Wednesday)
Married Thurs last by Rev J. S. Ebaugh, William Sanderson to Miss
Hannah Wolf, both of North Middleton twp of this co.
- Same day by Rev D. Hassinger, Fred Reib, to Miss Maria King,
both of Newton twp.

237. Feb 16 1825 (Wednesday)
Died Sun evening last at an advanced age, Peter Black, of this
co.
- Yesterday at the residence of his mother, Jacob Miller, sadler
of this borough.
- This morning, Peter Fishburn, an old inhabitant of this co.

238. March 9 1825 (Wednesday) - Married Thurs last by Rev B.
Keller, Moses Brownsberger to Miss Mary Spanger, all of this
co.

239. March 16 1825 (Wednesday)
Married Tues evening last by Rev B. Keller, John Dunbar, of
Frankford twp to Miss Mary Rowland, of this place.
- On Sun evening last, Alexander P. Grimes, to Miss Jane Miller,
both of this borough

240. April 13 1825 (Wednesday)
Died Thurs last, James Carothers of West-Pennsboro' twp.
- On Mon, Henry Moudy, of this town.

241. June 15 1825 (Wednesday) - Died Sun last in South Middleton
twp, Mrs. Regina Belshoover, consort of George Belshoover, in
her 58th year.

242. July 13 1825 (Wednesday) - Died Sat 9th inst, Christian
Leonard, aged 75 years, officer of the Am. Rev.

243. July 27, 1825 (Wednesday) - Died Mon 17th inst in
Manchester twp, York co, Mrs. Witrecht, widow, at an advanced
age.

244. Aug 10 1825 (Wednesday)
Married on 4th ult by Rev B. Keller, John Hatten, to Miss
Elizabeth Sipplinger, all of South Middleton. -
On same day by same, John Saltzgeber, to Miss Catharine Dyse, all
of South Middleton.
- On Mon evening last by Rev Griffith, Mr. Lutz, Printer, to Mrs.
Harry, both of that place. - On Tues 28th ult by Rev Samuel
Helfenstein, Rev Augustus H. Lochman, of Harrisburg, to Miss
Ann Maria, dau of Mr. A. Partenheimer, of Phila.

245. Sep 7 1825 (Wednesday) - Died Thurs morning last, Mrs.
Nancy Goudy, dau of John Traugh of this place.

246. Oct 12 1825 (Wednesday) - Married on 6th inst by Rev B.
Keller, Samuel Meyer to Miss Rebecca Deerdorff, both of
Frankford.

247. Nov 2 1825 (Wednesday)
Married Wed evening, 19th inst by Rev George Duffield, Joseph H.
Kuhns, esq. of Greensburg, to Miss Margaret Elizabeth
Alexander, of this borough.
- On 18 Oct, inst, by Rev Platt, Rev James Williamson, of
Silverspring, to Miss Phebe Maria, youngest dau of Dr. Stephen
Hopkins, of Athens, Pa.
- On Tues 25th ult, George Spangler, to Miss Elizabeth Early, all
of this place.
- On Tues 25th ult, at Newville, by Rev Williams, Robert M'Cord
of this place to Miss Margaret Woodburn, dau of Major
Woodburn, decd, of the former.
- On Tues last by Rev A. M'Clelland, V. D. M., William Alexander,
to Miss Mary Lightcap, both of Kingstown, Cumberland co.
- On 20th ult by Rev B. Keller, Samuel Miller to Miss Elizabeth
Smyer.
- On same day by same, John Brownewell of Eastpennsboro' to Miss
Ann Krill, of Monroe.
- On 26th by same, John Rausch, of Liverpool Perry Co, to Mrs.
Catharine Koser of Frankford.
- On 27th by same, Peter Moers, of Reading to Miss Maria Rudisile
of this place.

248. Nov 9 1825 (Wednesday)
Married Thurs last, 3d inst by Rev B. Keller, John Fengal to Mrs.
Cath. Bailer, both of Tyrone twp, Perry co.
- On same day by same, George Longsdorf to Miss Eliza Hackett,
all of Silver-spring twp, Cumberland co.
- On same day by same, George Werts of York co, to Miss Maria
Lau, of Northmiddleton twp, Cumberland co.
Died Wed last, Mrs. Fosler, consort of George Fosler.
- On Fri morning last, Nicholas Swords, at an advanced age.

249. Nov 16 1825 (Wednesday)
Married 15th inst by Rev B. Keller, John Miller to Miss Margaret
Epply, both of Allen twp,
- On same day by same, Daniel Rudy, to Miss Catharine Wolf, both
of Monroe twp.

250. Nov 30 1825 (Wednesday)
Married 17th inst by Rev B. Keller, Abraham Miller, to Miss
Elizabeth Spang.
- On same day by same, George Zeigler, to Miss Sarah Sower.
- On 27th inst by same, John Malister, to Miss Mary Hays, both of
this place.
- On Thurs 10th inst by Rev Augustus H. Lochman of
Mechanicksburg, Isaac Greybill to Miss Polly Leidig, both of
Cumberland co.
- On Thurs last by Rev George Lochman, Furgus R. Kernan, to Miss
Elizabeth Shoemaker, both of this co.

251. Dec 7 1825 (Wednesday)
Married Thurs evening last by Rev J. S. Ebaugh, John Lechler, to

Miss Rebecca Cowfer, both of this place.
Died at Wilmington, Del, on 25th ult, Evan Thomas, Esq., of the
Bank of Wilmington and Brandywine.

252. Dec 14 1825 (Wednesday) - Married in Mechanicksburg, Thurs
last by Rev George Duffield, Matthew Moore of Southmiddleton
twp, to Miss Sarah Warren, formerly of Baltimore.

253. Dec 21 1825 (Wednesday) - Died Sat 17th inst after a short
but severe illness, George Wike, of this co, near Newville,
aged 44 years, 3 mos, 15 days, leaving a widow and 9 children.

254. Jan 11 1826 (Wednesday)
Married at Greensburg on 20th ult by Rev Speer, Maj. George
Gallagher, merchant of this place to Miss Mary Ann Horbach,
dau of Abraham Horbach of the former place.
Died Sun last, Robert Blean, old citizen of this co.
- On Tues 10th inst Francis Gaullagher, of a lingering illness. A
fatal quarrel took place on Christmas day, at Mr. Hughes'
Mount Alto Iron Works, between a white man name Pennell and a
black man, slave of Mr. Hughes. Pennell apparently attempted
to strike the black with a shovel who seized what is termed a
ravel, and gave a stroke upon the head of Pennell which
fractured his skull. He lingered until Friday morning
following, leaving a wife and 6 children. The black fellow was
committed to the jail of Franklin co on Fri last.
Gettysburg Sentinel. Gettysburg - An inquest was held Thurs
morning last by Charles F. Kenner, Esq. on the body of William
Young, found dead in Samuel Diehl's mill dam, Menallen twp.
Jury found his death was occasioned by intemperance.

255. Jan 25 1826 (Wednesday) - Died Sun morning last after a
lingering illness, Mrs. Jourdon, old inhabitant of this
borough.

256. Feb 1 1826 (Wednesday)
Died Sun last, Michael Pupp, of this co.
- On Sun evening last, Mrs. Putto an old inhabitant of this
place.
- On Thurs last, Mrs. Isabella Wills, consort of Alexander Wills,
Esq. of Cumberland co.
- On Mon evening last, Abraham Rupley [innkeeper - Am. Vol.], of
North Middleton twp, Cumberland co.
- On Tues morning last, Miss Jane M'Clelland, of this place [age
about 18 years - Am. Vol.].

257. Feb 8 1826 (Wednesday)
Died on Sat morning last, Reuben Clippinger, aged about 15 years,
son of John Clippinger, Sh'ff [after a few days illness - Am.
Vol].
- On Mon morning last, Margaretta Porter, aged about 8 years, dau
of William Porter, late of this borough, decd.
- Fri morning, 3d inst, Mrs. Mary Veasey, late of the Eastern

Shore of Md.

258. Feb 15 1826 (Wednesday)
Died this morning, Mrs. Margaret Pringle, wife of Rev F. Pringle,
of this borough, aged 77 years.
- On Fri morning last at an advanced age, Mrs. Kernan, old
inhabitant of this place.

259. Feb 22 1826 (Wednesday)
Died Thurs last of a short illness, John Hershey, aged about 3
years.
- In Shippensburgh on Fri morning last, Dr. Simpson, of that
place.
- On Sat morning last, Mrs. Line, consort of William Line, Esq.

260. March 8 1826 (Wednesday) Col. Stephen Kerr, and his brother
William Kerr, lately of this place, were both drowned in
attempting to descend the Conodoguinet in a boat.
Died Sun morning last, Hugh Johnston, a soldier of the Rev;
interred with military honours.
- On Tues morning last, Mrs. Lease, consort of George Lease,
merchant of this place.

261. March 15 1826 (Wednesday)
Married 9th inst by Rev B. Keller, John Gramlich, to Miss
Catharine Law, both of North Middleton twp.
- On same day by same, William Gill, to Miss Sarah Mussleman,
both of Westpennsborough.
- On 22d ult by Rev James Snodgrass, Wm. F. Geddes, Printer,
formerly of this place, now of Phila to Miss Nancy M'Cormic,
dau of Henry M'Cormic, decd, late of West Hanover, Dauphin co.
Died Sat evening last, Robert M'Cord, of this place.
More details on the deaths of Col. Stephen Kerr and his younger
brother William Kerr. Col. Kerr and his brother, were
reconnoitering in a skiff, the practicability of descending
the Conodoguinet with produce, when they reached
Shallaberger's dam, Col. Kerr was landed, and proceeded ahead,
to ascertain the best mode of passing the fall; while William
who as a skillful boatman, determined to venture alone with
the skiff, in going over the pitch. The boat passed the fall
with great velocity but safely, and William made one or two
pulls with the oars, to carry him beyond the edying current -
It was in vain, the boat was carried back into the deep and
troubled water, immediately filled, and sunk. [Col. Kerr was
drowned in attempting to rescue his brother.] Col. Kerr left
a widow and 2 children.

262. March 29 1826 (Wednesday) - Married Thurs evening last by
Rev J. S. Ebaugh, James Hoffer, to Miss Ann Eliza Kaufman
[Caufman - Am. Vol.], all of this place.

263. April 12 1826 (Wednesday)
Married Wed last by Rev J. Williams, James G. French, of Vevay
(?), Indiana, to Miss Jane Cowen of Cumberland co.

Died Wed last, Miss Nancy Miller, dau of Michael Miller of this
   place.
- Suddenly this morning, Capt. Domminick Cornyn, late of the U.
   S. army, and for many years an active politician of this co.
   He was a native of the county Leitrim, Ireland, where he
   received a liberal education.

264. April 19 1826 (Wednesday)
Married 5th inst by Rev B. Keller, Malon Greist, to Miss Martha
   Pawling, both Harrisburg.
- On 11th inst by same, John Dunbar, to Miss Jane Elizabeth, dau
   of Walter Bell of this place.
- On 13th inst by same, Jacob Ward, to Miss Mary Fister, both of
   North Middleton.

265. April 26 1826 (Wednesday) - Died suddenly on Sabbath, 23d
   inst, while at church, Mrs. Rebecca M'Clure, of this borough.

266. May 3 1826 (Wednesday) - Married 31st ult by Rev B. Keller,
   William Armstrong, to Miss Matilda Agres, both of Harrisburg.

267. May 10 1826 (Wednesday)
Died Sun evening last, Mr. Ogue, Music Master, of this place.
Meeting of relatives of those interred in Old Grave Yard, best
   known by name of the Meeting House Springs, at house of James
   Bell, to chose committee for constructing fence around the
   grave yard.

268. May 17 1826 (Wednesday) - Died in City of Phila, Sun 30th
   ult, Gunning B. Bedford, Editor of the Lancaster
   Intelligencer, in his 26th year.

269. May 24 1826 (Wednesday)
Married on 16th inst by same, John Wolf to Miss Magdalena
   Handshoe, both of North Middleton.
- On 18th by same, Frederick Shally to Miss Sarah Frees, both of
   South Middleton.
- On same day by same, William Morrison, to Miss Catharine Weise,
   both of South Middleton.

270. May 31 1826 (Wednesday)
Married 25th inst by Rev B. Keller, Michael Spangler, to Miss
   Isabella Kerr, both of this place.
- On same by same, Christian Crall, of Dauphin co, to Miss
   Elizabeth Handshoe of Northmiddleton twp.
- On Thurs evening last, by Rev Griffith, William Crop, to Miss
   Rachel Fetterman, all of this place.

271. June 7 1826 (Wednesday)
Married 2d inst by Rev B. Keller, Michael Livingston to Miss
   Susanna Stauffer, of Mechanicsburg.
- On same day by same, Henry M. Brown to Miss Sarah Garman, both
   of North Middleton.
- On 30th ult by Rev B. Keller, Samuel Morret to Miss Mary Grable

[Grebill - Am. Vol.] - near Churchtown.
From the Steubenville Herald. - On Tues evening by Rev Joshua
Monroe, John Hall, to Miss Mary Wampler, dau of Rev Joseph
Wampler, all of this town.

272. June 14 1826 (Wednesday)
Died Sat last, Mrs. Mary Scobey, after a lingering illness, aged
86 years.
- On Sun morning last, John Smith, old inhabitant of this place,
aged 74 years.
- On Sun morning last, Mrs. Catharine Wolf, of this place.
- On Tues last, George Natcher, after a lingering illness, aged
35 years.

273. June 28 1826 (Wednesday)
Married 22d inst by Rev B. Keller, John Shade, to Miss Susan
Allspach, both of Northmiddleton.
- On same day by same, Andrew Hecker, to Miss Charlotte Wahl,
both of this place.

274. July 5 1826 (Wednesday) - Married on Thurs 24 June, by Rev
J. Niblock, Robert Kelley of Baltimore, to Miss Isabella
Patterson, of Perry co.

275. July 12 1826 (Wednesday)
Died Fri evening last, Patrick Fitzimons of Miffin twp,
Cumberland co.
- On Sat last, Mrs. Mitchell of this place.
- On Mon morning last, Rev George Lochman, Pastor of the
Evangelical Lutheran Congregation of Harrisburg.

276. July 19 1826 (Wednesday) -
Married 13th inst by Rev B. Keller, Joseph Kneisely to Miss
Margaret Smith, both of this place.

277. July 26 1826 (Wednesday) - Died Mon afternoon last, Jacob
Keigley, Esq. at an advanced age, old inhabitant of this
place.

278. Aug 9 1826 (Wednesday)
Married 3d inst by Rev B. Keller, Jacob Hershe, of Lancaster co,
to Miss Elizabeth Klepfer of Carlisle.
- On same day by same, Nehemia Underwood Reed, to Miss Julian
Fairs, Perry co. Rev Lochman, D. D. Pastor of Lutheran
congregations of Harrisburg and its vicinity died at his
residence in Harrisburg, Mon morning, 10th ult, in his 53d
year, more than 30 of which had been occupied in the service
of the church; buried in the area in front of the Lutheran
church.
Died in Wayne twp, Mifflin co, 4 July, William Ross, aged 109
years, soldier of Braddock's field in 1755 where he was
slightly wounded. He enlisted at the commencement of the rev
war and was in most of the engagements. Although poor, he
never received a pension. Those with whom he had served were

all dead; his discharge was lost; the pension officers at
Washington were scrupulous.   Juniata Gazette.

279. Aug 16 1826 (Wednesday)
Married at Chambersburg on 1st inst by Rev M'Cosker, Michael
  Boyle, to Miss Sarah Krider, both of Carlisle.
- On Thurs 20 July, by Rev Henry Habliston, George Saderson to
  Miss Louisa Smith, both of Shippensburg.
Died Sun 6th inst after a short illness, Henry Peffer Jr. aged
  about 22 years, son of Henry Peffer of Dickinson twp.
- On Fri last, Solomon Stouffer, near Carlisle. Yesterday
  morning, Mrs. Eyler, wife of Peter Eyler, of this place.

280. Aug 23 1826 (Wednesday)
Married Thurs evening last by Rev Duffield, Andrew Comfort, to
  Miss Priscilla Murray, both of this place.
- On 10th inst by Rev B. Keller, Elias Berlin, to Miss Hannah
  Brancher, both of South Middleton.
- On 17th inst by same, Christian Klink, to Miss Maria Failor,
  both of North Middleton.
- On Tues 15th inst by Rev Hoffmeir, Capt. Daniel R. Keller, of
  Lebanon and lately of this place, to Miss Mary Heitshu, dau of
  Philip Heitshu, Esq. of Lancaster, Pa.
Died Fri last in Allen twp, Mrs. Shaw, at an advanced age.

281. Aug 30 1826 (Wednesday)
Married Thurs evening last by Rev B. Keller, Andrew Brumbaugh, to
  Miss Rosanna Kauffman, both of this place.
- On same day by Hugh McMullin, Levi Gribble of Allen twp,
  Cumberland co, to Miss Mary Wilson, of Monaghan twp, York co.

282. Sep 6 1826 (Wednesday)
Died suddenly near Newville, Sun morning last, Mrs. Lacy Conally,
  relict of Joseph Conally, decd. He was born about 7 miles
  west of Carlisle in 1743, when there was scarcely a white
  inhabitant west of this town; her father, Adam Hays, having
  been one of the first settlers.
Married Sun last by Rev B. Keller, Jacob Kutz, to Miss Sarah
  Fought, both of North Middleton twp.

283. Sep 13 1826 (Wednesday) - Married last evening by Rev
George Duffield, Peter B. Smith, Esq. to Miss Mary Scoby, both
of this place.

284. Sep 20 1826 (Wednesday)
Married Thurs last by Rev J. S. Ebaugh, John Brown, to Miss
  Catharine Shombarger.
- Same day by same, J. Hartman, to Miss M. Roudebaugh. - Same day
  by same, Baltzer Lutz, to Miss Nancy Ebey.
- On 17th by same, Christian Waltzer, to Miss Eve Cairns.
- On Thurs evening last by Rev Dr. Neil, John Rudecill, to Miss
  Elizabeth Sharretts.
- On Thurs evening last by Rev G. Duffield, Mr. Flemming, to Miss
  Elizabeth Henwood.

285. Oct 4 1826 (Wednesday)
Died Wed Sep 27, after a short illness, Mrs. Isabella Barkley,
    wife of Robert Barkley, of this place, in her 74th year.
- On Tues morning last, John Butterfield, esq., Post-Master at
    Landisburg, Perry co.

286. Oct 11 1826 (Wednesday)
Died Tues morning last, at an advanced age, Mrs. Myers, of this
    place.
- On Wed last in Richmond twp, in Berks co, Thomas Dum killed
    John Fry by breaking his skull with the but of a gun. Dun
    has fled and not seen since. Times.

287. Oct 25 1826 (Wednesday)
Married Thurs last by Rev Benjamin Keller, Jacob Weise to Miss
    Sarah Finegal, both of S. Middleton.
- Same day by same, John Anthony, to Miss Margaret Potts of North
    Middleton.
- On same day by same, Eli Miller, to Miss Eliza Frazier, both of
    Perry co.

288. Nov 8 1826 (Wednesday)
Married 22d by Rev B. Keller, Michael Wauger, to Miss Sophia
    Weber, both of this co.
Died Tues last, after a short illness, James Baxter, of this
    place.
289. Nov 15 1826 (Wednesday)
Married 7th inst by Rev B. Keller, Michael Weber of South
    Middleton to Mrs. Ann Reiff of Silverspring twp.
- On 10th inst by same, Jacob Schleider to Mrs. Fanny Gosweiler,
    both of Mechanicsburg.
- On same day by same, Adam Luts of Lancaster co, to Miss Lydia
    Sensaman of Silverspring.

290. Nov 29 1826 (Wednesday)
On 18th inst James Quinn was found guilty of murdering in the
    first degree in Lebanon, Pa, of murdering his wife; sentenced
    to death.
Married by Rev A. H. Lochman of Mechanicksburg on 7 Nov, Jacob
    Schwartz, to Miss Maria Longanecher both of Eastpennsboro.
- On 14th by same, Abraham Dehoff of York co to Miss Maria Lynch,
    of Cumberland.
- On 23d inst by same, Robert Dunbar, to Miss Christina May, both
    of East Pennsborough twp, Cumberland co.
- On Tues evening last by Rev Dwen, Jacob Faust, to Miss
    Elizabeth Lechler, dau of Henry Lechler, Esq., all of this
    borough.

291. Jan 10 1827 (Wednesday) - Died Mon 1st inst in Dickinson
    twp, of a pulmonary disease, Mrs. Sarah Lamb, consort of David
    Lamb, in her 35th year, leaving husband and 4 small children,
    sister and brothers.

292.   Jan 17 1827 (Wednesday) - Died Tues 9th inst at his late
residence about 4 miles West of Carlisle, John Line, old
inhabitant of this co.

293.   Jan 24 1827 (Wednesday)
Married 11th inst by Rev B. Keller, Lewis Kline, to Miss Barbara
Glime, both of Monroe twp.
- On same day by same, George Group of Hundington twp, to Miss
Lehna Mowrer, of South Middleton.
- On 18th inst by same, George Beltzhoover of Monroe twp, to Mrs.
An Maria Gross, of Eastpennsboro.
Died Tues morning last, John R. Lockerman, bookseller, of this
place.
- On Sat 13th inst in East Pennsborough twp, George Sailor,
formerly Innkeeper of this place, of a pulmonary complaint.

294.   Jan 31 1827 (Wednesday)
Married 23d by Rev B. Keller, Christian Fehler, to Miss Margaret
Stoneberger, both of Frankfort twp.
- On 25th inst by same, Henry Kryder, to Miss Elizabeth
Hauenstine, both of West Pennsborough.

295.   Feb 7 1827 (Wednesday) - Married Tues last by Rev George
Duffield, Daniel Holmes, to Miss Mary Giffin, dau of James
Giffin, Esq., all of North Middleton twp.

296.   Feb 14 1827 (Wednesday)
Married Wed evening 7th inst at residence of John De Pue, esq. in
Harrisburg by Rev John Herbst, of Gettysburg, Andrew G.
Miller, Esq. Atty at Law, of Gettysburg, to Miss Caroline E.
Kurtz, dau of Benjamin Kurtz, Esq. formerly of Harrisburg.
Died suddenly on Fri, 9th inst, Danial N. Pumroy, of
Shippensburg, of Erysipelas.

297.   March 7 1827 (Wednesday)
Married Wed last by Rev B. Keller, Jacob Musselman of West Penns-
borough twp, to Mrs. Sarah Tobias, of Frankford twp.
Died Wed last, Michael Ege, proprietor of Spring Forge.

298.   March 14 1827 (Wednesday)
Married 27th ult by Rev B. Keller, Robert Ruppley of South
Middleton, to Miss Margaret Fought of North Middleton.
- On 6th inst by same, Christian Dumma, to Miss Hannah Coler,
both of North Middleton.
- On 8th inst by same, Henry Zearing of Newburg, to Miss
Elizabeth Eigleberger, of East Pennsborough.

299.   March 28 1827 (Wednesday)
Married Thurs evening last by Rev Grifith, Thomas Brown to Miss
Margaret Phillips, both of this place.
- On 13th inst by Rev B. Keller, Rudolph Hess, to Miss Ann Maria
Wild.
- On 15th inst by same, George Heckman, to Miss Catharine Stum,
both of this place.

- On same day by same, Andrew M. Carney to Miss Catharine M'Fadden, both of this place.
- On 20th by same, Adam West to Miss Agnes Barnet of Mifflin twp.
- On 22d by same, Joseph Brownewell to Miss Fanny Brand.
Died Sun morning last after a lingering illness, Wm. Walker of this place.
- Yesterday morning about 5 o'clock, Frederick Emanuel, infant son of Rev Benjamin Keller.

300. April 4 1827 (Wednesday)
Married Mon evening last by Rev B. Keller, Gabrial Line, to Miss Mary Peffer, both of Dickinson twp.
Died suddenly Thurs evening last, Mrs. Jane Alexander of this place. Cross-creek twp, Washington co, Pa.
- On Sat evening, 17th inst, about midnight, Mrs. Hannah Buchanan, left her residence in a disordered state of mind and has not been seen since. Any information on her given to any person in West Middletown will relieve a number of distressed relatives and an anxious neighborhood. She is about 42, of middle stature, black eyes and hair.

301. April 11 1827 (Wednesday) - Died Mon evening last, Christian Leib, of this place.

302. April 25 1827 (Wednesday)
Married Tues evening last by Rev Joseph Spencer, Captain Samuel A. M'Coskry, to Miss Eliza Montgomery, both of this place.
- On 19th by Rev B. Keller, Moses Mundorff, of York co, to Miss Cosiah Coopperstone, near this place.

303. May 2 1827 (Wednesday)
Married in this place on Tues 24 April by Rev Joseph Spencer, Samuel A. M'Coskry, Esq. to Miss Eliza L. Montgomery, dau of the late Dr. Thomas W. Montgomery of N.Y.
- On Tues 17th ult by Rev Hassinger, Henry Givler, of Westpennsborough, to Miss Rebecca Line, of Dickinson twp.

304. May 9 1827 (Wednesday)
Married Tues 17th ult by Rev D. Stroh, (and not by Rev Hassinger, as stated in our last) Henry Givler of Westpennsborough, to Miss Rebecca Line, of Dickinson twp.
Died Sat last Miss Mary Brandt, dau of William Brandt, of this borough. In Phila, at midnight 29th ult, Hon. Wm. Tilghman, chief justice of the Supreme Court of Pa, in his 71st year.

305. May 16 1827 (Wednesday)
Married on 3d inst by Rev Benjamin Keller, Jacob Forney, to Miss Elizabeth Senseman, both of Silverspring.
- On 8th by same, Ephraim Colestock, to Miss Hannah Boon, both of Harrisburg.
- On same day by same, John Bauman, to Mrs. Maria Shamback, both of Frankford.

306. May 23 1827 (Wednesday)
Married in Dillstown on Thurs evening last by Rev Williamson of
    silver spring, John Cresler, of Carlisle, to Miss Mary Jones
    of the former place.
- In Baltimore on Sun evening 15th inst, by Right Rev Bishop
    Kemp, Geo. Leas, merchant of Carlisle, to Hester Maria,
    youngest dau of the late Dr. Jacob Ringgold of Baltimore.
Died Thurs morning last of a consumption Catharine Miller, dau of
    Michael Miller of this place.

307. May 30 1827 (Wednesday) - At a late military training in
    Pike twp, Bradford Co, Pa, a man named Evetts, aged 73, was
    killed by Nathaniel Platt. Previous to the murder, Platt had
    nearly gouged out the old man's eyes.

308. June 6 1827 (Wednesday)
Married 31st ult by Rev B. Keller, Thomas M'Quoid, to Margaret
    Wall, both of Harrisburg.
- On same day by same, Jacob Biship to Miss Margaret Sweitzer, of
    Allen twp.
- In Harrisburg on Thurs last by Rev De Witt, Rev Daniel McKinley
    of Bedford to Miss Mary Wyeth, dau of John Wyeth, editor of
    the Oracle.
Died Sat morning 26th ult, James Carothers of this place.
- In Martinsburg, Va., Tues 29th ult, aged about 27 years,
    William Delancey, son of John Delancey, Esq. of this borough.

309. June 13 1827 (Wednesday)
Died Thurs last, Mrs. Wright, wife of Robert Wright of this
    place.
- On Sat last, William Levis, Esq., aged 85, soldier of the
    revolution; buried with military honours.
- Fri last at Spring Forge, John Filey; bur. with Masonic honors.

310. June 20 1827 (Wednesday)
Married Thurs evening last by Rev George Duffield, Parker
    Simison, to Miss Maria Humerich, dau of Christian Humerich,
    all of this place.
- On 16th by Rev B. Keller, John Whealer, to Miss Ann Kenny, both
    of York co.
Died Tues morning last of consumption, aged 64 years, Mrs. Sarah
    Blair, relict of William Blair, formerly of this borough.

311. June 27 1827 (Wednesday) - Died Fri last of consumption,
    aged about 48 years, Dr. John Fahnestock, of this borough.

312. July 4 1827 (Wednesday) - Died Fri 29 June, aged 53 years,
    Mrs. Rachel Bovard, wife of Charles Bovard, Esq. of Perry co,
    wife and mother.

313. July 11 1827 (Wednnesday) - Died suddenly from the kick of
    a horse at his residence near new London Cross Roads, George
    Duffield, Esq., late Comptroller General of Commonwealth, many
    years an inhabitant of this city, in 61st year. Lanc. Exam.

314. July 25 1827 (Wednesday) - Married on 19th inst by Rev B. Keller, Daniel Rupp, to Miss Caroline K. D'Aristede, both of Mechanicksburg, Cumberland co.

315. Aug 1 1827 (Wednesday)
Married in Newville Thurs evening last by Rev Williams, John Halbert, of this borough, to Miss Eliza Ann Crotzer, of the former place.
- On Fri evening last, William S. Vanderbelt, returning home from the river with a load of shingles, stopped his wagon about 1 mile this side of Newville, for the purpose of locking the wheel, when going to descend a hill; the horses started before he was prepared, when running forward to stop them, he was thrown down and the wheels passed over him which caused his immediate death.

316. Aug 22 1827 (Wednesday) - Died at Pittsburgh, Sun morning, 12th inst, in his 30th year, Col. John M'Farland, editor of the Allegheny Democrat.

317. Aug 29 1827 (Wednesday)
Married at Lancaster, on 18th inst, by Rev Dr. Endress, Rev Ludwig Mayer, Professor in the Theological Seminary at Carlisle, to Miss Maria Smith, of Lancaster.
- On Thurs 22d inst, by Rev J. S. Ebaugh, Capt. John Sailor, to Mrs. Susan Westheffer, of this co.

318. Sep 12 1827 (Wednesday)
Died Fri last of consumption, in her 20th year, Miss Eliza Crain, of this borough.
- On Mon morning last, in his 52nd year, Joseph Knox, merchant, of this borough.
- On 8th inst, Mrs. Nancy Hays, consort of Joseph Hays of this borough, aged 55 years.

319. Sep 19 1827 (Wednesday)
Died 3d inst at Williamsport, Washington co, Pa, in his 72d year, Hugh Wilson, formerly a merchant of this place.
Married Thurs morning, 6th inst in St. John's Church in this place, by Rev Professor Spencer, Frederick Watts, Esq. of this borough, to Miss Eliza Marcia Gold Cranston, of Mervan, Newcastle co, Del.
- On Tues 4th inst at Harrisburg, by Rev A. H. Lochman, Valentine Kettering, to Mrs. Mary Lechler, both of the vicinity of this place.
- On 5th inst by Rev B. Keller, Geo. Waler, to Miss Mary Sherer.
- On 6th inst by same, Mathew Bags, to Miss Elizabeth Hardy.
- On same day by same, Samuel Miller, to Miss Hetty Sloneaker, both of Kinstown.

320. Oct 10 1827 (Wednesday)
Married Wed 26th ult by Rev Dr. J. M. Mason, Rev Erskine Mason, pastor of the First Presbyterian Church in Schenectady, N.Y.

to Mary, dau of the late Dr. Samuel A. M'Coskry, of this
place.
Died Sun morning, 30th Sep, after a short severe illness, Rev Dr.
Endress, pastor of the Lutheran church of Lancaster city, in
his 53d year, leaving widow and children.

321. Oct 24 1827 (Wednesday)
Married Thurs 11th inst at Springfield by Rev A. Sharp, Samuel
Henry of Dickinson twp, to Miss Eliza M'Neal of
Westpennsborough, all of this co.
Died Sat morning 13th inst, Jacob Goodhart, sen, old inhabitant
of Dickinson twp.

322. Oct 31 1827 (Wednesday) - Married at Williamsport, Lycoming
co, Tues 16 Oct, by Rev Henry Lenhart, James P. Bull (Editor
of the Bradford Settler) of Towanda, Bradford co, to Miss Ann
E. Wallis, of Williamsport, dau of Major Joseph J. Wallis.

323. Nov 14 1827 (Wednesday)
Married 8th inst by Rev Benjamin Keller, George Bander to Miss
Mary Ann Snyder, both of East Pennsborough.
- Same day by same, Jacob Bosler, to Miss Margaret Long,
Dickinson twp.

324. Nov 21 1827 (Wednesday) - Died in Newville, Fri last, about
40 years of age, Miss Ann Gillaspie.

325. Nov 28 1827 (Wednesday) - Died Sun 4th inst at Col. Noble's
Hotel in Lancaster, Ohio, J. C. Hippius, a stranger. He
arrived at Col. Noble's in very ill health, in the Columbus
hack on Tues evening 30th ult. On the same night he was
seized with a species of appoplexy at which time he spoke but
once when he mentioned his name. From his papers he appears
to have been a travelling trader in Pa, Ohio, and Indiana,
about 40 years of age, about 6 feet, German or Swiss.

326. Dec 5 1827 (Wednesday)
Married 25 Oct last by Rev J. S. Ebaugh, John Heagy to Miss Sarah
Weibley.
- On 30th by same, Henry Stump, to Miss Margaret Beistlein.
- On 8 Nov by same, John Suesholz, to Miss Leah Hinner.
- On 15th by same, Jacob Sholly, to Miss Sophia Steinauer.
- On 22d by same, Andrew Washmood, to Miss Eliza Greason.
- On 29th by same, Wm. Smith, to Miss Catharine Crocket, all of
the vicinity of Carlisle.
Died in Haines twp, Centre co, Fri 23 Nov, Adam Harper, Esq. one
of the Assoc. Judges of that co, aged upwards of 70 years.
- On Wed 28th Nov. Samuel Mohler, esq. a Rep elect from Lancaster
co, in the State Legislature.

327. Jan 2 1828 (Wednesday)
Married on 27th ult by Rev B. Keller, John Eby to Miss Elisabeth
Schaeffer, both of South Middleton.
- On same day by same, Jacob Frees, to Miss Mary Ann Baker, both

of West Pennsborough.

328. Jan 30 1828 (Wednesday)
Married on 22nd inst by Rev B. Keller, David Swanger, to Miss
Rebecca Welch, near Churchtown.
- On 24th inst by same, Solomon Brendle, to Miss Mary Ann Smith,
of Monroe twp.
- On same day by same, Henry Gosler, to Miss Mary Switzer, of
Allen twp.
- On same day by same, James How, to Miss Mary Pennrose, both of
Dickinson twp.
- In this place on same day by same, Jacob Martin, of Elizabeth
twp, Lancaster co, to Miss Catharine Forry, of Berlin, Adams
co.

329. Feb 20 1828 (Wednesday)
Died Sat 16th inst, James Tizzard, lately one of the Editors of
the Democratic Republican, in his 35th year. He ruptured a
blood vessel about a year ago which ended in a pulmonary
complaint. He has been a long time resident of our town. He
left a widow and 6 small children.
Died at Eaton, Ohio, 31st ult, Samuel Tizzard, Sen. in his 72nd
year. At Harrisburg, Mon morning, 11th inst of a pulmonary
complaint, Mrs. Eliza Boyd, eldest dau of Peter Keller.

330. Feb 27 1828 (Wednesday)
Married Thurs last at Harrisburg by Rev Dewitt, Jesse Duncan, to
Miss Sophia Cart, all of this place.
Died at Harrisburg, Sat 16th inst, Mrs. Mary Gotts, late widow of
H. Rheem, decd, formerly of this place.

331. March 5 1828 (Wednesday)
Died Thurs last of a pulmonary complaint, Daniel Fisher, aged
about 33 years.
- On Mon last, Miss Mary Sanderson, of this place.

332. March 19 1828 (Wednesday) - Died Fri morning last, Robert
White, cabinet maker of this place.

333. March 26 1828 (Wednesday)
Married Thurs 13th ult by Rev Williamson, John Wolf, of
Shippensburg to Miss Jane Orr, of Eastpennsborough.
Died Sun morning last, Mrs. Swigart, consort of Geo. Swigart of
Frankford twp.
- On Tues morning last, Mrs. Hake, consort of Daniel Hake, of
Frankford twp.

334. April 2 1828 (Wednesday)
Married Thurs evening last in Perry co by Rev Niblock, Dr. John
M. Laird, of Millerstown, to Miss July Ann Power, of Juniata
twp.
- On Thurs 27th ult in Harrisburg, by Rev Lochman, Charles A.
Snyder, Esq. to Miss Barbary Ann Keller, both of that place.
Died this morning, John, son of Michael Mathews, of this place,

aged about 14 years.

335. April 9 1828 (Wednesday)
Married by Rev J. S. Ebaugh, on 18th ult, Wm. Croll, to Miss
    Catharine B. Starry.
- On 20th ult by same, Thomas Matthews, to Miss Hetty M'Hose.
- On 25th ult by same, Jacob Mauntz, to Miss Elizabeth Shoch.
- On same day by same, Christian Lehmer, to Miss Fanny Cockley.

336. April 16 1828 (Wednesday)
Married 3d inst by Rev Wm. R. De Witt, Jesse M'Quaid, of this
    place, to Miss Mary Edwards, of Harrisburg.
Died on Tues last, Mr. J. W. L. Hogue, inhabitant of this place.
- On Mon morning last at his residence, in Hopewell twp, John
Wherry, Esq., one of the commissioners of this co.

337. April 23 1828 (Wednesday)
Died Thurs evening last of a lingering complaint, John Zeigler,
    inhabitant of Westpennsborough.
Married Wed evening last by Rev Geo. Duffield, Robert Kenyon to
    Miss Eliza Halbert, dau of Capt. Joseph Halbert, late of this
    borough, decd.
- On Thurs 10th inst by Rev J. S. Ebaugh, John Henderson to Miss
    Elizabeth Jones.
- On Thurs 17th by same, Jacob Stein, to Miss Elizabeth Leephart.
- On Tues 22d inst by same, James R. M'Mullin, to Miss Rebecca
    Brady, all of the vicinity of Carlisle.

338. April 30 1828 (Wednesday) - Died Fri morning last, Mrs.
    Barbara Housnett, at an advanced age.

339. May 14 1828 (Wednesday) - Married Thurs 1st inst by Rev J.
    S. Ebaugh, Thomas Harris, to Miss Julia Ann Lechler.

340. May 21 1828 (Wednesday) - Died suddenly on Fri evening
    last, Mr. Horner, son of Michael Horner of North Middleton
    twp.

341. May 28 1828 (Wednesday) - Died on Tues 13th inst in
    Newlonsburg, Westmoreland co, of the typus fever, William
    Wilson, of this co.

342. June 4 1828 (Wednesday)
Married 13th ult by Rev E. Keller, Daniel Pickard, to Miss
    Elizabeth Sword, both of Silverspring twp.
- On 29th ult by same, John Ockerman, of Perry co, to Miss
    Elizabeth Pickard of East Pennsborough.
- On 1st ult by Rev Geo. Duffield, John Davidson, to Miss Eliza
    Wilson, all of this co.

343. June 11 1828 (Wednesday)
Married Tues evening last by Rev Dwen, Joseph Faust, to Miss
    Margaret Grimes, both of this place.
Died Thurs last, Philip Zeigler, an old inhabitant of North

Middleton twp.

344. July 2 1828 (Wednesday) - Married in Harrisburg on Thurs
last by Rev Duffy, David E. Lechler, to Miss Maria Shindle,
both of Lancaster.

345. July 9 1828 (Wednesday)
Married 10th ult by Rev J. S. Ebaugh, Joseph Watson, to Miss
Barbara Bender.
- On 12th ult by same, George Sigler, to Miss Ann Heagy.
- On 26th ult by same, Wm. Nicholson, to Miss Jemimah Furguson.
- On 29th ult by same, Michael Wagner, to Miss Mary Brown.
- On 1st inst by same, Samuel Minmich, to Miss Mary Askins.
- On 8th inst, David Stephenson, to Miss Leah Schreiner [See
Amer Vol.]

346. Aug 27 1828 (Wednesday) - Married Tues 26th inst by Rev J.
Sheppard, Robert Nelson, to Miss Ann Wilson, both of Monaghan
twp, York co.

347. Sep 10 1828 (Wednesday)
Married 24th ult by Rev E. Keller, Christian Bishop, to Miss
Catharine Coover, both of Cumberland co.
- On 31st at Mechanicsburg, by same, Alexander Creigen, to Mrs.
Susanna Caston, both of Cumberland co.
- On 4th by same, Thomas Bruner, of Perry co, to Miss Mary
Burkholder, of Cumberland co.
- On 4th inst by Rev F. Heyer, Samuel Diller, to Miss Catharine
Ritchwine, both of this co.

348. Sep 17 1828
Died suddenly on Sun morning last, at Middlesex, Miss Heagy.
- On Sun evening last, at Clarks ferry, of the prevailing fever,
Jacob Switzer, of Dickinson twp, aged about 40 years.
- On Tues morning last, Neal M'Laughlin, aged about 58 years.

349. Oct 8 1828 - Married Thurs 2d inst by Rev F. Heyer, John
Fister, to Miss Agnes Weaver, all of this co.

350. Oct 22 1828
Died Wed morning last, Jacob Wetzel, of N. Middleton twp.
- On Sat evening 17th inst, Mrs. Catharine Bowman, of west
Pennsborough.

351. Nov 6 1828 - Died Fri 24th ult, Mrs. Martha Orr, consort of
William Orr, of East Pennsborough, aged 42 yers.

352. Nov 20 1828 - Married Thurs 13th inst by Rev J. Moody,
James Lewis to Miss Elizabeth Tritt, dau of Jacob Tritt, all
of Newton twp.

353. Nov 27 1828 - Died Fri last, John Huston, Sen. of Dickinson
twp, at an advanced age.

354. Dec 25 1828 - On Thurs evening last by Rev Heyer, Isaac
    Shafer, to Miss Henrietta Sanno, both of this place.
    - On 11th inst by same, Jacob Weir, to Miss Sarah Sholl, both of
    the vicinity of Carlisle.

355. Jan 1 1829
Married 16th ult by Rev E. Keller, Robert Hall, to Miss Susanna
    Hunt, both of Silver Spring twp, Cumberland co.
    - On 18th ult by same, John Hallaugher, to Miss Elizabeth Shelly,
    of Allen twp.
    - On 18th ult by Rev J. S. Ebaugh, George Shambaugh, to Miss Mary
    Sneider.
    - On 25th ult by same, Andrew Rauhauer to Miss Mary Hopple

356. Jan 29 1829
Married Thurs last, 22d inst by Rev Heyer, Christian Frank, to
    Sarah Minning, both of this co.
    - On Tues evening last by Rev C. Davis, Frederick Sannon, to Mrs.
    Nancy Natcher, both of this place.

357. Feb 5 1829 - Died at Bloomfield on morning of 2d inst,
    Charles D. Davis, esq., atty at law, native of Chester co, Pa,
    and for some time practiced law in this borough, from whence
    he removed to Perry co.

358. Feb 26 1828 - Married Thurs 19th inst by Rev E. Keller,
    John Pollinger, of York co, to Miss Ann Bishop, of Monroe twp,
    Cumberland co.

359. March 12 1829
Married 19th ult by Rev F. Heyer, Conrad Westphal to Miss Polly
    Frieze. - On 5th inst by same, Henry Bohr, to Miss Mary
    Snyder. - On same day by same, Daniel Eckles to Miss Martha
    Barbour. - On 10th inst by same, David Rine, to Miss Ann
    Gevler. - All of this place and vicinity.
    - In Shippensburg, on 19th ult by Rev H. R. Wilson, Wm. M. Grier,
    esq., Atty at Law, to Miss Sarah Mahon, all of that place.
    - In the same place on 24th ult by same, Jesse Carothers,
    merchant of this borough, to Miss Mary Williamson, of ths
    former place.

360. March 26 1829
Married Thurs 19th inst by Rev F. Heyer, Michael Watson, to Miss
    Mary Grier, both of this co.
    - On Thurs evening 19th inst by same, Rev John Crawford, to Miss
    Maria Spotswood, all of this place.

361. April 2 1829
Married Thurs 26th ult by Rev F. Heyer, John Lippert to Miss
    Elizabeth Watson, both of this co.
    - On same day by same, Alexander F. Topley of Perry co, to Miss
    Susan Ziegler, of this co.
Died Sat last at Harrisburg, Eben S. Kelley, Esq., member of the
    Senate from Armstrong co.

- On Fri morning last, at an advanced age, Mrs. Elizabeth Pence, of this place.
- On Sat last, John Sheffer, of N. Middleton twp.
- Yesterday morning, Mrs. Gould, wife of Andrew Gould, of this place.
- On Sun last, at an advanced age, Mrs. Betsy Cain, of this place.
- On 26th ult, Martin Kraber, citizen of Baltimore, after a painful and protracted illness, in his 72d year.

362. April 16 1829
Died Tues evening last, of typhus fever, in his 12th year, Samuel Gray, son of John Gray, merchant of this place.
- On Fri moning last at Downingtown, Chester co, Pa, George A. Fairlamb, M. D. Senior editor of the Independent Journal.

363. April 23 1829 - Died Mon evening last, Mr. Dunbar, of this borough.

364. April 30 1829
Married 23d inst by Rev E. Keller, Samuel Duey, to Miss Carolina Craut, both of Cumberland co.
- On Thurs 2d inst by Rev F. Heyer, Isaac Curt to Miss Maria Ward, both of this co.
- On 23d by same, Jacob Stickle, to Miss Catharine Witcom, both of this co.
- On same day by same, George Sweigert, to Mrs. Margaret Cornman, both of this co.
Died Wed, 22nd inst, in Monaghan twp, York co, John Cavanaugh, aged 78 years, old revolutionary soldier.

365. May 14 1829
Married Thurs, 30th ult by Rev A. Griffith, James M'Clune, to Miss Rebecca Mehaffey, both of South Middleton twp.
Died 24th ult, aged 72 years, Mrs. Margaret M'Keehan, consort of Benjamin M'Keehan, decd, of Westpennsborough twp.
- On Tues morning last, aged 41 years, James Elliott, of South Middleton twp.
- On Sat last in South Middleton, John Randolph, farmer. Of apoplexy, at his late residence, Cochranville, in Chester co, on morning of 3d inst, Gen. Samuel Cochran, for many years Surveyor General of this commonwealth.

366. May 21 1829
Married 12th inst by Rev John S. Ebaugh, Michael Clark, to Miss Catharine Starner.
- On 14th by same, Joseph Wonderlich, to Miss Mary Wonderlich, both of this co.
Died Thurs morning last, John Roads, in his 84th year, inhabitant of Westpennsboro' twp.

367. May 28 1829
Married Thurs 14th inst by Rev Joseph Anderson, Robert H. Miller, sen., editor of the St. Clarisville Gazette, to Miss Mary

Barton of Ohio.
- On 7th inst by Rev E. Keller, Joel Miller to Miss Sarah Eichelbarger, of this co.
- On 21st inst by same, Peter Siechrist to Miss Elizabeth Short of this co.
- On same day by same, at Mechanicksburg, Nicholas Sword to Miss Mary Ann Shupp, of this co.

368. June 11 1829 - Married Thurs last by Rev F. Heyer, Solomon Wolf, to Miss Elizabeth Hoppel, both of this place.

369. June 25 1829
Married Tues 9th inst by Rev J. S. Ebaugh, Jacob Hippel to Miss Susanna Hekman.
- On Thurs 11th by same, Jacob Severs, to Miss Rachel Wolf.
- On same day by same, John Hasler, to Miss Catharie Becker.

370. July 2 1829
Married Thurs 11th ult by Rev F. Heyer, Abraham Miller, to Miss Elisabeth Scub (Scuh?).
- On same day by same, Samuel Gowday, to Miss Eliza Savage.
- On Fri morning 12th ult by same, Eli Egner, to Miss Dorcas Sowerbeck.
- On Tues 23d ult by same, John Weiser, to Miss Susan Finnacle.
- On Thurs 25th ult by same, John Fehler, to Miss Anna Lorish.

371. Jul 16 1829 - Died Mon last, David Cryder, soldier of the rev; interred with military honors.

372. July 23 1829
Died Sat 11th inst, William Vance of this place, aged 24 years.
- On Wed 15th inst, Daniel Vance, aged about 27 years.

373. Aug 6 1829
Died Fri last, Peter Vance, of this place, at an advanced age.
- On Sat last, after a lingering illness, John Duffy, of Westpennsborough twp.

374. Sep 10 1829
Died Sat last in his 23d year, Charles Curtz, of this borough.
- On same day, aged about 38 years, Thomas Hays, of the borough.
- On same day at an advanced age, Mr. Davis, of South Middleton twp.
- On Mon last, aged about 37 years, Louis De Gal, of this borough, native of France.

375. Sep 24 1829
Married 10th inst by Rev F. Hyer, Michael Low, to Miss Susannah Hartman, both of this co.
- On 3d inst by Rev E. Keller, Andrew Diven, to Miss Martha Feiler, both of Mechanicsburg.
- On 10th by same, John Renaker, to Miss Ann Herst, both of this co.
- On above day by same, Peter Feidel, to Miss Mary Bishop, of

this co.
- On Tues 8th inst by Rev Stroh, Henry Slaybaugh, to Hannah
Hower, all of the borough of Newville.

376. Oct 16 1829 (Friday) - Married Thurs evening, 1st inst by
Rev J. S. Ebaugh, James Davis, to Miss Eliza Sponsler, of North
Middleton.

377. Oct 22 1829 (Thursday) - Died Mon morning last of typus
fever, John Nevin of the vicinity of Shippensburg in this co.

378. Nov 5 1829 (Thursday)
Married Tues evening 20th ult by Rev David Crall, Thomas Devor of
the borough of Shipensburg to Miss Jane Patterson, of Perry
co.
- On Thues 3d inst by Rev F. Hyer, Joseph Shrom, jr. of this
place, to Miss Rebecca Kenower, of South Middleton.

379. Nov 12 1829 (Thursday)
Married Thurs 29th ult by Rev George Duffield, Henry L. Baugher,
V. D. of Boonsborough, Md. to Miss Clarissa M. Brooks, of this
borough.
- On Tues last 5th inst by Rev Niblock, John Grier, of Dickinson
twp, Cumberland co, to Miss Maria, dau of col. Charles Bovard,
of Rye twp, Perry co.
- On Tues last in Dickinson twp, by Rev A. Griffith, George L.
Line to Miss Maria, dau of Emanuel Line.

380. Nov 19 1829 (Thursday)
Died Sat last, Job Randolph, of North Middleton twp.
- On Mon last, aged about 40 years, Joseph Briggs, of Silver
Spring twp.

381. Dec 3 1829 (Thursday)
Married 19th ult by Rev F. Heyer, Benjamin Rieber, of Perry co,
to Miss Sarah Low of this co.
- On 26th ult by Rev F. Heyer, George Stenhower, of Adams co, to
Miss Susan Seip, of this co.

382. Dec 10 1829 (Thursday) - Married Thurs last by Rev F.
Heyer, Adam Humerich, to Miss Mary Zigler, both of this co.

383. Dec 17 1829 (Thursday)
Married Tues 8th inst by Rev Heyer, John friese, to Miss Sarah
Miller.
- On Thurs 10th by same, Abraham Hartzell to Miss Nancy Eberle,
all of this co.
Died Fri morning last, suddenly, John Markley innkeeper at
Trindle's Spring, Silver Spring twp.
- On Wed morning last at 4 o'clock, Andrew Gray of this place, in
his 89th year.

384. Jan 7 1830 (Thursday)
Married Fri morning last at the residence of Gen. Spangler, by

Rev Mayer, Mr. Timmons of Carlisle, to Miss Catharine
Swartzbauch, of York.
- On 24th ult in Phila, by Rev Engles, William Martin Crouce,
  formerly of this place, to Miss Rachael Campbell, of that
  city.
- On Thurs evening last by Rev Lochman, William Wendel, to Miss
  Ann Stakemiller, of Eastpennsborough.

- - - - -

CARLISLE WHIG (Issues held by Cumberland County Historical
Society)

385. Wed 10 Jul 1822, No. 27, vol. 5
My wife Hetty has left my bed and board without just cause. Neal
M'Laughlin, Carlisle.

- - - - -

CARLISLE GAZETTE (Issues held by Cumberland County Historical
Society)

386. Tuesday Aug 19, 1823.
Married Tues evening last by Rev John S. Ebaugh, Daniel Leonard
  to Miss Elizabeth Burney, of this borough.
- In Virginia by Rev. T. Burkby, David Bealle, age 69, to Miss
  Hannah Saunders, aged 46.
Died suddenly on Thurs last at 11 o'clock, Miss Emeline Hamilton,
  of an inflamation of the stomach, youngest dau of late Judge
  Hamilton of this Borough.
- At his country seat in Franklin Co., Isaac Eaton, Esq. one of
  the assoc. judges of the courts of that co.
- At Phila on Wed the 6th inst, Peter C. Konkle, printer, in his
  45th year.

387. 19 Aug 1823
Married Tues evening last by Rev George Duffield, George Fleming,
  editor of the "Religious Miscellany," to Miss Margaret Brandt,
  both of this borough.
Died Tues afternoon, after a short, but severe indisposition, at
  his residence on the Frankford Turnpike, Jacob G. Tryon, Esq.,
  High Sheriff of city and co. of Phila, in his 34th year.
- At Greneda, of which place he was a native, F. A. Webster,
  Esq., aged 43. His corpse weighed 555 pounds, and it was
  necessary to put his body into the coffin outside of the door
  - borne to the grave by twenty persons.

388. 2 Sep 1823
Died Fri last, Mrs. M'Kinney, wife of Philip M'Kinney.
- On Sat last Mrs. Eckard, of a lingering disease, wife of Dr.
  Eckard, of this borough.
- On same day Mrs. Smith at an advanced age, of this borough.
- On same day Richard Forbes, of West Pennsborough.
- On 27th ult. Henry Bearbower, wagon-maker, of this borough.

- In this borough on 25th ult, Mr. Joseph M'Coy, Cooper.

389. 9 Sep 1823
Married at Harrisburg on Thurs evening last by Rev Dr. Lochman,
    Joseph Lawrence, esq. Speaker of the House of Rep, to Miss
    Maria M., dau of Judge Bucher of that place.
Died Sat evening last, Isaac Wynkoop, of East Pennsborough
    township.
- On Sat morning last, Elizabeth, youngest dau of John Wyeth, of
    Harrisburg.

390. 16 Sep 1823
Married Thurs evening 4th inst, by Rev. J. S. Ebaugh, Conrad
    Nunamacker, to Miss Catharine Quigley, both of this borough.
Died at late residence of his father, Richard Snowden, Prince
    George's Co., MD, on 5th inst, Charles A. Snowden, late
    student of Dickinson College, at Carlisle, aged 18. [long
    obit.]
- At his residence in West Pennsborough Twp, General Andrew
    Mitchell, late Sheriff of this co., soldier of the late war,
    excellent officer, in the battles of Chippewa, Bridgewater;
    buried in the burial ground at Newville.
- At Springfield, Tues last, Robert Young, for many years
    resident of this borough.
- In North Middleton twp, Sat last, Mrs. Wise, consort of George
    Wise.
- In Washington Co., Sun 7th inst, Mrs. Isabella Walker, aged
    near 70 years, consort of John Walker, esq. late of this co.
- At Bedford, Sun 31st ult, very suddenly, Wm. Littlejohn, esq.
    of this co., formerly a captain in the 1st regt, of U.S.
    Dragoons.
- On 5th inst, in South Middleton, Miss Sarah Maxwell.

391. 30 Sep 1823
Died Fri evening last, John M'Coy, eldest son of Gen. M'Coy, aged
    about 9 years, 6 mos. He had just left his school about 5
    o'clock in the evening as was about to proceed to the
    Garrison, residence of his father, with his uncle, who was in
    town with a horse and cart. He was killed when the horse took
    fright and ran about 40 yards when the cart overturned on top
    of the boy.
- On Fri last of a billious cholic, William Munro, of Dickinson
    twp.
- On Sat last, Mrs. Donally, of this borough.
- On same day, Mrs. Morrison, of this borough, at an advanced
    age. - On yesterday morning, of a typhus fever, Edward
    M'Gonigal, of this borough, in his 36th year, leaving widow
    and 4 children.
- On yesterday morning, John, infant son of col. Kerr, of this
    borough.
- On Sun last at the residence of her father in Dickinson twp,
    Mrs. Rachel Sterrett, dau of Mr. Woodburn.
- On 22nd inst, at the residence of Commodore O'Brian, Samuel

Gray, in his 60th year.

392.   14 Oct 1823
Died Thurs week, Mrs. Ann Mahon, sister to the hon. Thomas
Duncan. [See item #5.]
- On Fri week, Mr. Plunket Hackett (hatter) of this borough.
- At Mechanicksburg, Tues 7th inst, after a severe illness, Mrs.
Jane Foulk, consort of Stephen Foulk, consort of Stephen
Foulk, residence of that place.

393.   21 Oct 1823
Married Tues evening 14th inst, Jacob Shrom, of this borough, to
Miss Suaan Bear, of the borough of Hanover, York Co.
- At Princetown, New Jersey, Tues 7th inst, by Rev Bayard,
William Augustus Washington, of Haywood, VA, to Miss Juliet
Elizabeth, eldest dau of Samuel Bayard, esq.

394.   28 Oct 1823 - Died Tues 21st inst, Mrs. Mary Lee, consort
of Richard H. Lee, esq. of Leesburg, VA. [See item #5.]

395.   11 Nov 1823 - Married in Perry Co. Tues 4th inst by Rev
Jacob Shull, Henry Gould, to Miss Elizabeth Rice, both of this
place.
396.   25 Nov 1823 - Married Thurs evening last, George Reisinger,
of this borough, to Miss Mary Munholm, of Mechanicksburg. [See
item below]

397.   2 Dec 1823 - Married Thurs evening 20th inst by Rev. H. R.
Wilson, George Reisinger, of this borough, to Miss Maria
Munhall, of Allen twp, Cumberland co., and not to Mary Munholm
of Mechanics-burg as erroneously published in our last.

398.   16 Dec 1823 - Died Fri last, Jane Hays, of a consumption,
wife of John Hays, of Frankford twp, and dau of George
Pattison, esq. of this borough. [See item # 11]

399.   30 Dec 1823 - Died on Mon 29th inst after a lingering
illness, James M'Braerty, of this borough.

400.   20 Jan 1824
Married Sat last by Henry Titzel, Esq., George Shuler, to Miss
Lydia Saul, all of Tyrone twp, Perry co.
Died Fri last, Adam Matthews in 71st year of his age, member of
M..E. Church.
- On Sat night last suddenly, Hugh Levingston, of York co. [See
item #14]

401.   27 Jan 1824 - Married at Chambersburgh, PA, Tues 6th inst,
by Rev D. Denny, Patrick Gallagher, of Westmoreland co, to
Miss Martha M'Kee, of that vicinity.

402.   3 Feb 1824
Married Tues evening last by Rev. Prof. Spencer, Col. Charles J.
Jack, of Phila, to Miss Leonora, youngest dau of Commodore

Richard O'Brien, of Tarra Plains, near this borough. [See
item #15]
- On Tues 10th ult by Rev Moody, David Ritchey, of Stoughstown,
to Miss Elizabeth Kelso of Westpennsbro.
Died at Newville, on Mon evening last, William Graham, Wheelright
and Chairmaker, formerly of this borough.
403. 10 Feb 1824
Married at Hampton, Virginia, Thurs 29th ult by Rev Gilliam, Dr.
George P. French, to Miss Elizabeth, 3d dau of Commodore James
Barron.
Died Mon 26th ult, Henry Quigley, of Lisburn, Cumberland Co.
- On Mon 2d inst in the city of Lancaster, Joseph Russell, in his
29th(?) year, formerly a residence of this borough.
- On 19th ult in Washington city, John Erskine, printer, aged
about 40 years.

404. 24 Feb 1824 - Married Thurs last by Rev Williams, William
Wightman, to Miss Mary Dunfee, of Newville.

405. 2 Mar 1824 - Married at Bedford Tues last by Rev Yager,
William M'Dowell, one of the editors of the Bedford Gazette,
to Miss Ellen Smith, dau of Mr. H. Smith, of Colerain twp.

406. 9 Mar 1824
Married Thurs evening last by Rev George Duffield, Samuel Hays,
saddler, to Miss Isabella Phillips, dau of George Phillips,
editor of the Carlisle Herald.
Died Sat evening last of consumption [after a lingering illness -
Am. Vol.], Miss Jane Hutton, member of the M.E. church, and
only remaining child of James Hutton of this borough.

407. 23 Mar 1824
Married Thurs last by Rev Winebrenner, John Hinny, to Mrs.
Elizabeth Huber, both of Mechanicksburg.
- On 3d inst at west Chester, by Rev William Hodson, Isaac
Thomas, M.D. to Ann Charlton Miner, dau of Charles Miner, esq.
senior of the Village Record.
- At New York on Mon evening the 15th inst by Rev Duboise,
Captain Joseph Plympton of the 5th Regt., U.S. Army, to Miss
Eliza Matilda Livinston, dau of P. W. Livinston, esq. of that
city.

408. 6 Apr 1824
Married - Thurs evening 4th inst by Rev Pearce, John Brown, to
Miss Mary Ritchey, all of this co.
- At Landisburg, Thurs week, by Rev J. Shull, Jesse Miller, esq.
Sheriff of Perry Co., to Miss Eliza Sample, both of that
place.

409. 13 Apr 1824 - Died on Tues after a short illness, Rev
Philip Larassy, of St. Augustine Church, aged 42 years.

410. 27 Apr 1824
Died in Phila on Sun 18th inst, of a consumption, John J. Smith,
in his 22d year, son of Patrick Smith, late of this borough.
- In Savannah, GA, on 30th Mar last, Charles Walters, watchmaker,
formerly of this place. [See item #26]

411. 8 Jun 1824 - Died at York, PA, on 28th ult after a
protracted illness, David Cassat, Esq. in his 56th year.

412. 29 Jun 1824
Married Tues 15th inst, by Rev Williams, William Kerr, jr. of
Huntingdon co., to Miss Eliza Sterrett, of this co. [See item
35]
Died Fri last in this borough, of consumption, about 35 years of
age, James Feris, schoolmaster, native of county Armagh,
Ireland.

413. 27 Jul 1824
Married at Bloomsburg Tues 6th inst by Rev Kesler, Captain Edward
S. Moore, to Miss Mary, dau of Joseph Prutzman, Esq. all of
Danville, Columbia Co., PA.
Died Sat evening last after a few days sickness, in his 55th
year, John Wolf, of North Middleton twp.
- In Harrisburg twp, on 23d inst at about 2 o'clock in the
morning, Mrs. Susan Sloan, dau of Peter Wenrich, Esq., 8 weeks
after her marriage, leaving father, mother and husband.
- On Thurs evening last, Geo. Fisher, son of Geo. Fisher, Esq.,
aged 22 years (Har. Penn.)

414. 17 Aug 1824
Married last evening by Rev Williams, Rev John V. E. Thorn of
Long Island, to Miss Susan Hamilton, second dau of hon. James
Hamilton, decd, late of this borough.
- On Thurs evening last, by Rev R. S. Vinton, Jacob Spangler, to
Mrs. Elizabeth Watterberry, both of this borough.
Died at the residence of his sister in White Deer twp, Union co.,
PA, James Flemming, schoolmaster, formerly of this place, in
his 65th year.
- At Phila on Wed evening, 11th inst, Rev John Plitt, in his 61st
year.

415. 24 Aug 1824
Married 12th inst by Rev John S. Ebaugh, Wilson Fisher, to Miss
Hoover, both of North Middleton twp. Same day by same, George
Berger, to Miss Nancy Tate, both of Allen twp.
- On Tues last by same, Abraham Henwood, to Mrs. Sarah Jackson,
both of this borough.
- On Tues evening last by Rev De Witt, Rev Alexander Sharp, to
Miss Elizabeth Bryson, both of this co. Whereas my wife
Catharine having left my bed and board... Valentine Kettering.
Newville.

416. 31 Aug 1824
Married at Norfolk, VA, Wed evening last by Rev Wingfield, John

P. Tuttle, of the U.S. Navy, to Miss Margaretta, second dau of
Com. James Barron.
Guardianship accounts: John Davidson and Ruth Thompson exec of
Matthew Thompson, decd, who in his life time was guardian over
John Boyd, Adam Boyd, Elizabeth Boyd, James Boyd and Wm. Young
Boyd, minor children of Wm. Boyd, late of Newton twp, decd.
- David Lamb and Thomas Bell, guardians over Polly Pattison,
minor dau of James Pattison, late of the state of Md.

417. 7 Sep 1824
Married Thurs last by Rev Augustus H. Lochman, David Miller to
Miss Sarah Smith, both of this co.
- Same day by Rev J. Winebrenner, Frederick Weiser, to Miss
Elizabeth Kisel, both of this co.

418. 21 Sep 1824 - Married Tues last by Rev. De Witt, James A.
Mahanay, Esq., atty at law of the Northern Liberties, and
member of the House of Rep, from co of Phila, to Miss Hanna
Fahnestock, dau of Obed Fahnestock, Esq. of Harrisburg.

419. 28 Sep 1824
Married at Lancaster, PA, Thurs last by Rev Ashmead, Gunning
Bedford, Editor of the Lancaster Intelligencer, to Miss Ann
Eliza dau of late William Dickson, Esq. of that city.
Died Sun night last of a lingering and protracted disease, in his
23d year, William Lechler, of this borough, eldest son of John
Lechler, decd.

420. 5 Oct 1824
Married Sat last by Rev Dr. Lochman, Peter Radebach [Radeback -
Am. Vol.] to Miss Barbara Shelly, dau of Jacob Shelly of Allen
twp, both of this co.
- On Thurs morning last by Rev Babbet, Matthew M'Kelly, Esq.
Editor of the Lancaster Free press, to Miss Henrietta Michael,
dau of John Michael sen, of that city.
- On Thurs evening last by Rev Denny, Kenton Harper, editor of
the Staunton Spectator, to Miss Elenor dau of Capt. Samuel
Colhoun, of Chambersburg.

421. 11 Oct 1824 - Died Fri morning 25th ult at Newville, Miss
Isabella Dunbar, dau of John Dunbar, in her 25th year.

422. 26 Oct 1824 - Died Wed last at Hogne'stown, John Carothers,
Esq., aged 57 years. [See item # 47]

423. 9 Nov 1824
Married lately at the head of Lake Ontario, William J. Kerr, esq.
of Niagara, U.C. to Miss Brandt, dau of the late Col. Brandt,
Chief of the six nations.
- At Reading by Rev Herman, John Feary, aged about 76, to Mrs.
Drenkle, aged about 74, both of Berks Co.
Died Fri morning last, aged about 10 years, Robert Ferris, son of
James Ferris, decd.

424. 16 Nov 1824
Married Thurs evening last by Rev George Duffield, Andrew
Carothers, Esq., Atty at Law to Miss Isabella Alexander, dau
of Col. John Alexander, decd, formerly of this co. [See item
#50]
- On same evening by Rev. Patrick Dwenn, Neal M'Ginley to Miss
Harriet L. Purcell, both of this borough.
- On Tues week, at Littlestown, Adams co. by Rev Debarth, Dr.
Joseph A. Shorb, to Miss Louisa Josephine, dau of Dr. E.
Davis, both of that place.
- At York, Sun evening last, by Rev Williams, Daniel Sleeger,
printer, to Miss Sarah Sedgewick, both of that borough.
- At Litiz, Tues week by Rev John Bechler, Jacob Grosh, Esq. late
of member of the Senate from Lancaster co. to Miss Margaret
Marwell of Latiz.
- On Thurs 21st ult at Hanover, by Rev Melsheimer, Eli Lewis,
late editor of the York Recorder, to Miss Rebecca Farney, of
Hanover.
- On Mon week by Rev Dr. Lochman, Benjamin H. Musser, of York co.
to Miss Elizabeth Rupley, dau of John Rupley, Esq. of this co.
[See item #50]
Died 3d inst in Menallen twp, Adams co, George Hartzell, sr. He
had 17 children (13 of whom were married), 100 grandchildren,
12 great grand children, in all 129 - of whom only 6 have
died, leaving 123 living descendants at the time of his death.
- On Tues last, Mrs. Catharine Rupley, wife of John Rupley, jr.,
of this co.

425. 23 Nov 1824
Married Tues evening last by Rev Patrick Dwen, James Johnston, of
Lebanon co, to Miss Johana Beelen, dau of Francis Beelen, esq.
of Perry Co.
Died on 1st inst in Cumru twp, Berks co, PA, Michael Bear, born
20 Feb 1720.

426. 30 Nov 1824
Married at - Athens, OH, on 2d inst by Rev Dr. R. G. Wilson, Rev
John Pitkin, of Waterford, to Miss Eliza Wilson.
- At the same time and place by same, William Johnston, M. D. of
Greenfield, to Miss Fanny Wilson, dau of Rev. R. G. Wilson,
principal of Athens College.
Died yesterday morning of dropsy, at the Poor House of this
borough, John Hall, native of England, and a soldier of the
late war in his 37th year.

427. 14 Dec 1824
Married Mon evening 6th inst by Rev Marmaduke Pearce [by Rev.
Vinton - Am. Vol.], Rev Jasper Bennet, of the M.E. Church to
Miss Eliza Thompson, of South Middleton twp, Cumberland co.
[See item #53]
Died yesterday evening after lingering consumption, at residence
of his brother in East Pennsboro' twp, in his 28th year,
Samuel Alexander, jr., member of ME. Church of this borough.

CARLISLE GAZETTE (Held by Cumberland Co. Historical Soc.) 75

428. 21 Dec 1824 - Married at Chambersburg on 14th inst by Rev
Denny, Mr. B. M. Jones, merchant, to Miss Ann Lindsay, dau of
Thomas Lindsay, all of that borough.

429. Oct 3, 1827 (Wednesday) - Married Thurs evening last by Rev
Dr. Mason, Rev Erskine Mason, to Miss Mary M'Coskry, dau of
Dr. Samuel A. M'Coskry, late of this borough, decd.

- - - - -

AMERICAN VOLUNTEER

(Issues held by Cumberland County Historical Society)

430. 1 Feb 1821 - Died 28th inst at the late residence of his
deceased son Philip, at Conewago, Adams Co., Bryan Cornyn,
aged 78 years.

431. 8 Feb 1821
Married Thurs 25th ult by Rev Coulter, Alexander M'Clure of
Tyrone twp, to Miss Isabella Anderson, dau of hon. Wm.
Anderson of Toboyne twp, Perry co.
- On same day by Rev Smith, John Jacobs, to Miss Elizabeth Baker,
both of Saville twp, Perry co.

432. 22 Mar 1821 - Married in Washington co., Pa, Thurs evening
8th inst, by Rev Andrew Wylie, pres of the Washington college,
David Quail, of Strabane twp, to Miss Margaret R. Walker, dau
of John Walker, esq. late of Cumberland co., now of Chartiers,
Washington Co.

433. 29 Mar 1821 - Married Wed evening 21 Mar by Wm. M'Donald,
esq. Andrew Snyder to Miss Margaretta Murphy, both of
Springfield, West Pennsborough twp.

434. 5 Apr 1821 - Died last week near Harrisburg, Miss Ann Maria
Reehm, aged about 18 years, dau of Henry Reehm, tanner,
deceased.

435. 12 Apr 1821
Married at Sacket's Harbour, N.Y. on 21 March, Dr. Samuel H.
Littlejohn, of the U.S. Army, to Miss Elizabeth M. Harrison,
dau of late John Harrison, of New York.
Died Sat evening last in this borough, aged about 62 years, Mrs.
Abigail Reilley, late of Westmoreland co., whence she had come
to this place in apparent perfect health but a few days
before; member of the Meth church upwards of 30 years, mother
of James Reilly who officiated the last two years as one of
the clergy to the society in this district.
- On Mon last suddenly, Mrs. Eleanor Johnson, wife of Hugh
Johnson of this town, for some time in a lingering state.
Greensburg, Apr 5, 1821. William Findley of Westmoreland died at
his house in Unity twp, at 10 o'clock the night before last.

436. 19 Apr 1821
Died 5th inst near Huntingdon, PA, Mrs. Sarah Ker, in her 22d
year, consort of John Ker, and sister of Samuel Woods, jun. of
this co. [See item in 26 April issue below.]
- On Fri evening last, near Springfield, Mrs. Lydia M'Neal, wife
of Mr. S. M'Neal of that town, leaving husband and a number of
children.
- On Sat last in Frankford twp, Miss Eleanor Logan.
- On Sun evening last of a pulmonary complaint, Mrs. Elizabeth
Foster, consort of Crawford Foster of this borough, and dau of
George Pattison, esq., leaving a husband and two infants.

437. 26 Apr 1821
Married at Phila on Tues evening 17th inst by Rev Ned, John D.
Mahon, esq. of Carlisle, to Miss Mary E. dau of Thomas Duncan,
esq. of that city.
Died Tues night last, Daniel Hoomer, of South Middleton twp, aged
47 years, 9 mos, 22 days.
Died at Harrisburg last Sat week, after a long spell of sickness,
John Benjamin, aged 46 years, 9 mos, 19 days, elected sergeant
at arms to the House of Representatives for a number of years.
In announcinbg the death of Mrs. Sarah Ker, wife of John Ker,
of Huntingdon co., we stated that she was the sister of Samuel
Woods, jr., which was an error. She was the dau of Samuel
Woods, sr. of this co.

438. 2 May 1821
Died at Landisburg, Mon 23d ult, Michael Franks, in his 23d year.
At his res in Rye twp, Perry co. in Tues 24 Apr, Rev Joseph
Brady, for many years a zealous minister for several
Presbyterian churches in the lower end of that co. Forester.
Suicide. John Stanley, schoolmaster, in Westpennsborough twp,
near Mr. Palm's tavern, on Tues 24th inst, cut his throat and
stabbed himself in several places with a pen knife. He was
found, alive, in the schoolhouse, where he perpetrated the
act, in the evening, having been absent from his boarding
house about three hours. He assigned no reason for the
commission of the deed, and appeared penitent. He died on Mon
evening last. He had taught school 16 or 18 years in the
settlement, and was considered a civil, inoffensive man.

439. 17 May 1821 - Died Fri last, aged 75 years, Stophel Gould.

440. 24 May 1821 - Married in Allen twp, on 12th ult by Patrick
Laverty, esq. Joseph Anderson, son of John Anderson of
Dillsburg, York co., to Miss Margaret Swanger, dau of Abraham
Swanger, deceased.

441. 31 May 1821
Died in this borough, Sat morning last, after a lingering
illness, Mrs. Elizabeth Conner, consort of Francis Conner.

442. 14 Jun 1821
Married Thurs last in this borough, Charles Walters, of

Lewistown, to Miss Jane M'Dannel, of Carlisle.
Died yesterday morning about 5 o'clock at the barracks near
  Carlisle, in the prime of life, George Hackett, esq., for many
  years barrack-master and military storekeeper, leaving wife
  and some young children.
- At Harrisburg, Mon week last of consumption, in her 24th year,
  Miss Harriet Henry, dau of late judge Henry, deceased.

443. 21 Jun 1821
Died yesterday morning about 9 o'clock, after a lingering
  pulmonary complaint, Thomas Hagan, esq., of this borough.
- Thurs last, aged about 80 years, Mrs. Martha Brown, of Allen
  twp.

444. 28 Jun 1821 - Married on 14th inst at Mercer, PA, by Rev
  James Dinwiddie, Jacob R. Stine, formerly of Carlisle, to Miss
  Emily P. dau of James Miller, esq.

445. 12 Jul 1821
Married Thurs evening last by Rev Reynolds, Dr. Robert P.
  Simmons, of Blairsville, Indiana co, PA, to Miss Jane
  Craighead, of this borough.
- On Tues evening last by Rev George Duffield, James Moore, to
  Miss Margaret Grayson, both of this borough.

446. 19 Jul 1821
Died Fri evening last at an advanced age John Hunter for many
  years of this borough.
- Same day Robert Pendergrass, native of this place, but who, for
  many years had resided in St. Charles Co., MO. He came here
  in March last on some business, was taken ill, and never able
  to return to his family.
- On Tues morning last, of a consumption, Andrew Keller, son of
  Leonard Keller, of this place.

447. 2 Aug 1821
Married Thurs 19th inst by Rev D. Helmuth, Rev George Schmucker
  of York Pa, pres of the German Lutheran Synod, to Mrs. Ann
  Weinert, of Phila.
Died in the vicinity of this borough on Thurs last, after a
  lingering illness, Mrs. Catherine Dewing, eldest dau of Mr. G.
  Fahnestock.
- Same day of a cholick, Miss Catharine Snyder, dau of John
  Snyder, near Carlisle.
- On Sun, Mrs. Greason, near Smoky town.

448. 9 Aug 1821
Died Sun 29th ult at Phila, Mrs. Mary Ann Elizabeth Hendel, in
  her 74th year, relict of Rev Wm. Hendel, D.D.
- At the residence of his brother, in New Berlin, Union co. on
  26th ult, Capt. Ralph Lashels, late of Gettysburg.

449. 16 Aug 1821 - Died 3 Aug inst, in Toboyne twp, Perry co, of
  a cholera morbus in his 20th year, Benjamin Taylor, son of

Henry Taylor, leaving parents, brothers and sisters.

450.   30 Aug 1821
Died Wed 22d inst, suddenly in East Pennsborough twp, Mrs.
   Elizabeth Stehman, aged 22 years, wife of John Stehman, and
   dau of George Kline, esq. late of this borough, decd.
- Suddenly on Mon last, Major John Kinkead, of North Middleton
   twp.

451.   6 Sep 1821
Married Thurs 23d ult, Philip Dorsheimer, of Cumberland, to Miss
   Sarah Gorgas, of Dauphin co.
Died about 3 o'clock on Tues morning last, John Stehman, of East-
   pennsborough twp. We recorded the death of his wife last
   week.

452.   13 Sep 1821
Died about half past eleven o'clock on Tues evening last in the
   prime of life, Miss Matilda French an only dau, of typhus,
   which confined her about 4 weeks.
Harrisburg, Sep. 7 - Died in this borough on Wed night last, of
   typhus fever, Samuel Cochran, junr, son of the surveyor
   general, in his 24th year. We are informed that out of about
   70 families in Millersburg, Dauphin co, not more than 6 or 8
   are entirely healthy. Intel.
Died at Green-Castle on Wed 5 inst, in his 69th year, George
   Clarke, Esq., late Collector of the United States revenue for
   ths dist. Franklin Repos.

453.   20 Sep 1821
Married by Rev Benjamin Keller, 11 inst, George M. Baer, to Miss
   Elizabeth Richter.
- On 13th by same, Wm. Brennizer, to Miss Susan Kreitzer, of
   Eastpennsborough.
- On Thurs last by same, James Eagen, to Miss Maria Zarman, both
   of Carlisle.
- Same day in Carlisle, by Rev Ebaugh, Daniel Stine, esq. of
   Harrisburg, to Miss Anna Maria Kleiss, of Lancaster.
Died at Mifflin town Thurs 6 inst, col. Thomas Beale, high
   sheriff of Mifflin co. in his 34th year.

454.   27 Sep 1821
Married Thurs last by Rev Dr. Lochman, George Balmer, to Miss
   Mary Spansler, both of Allen twp.
Died at Harrisburg, Thurs last, Joseph A. M'Jimsey, esq for a
   number of years chief clerk of the senate of this state.
- Mon last of a consumption, Mrs. Mary Trimble, wife of Thomas
   Trimble of Dickinson twp, and dau of Samuel Woods, senr.
- 19th inst, Samuel Rowan, of this borough.

455.   4 Oct 1821
Married Thurs evening last by Rev Reynolds, Nathan Reed, of
   Newville, to Miss Elizabeth Hoffer, dau of Melchor Hoffer, of
   this borough.

Died Fri last, Andrew Martin of this borough.

456. 11 Oct 1821
Married 29 ult by Rev Clarkson, Frederick Eichelberger, of the
Senate of this state from York Co, to Miss Catharine Baker,
dau of late Frederick Baker, esq. of Lancaster, decd.
Died at Thomsontown, Miffin co. Sep 29th in his 33d year, Dr.
John B. Smith, son of Capt. John Smith, of this place.
- At Pensacola, Lieut. Joseph Cassin of the U.S. Navy and at
Natchez, Dr. E. H. Bell, of U. S. army.
- On 3d Oct inst at his residence in Bellefonte, William
Petrikin, esq. in his 60th year.
- At Lancaster on 1st inst, George Price, editor of the Free
Press.

457. 25 Oct 1821
Died Tues last, Charles Herron, native of Ireland.
- Same day, Miss Jane M'Keown, of this borough, member of the
Meth Society.
- Same day, Mrs. Nancy Brown, wife of Robert Brown, of this
borough, aged about 70 years.

458. 1 Nov 1821 - Died in Toboyne twp, Perry co, Fri last,
captain David Moreland, citizen and soldier.

459. 8 Nov 1821
Died Mon 29th ult, Mrs. Margaret Rupley, wife of Frederick
Rupley, innkeeper, of this co., aged 50 years.
Married Thurs last by Rev Dr. Lochman, Thomas Fisher, to Miss
Eleanor Gill, both of this co.
- On Mon morning last by Rev F. Pringle, John Moore, of
Baltimore, to Miss Cinthia Moore of this place.

460. 15 Nov 1821
Married Thurs last by Rev Ebaugh, Jacob Wise, son of col. John
Wise, of South Middleton twp, to Miss Margaret Moore, of the
same twp.
- On same day by Rev B. Keller, Richard Waugh, of this place, to
Mrs. Margaret Holmes of North Middleton.

461. 29 Nov 1821
Married at Harrisburg on 20th inst by Rev Dewitt, Samuel White to
Miss Sarah Hills, dau of Stephen Hills, architect, and on
Thurs last, Nathaniel Henry, printer, to Miss Maria Ingram,
all of that place.
Died of a dropsy on Sun last, John Keith, merchant of this
borough, aged about 50 years.

462. 6 Dec 1821 - Married Thurs evening last by Rev G. Duffield,
John Agnew to Miss Margaret Brown, both of this borough.

463. 13 Dec 1821
Death of Dr. Charles N. M'Coskry of the U.S. army, a young
gentleman, a native of this place. He died at St. Augustine,

Florida.
Married at Lewistown, PA, Mon evening 3d inst, Alexander
Brackenridge, esq. to Miss Mary M. Porter, both of Pittsburg.

464. 17 Jan 1822 - Died about 3 o'clock yesterday morning
Alexander Galbraith, soldier of the rev, many years a citizen
of this borough.

465. 24 Jan 1822 - Died in this borough on Mon morning last,
about 6 o'clock, Mrs. Isabella Phillips, in her 77th year, of
Carlisle.

466. 31 Jan 1822 - Died 18th inst, Mrs. Elizabeth M'Allister,
wife of Archibald M'Allister, esq. of Fort Hunter, Dauphin co.

467. 21 Feb 1822
Married Tues evening last by George Duffield, V. D. M., John
Duncan, esq. to Miss Margaret Sterrett, both of this borough.
Died near this borough, Sat day night last, aged upwards of
seventy years, Mrs. Ann Laughridge, relict of Abrahamn
Loughridge, of this borough, inhabitant of this borough about
a half a century.

468. 28 Feb 1822 - Died 7th inst Zalmon Towsey, of Toboyne twp,
Perry co.

469. 7 Mar 1822
Married Thurs evening last by Rev Benjamin Keller, Gilbert
Seawright, to Miss Sarah Kerr, dau of Andrew Kerr, of this
borough.
Died of a lingering illness, Mon 18th ult at the residence of her
son, Capt. James Piper, at Big Spring, Mrs. Jane Piper, in her
68th year.
- 21st inst, Dr. John B. Arnold, of Adams Co., in his 47th year.

470. 21 Mar 1822
Died in this borough on Sun morning last, Miss Margaret Crain,
dau of Richard Crain, jr. late of N. Middleton twp, decd.
- On Mon last at an advanced age, David M'Gowan, of Allen twp,
soldier of the rev.

471. 28 Mar 1822
Married Thurs 14th inst by Rev Peter Hall, Rev John W. Hamm, of
Newville, to Miss Esther Lefever, of Westpennsborough twp.
Died Mon morning last in this borough, of a morbid affection of
the breast, Rev George H. Woodruff, pastor of the Epis church.
Mar 21, 1822, at the house of Daniel Sharbon, in Eastpennsborough
twp, Cumberland co., George Bennet Mountain, recently arrived
from England and was on his way to his sons, at Mayville, KY.
- Landisburg, March 21 - On Sun morning last, Peter Solenberger,
senr, found dead in bed, at the house of John Strawbridge.
- 25th inst in Dauphin co., Capt. John Brisbin, aged 92 years,
officer in the rev war.
- Of an apoplectic fit in Petersburg, Adams Co., on Fri last,

Thomas A. Bigham, formerly of this co.

472. 4 Apr 1822
Married Thurs last by Rev Caleb Reynolds, Charles Parker, to Miss
    Isabella Smith, both of this place.
- On the evening of the same day by Rev. Ebaugh, Rev. Shall, of
    Perry Co., to Miss Catharine Keller, dau of Leonard Keller of
    this borough.
Died Wed 27th ult, Mrs. Jane Smith, wife of Thomas G. Smith,
    merchant, of this borough, and dau of Charles Cooper, decd.
- 25 Mar between hours of 7 and 8, Rev George H. Woodruff, Rector
    of the Episc Church of St. Johns in the borough of Carlisle,
    and of St. Stevens, Adams Co. His illness was short but
    severe. [long obit.]
Sat night last in Harrisburg, Rose Wright, at an advanced age.
    She held the Post Office in that borough for several years.

473. 18 Apr 1822 - Died suddenly of as asthmatic complaint on
    morning of 12th inst, Samuel Piper, of Newton twp, in his 83d
    year.

474. 25 Apr 1822 - Died Fri morning last at Harrisburg, in his
    35th year, captain John Machesney, officer of the last war,
    and lately prothonotary of Dauphin co.

475. 9 May 1822
Died Sat night last in 83d year, William Harkness, senr of Allen
    twp, leaving widow and a number of children.
- Mon last, William Hoffman, of this borough, aged about 67
    years.
- Yesterday morning, Mrs. Mary Blair, relict of Wm. Blair, decd,
late of this borough, aged about 89 years.

476. 16 May 1822 - Died Sun evening 5th inst, after a lingering
    illness, in his 68th year, Thomas Truxton, late of the U.S.
    Navy.

477. 23 May 1822 - Married Thurs last, John Miller, to Miss
    Barbara May, both of this co.

478. 30 May 1822 - Died Thurs last, Thomas James, of this
    borough.

479. 6 Jun 1822
Married Thurs last by Rev. G. Duffield, Col. Stephen Kerr, to
    Miss Maria M'Kean, both of this borough.
Same day by same, George M'Carmick, to Miss Ann King, both of
    this co.
Died Fri last at his residence near this borough, John Lechler.
- On Sat last, dau of John Hackett, Sulphur Springs.

480. 13 Jun 1822 - Married Thurs last by Rev Winebranner, John
    Smith to Miss Catharine Snyder, both of Allen twp.

481. 22 Jun 1822 - Married Thurs evening last by Rev Ebaugh,
Walter A. Bayard, to Miss Susanna Armor, both of this borough.

482. 27 Jun 1822
Married 20th inst Jacob Clark, to Miss Catharine Longenecker,
both of East Pennsborough twp.
Died suddenly Wed 12th inst at his residence in Dickinson twp,
William Line, senr. in his 74th year, native of Lancaster Co,
citizen of this co. about 40 years, leaving a widow, 9
children and 40 grandchildren.
Died 21st inst at his res in Antrim twp, Franklin co., captain
James Poe. During the last war though far advanced in years,
marched with a number from this county for the defence of
Baltimore. Repos.

483. 8 Aug 1822
Died Mon last, Mrs. Jane Hammil, of this borough.
- On Tues last, George Miller, son of Michael Miller of this
borough.
- On 25 Jul 1822, at Mr. Landis' tavern, 3 miles below
Harrisburg, on the Reading road, Miss Maria Rickart, aged
about 20 years. The deceased came from Carlisle, and it is
believed, she has a brother- in-law keeping tavern, sign of
the Buck, 9 miles this side of Phila; it is also believed her
father resides near Elizabethtown, Lancaster co., PA.

484. 22 Aug 1822
Died Mon night last of the dropsy, Mrs. Eve Jumper, of this
place, relict of Conrad Jumper, deceased, at an advanced age.
- On Tues night last, John Brown, formerly tobacconist, of this
borough.

485. 29 Aug 1822 - My wife Catharine having left my bed and
board withou any just cause... Thomas Berry, Frankford twp.

486. 12 Sep 1822
Married Thurs evening last by Rev Reynolds, John Hubbard, to Miss
Elizabeth Guest, both of this borough.
Died at Chambersburg, Fri night last in her 29th year, after a
lingering consumption, Mrs. Nancy Greenfield, consort of Hugh
Greenfield.

487. 19 Sep 1822 - Died at Denton (Eastern Shore of Md.) on the
8th inst, Mrs. Susanna Oliver, of a bilious fever, in her 50th
year, of this borough.

488. 26 Sep 1822
Died Sun last of a consumption, Mrs. Lydia Miles, wife of Richard
Miles, of this borough.
Died Tues last at the res of R. Blaine, esq. near this borough,
Levi Wheaton.
- On Sun morning 15th inst at Harrisburg, David M'Cormick,
merchant, late of Lewistown, PA. He contracted the disease in
Phila where he had been on business, and had reached

Harrisburg on his way home.

489. 10 Oct 1822
Died Mon 30th ult, Mrs. Sarah Brumbaugh, consort of Andrew
Brumbaugh of this borough, in her 31st year.
On 5th inst after a lingering illness of several years, Andrew
M'Cullough of Newville, in his 75th year.

490. 17 Oct 1822 - Died Sun 6th inst in Harrisburg, Mrs. Rahm,
relict of late Melchior Rahm, aged 56.

491. 24 Oct 1822
Married Thurs evening last by Rev Joseph Spenser, George Lee of
Dickinson ...Wilhelmina Foster, dau of Thomas Foster of this
borough.
- On Tues week by Rev Dr. Lochman, George H. Bucher, merchant, to
Miss Rebecca Pool, both of Harrisburg.
- On Thurs last by same, Simon Cameron, printer and junior editor
of the PA Intelligencer, to Miss Margaret Brua, both of
Harrisburg.
Died at his late resience in Dickinson town on Fri last, aged
about 85 years, John Moore, for the last 11 years deprived of
his sight; buried in the grave-yard adjoining this borough.
- Very suddenly Tues last, Jacob Crever, esq. one of the oldest
citizens of this borugh. A few minutes before his death, he
was assisting workmen who were putting up a building on a part
of the lot on which he lived.
- On Sun morning last at his late res near this borough, John
Duncan, son of Thomas Duncan, esq. of Phila.

492. 31 Oct 1822
Married on the evening of Mon 21 inst, by Rev Gray, Dr. John
Parshall, of Landisburg, to Miss Ann Ross, dau of late colonel
Samuel Ross, of Tyrone twp, Perry Co.
- On Thurs week by Rev Gray, James Coyle, of Saville twp, to Miss
Mary Patterson of Toboyne twp, Perry co.
- Same day by Rev J. Shull, Henry Wax, to Miss Anna Painter, both
of Rye twp, Perry co.
Died Mon night last, suddenly, Robert Taylor, of this borough.
- On Thurs 17th inst in Toboyne twp, Perry co., Miss Ann Beams,
in 14th year of her age.
John E. Howard, jr., esq. the eldest son of our rev veteran of
that name, is no more; he died a few days since, at
Mercersburg, PA, of the fatal malady so prevalent at that
place. He attended his brother-in-law, the lamented M'Henry,
to that fatal spot, and both of these individuals, the pride
and ornament of their native city, expired at that place.
- Suddenly at the house of his brother, in Allen twp, Cumberland
co., on 18th inst. James Wills, merchant, of Pittsburg. He
had been to Phila, to lay in a fresh supply of merchandize,
was arrested by sickness on his return home - being unble to
proceed further than a few miles beyond Carlisle, was brought
back to his brother's, where he sunk under the hand of an
afflicting Providence. This affliction was the more

penetrating, as another brother, John Wills, also a merchant
in Pittsburg, died 16 days before, six miles beyond
Greensburg, on his return from Phila. They were in separate
business, both had families of two children each, were both in
the city of Phila at the same time; but John had started home
about a week before James, the delicate situation of his
family urging his return.
- On 17th inst, Ludwig Worman, esq., member of Congress, of Berks
  co.

493. 7 Nov 1822
Married Thurs 24 Oct, by Rev John S. Ebaugh, John Pritt, to Miss
  Catharine Line, both of this co.
Died Wed 23d ult. in East Pennsborough twp, Cumberland co., John
  Largan(?), in 22nd year, by a fall from an apple tree on the
  12th ult.
- On Thurs 24th ult John Eminger of the dysentery, farmer of the
  same twp.

494. 14 Nov 1822
Married Thurs last by Rev Lochman, Michael Smith, to Miss
  Catharine Miller, both of Perry co.
On 29th ult, by Rev J. Shull, Jonathan Gotscholl to Miss Anna
Maria Lacer, both of Toboyne twp, Perry co.

495. 21 Nov 1822
Died Fri evening last, Mrs. Hannah Loudon, consort of Archibald
  Loudon, of this borough. She was in her 55th year; had been
  in a delicate state of health. On Sat evening last of typhus
  fever, James H. Mason, son of Dr.Mason, Pres. of Dickinson
  college.

496. 28 Nov 1822 - Married Thurs evening last by Rev Joseph
  Spencer, Thompson Brown, to Miss Ann Givin, dau of James
  Givin, all of this borugh.

497. 5 Dec 1822
Died at Sunbury Tues week, Andrew Albright, esq., elected member
  of the Senate of this state from the counties of Union and
  Northumberland, at the late election.
- On 27th ult, Mrs. Elizabeth M'Gowan, widow of David M'Gowan,
  deceased, of this co.
- On Sun last Miss Ann Crane, of this borough.

498. 12 Dec 1822
Married in Mifflin co on 5th inst by Rev Coulter, John Piper of
  Cumberland co, to Miss Maria, dau of the late Nathaniel
  Randolph of Adams co.
- In Harrisburg on Thurs inst by Rev Wm. R. Dewitt, N. B. Wood,
  esq. to Miss Catharine Bender, both of that place.
Died suddenly on Sat night last capt. William Cook, late of
  Mechanicsburg. On Mon following he was interred at Silver's
  Spring with military honors.
- Recently at Millerstown, William North, Esq., formerly

commissioner of Cumberland co.

499. 19 Dec 1822
Married Thurs 12th inst by Rev Joshua Williams, George Skelly, to
  Miss Casindana Wilson, both of Newton twp, Cumberland co.
- On Tues evening last by Rev Ebaugh, John Ramsey, to Mrs.
  Elizabeth Hacket, both of this borough.
Died Fri last, after a short illness, Mrs. Charlotte Coffman, of
  this borugh, in her 82d year.

500. 26 Dec 1822
Married Mon evening last by Rev C. Reynolds, George Brown, of
  Allen twp, to Miss Ann Dodds of this borough.
Died on 28th ult in Millerstown, Juniatta, Dr. William
  Waterhouse, formerly of Hanterdon co., NJ, in his 29th year,
  leaving a wife and relatives.
- Suddenly on 18th inst, Miss Elizabeth Turner, dau of Joseph
  Turner, deceased, late of Dickinson twp.
- At Middletown, Dauphin co, on 22d ult, Theodore Burr,
  celebrated for his mechanical talents, but most for his
  extensive knowledge as a bridge builder.

501. 2 Jan 1823
Married 23 Dec by Rev Benj. Keller, Peter Swords, of Dickinson
  twp, Cumberland co., to Miss Isabella Adams, of Tyrone twp,
  Perry co. On 26 Dec by same, Henry Neal, to Miss Mary Butz, of
  East Pennsborough twp.
Died Fri last, after a short illness, Joseph Edwards, of this
  borough.
- On Sat last in his 63d year, Dr. Michael Leib, Prothonotary of
  the District Court for the City and County of Phila.
Fire - Fri evening last, a stable, property of the heirs of
  Joseph Logue, deceased in the neighborhood of the Seceder
  meeting house, in this borough, was destroyed by fire.

502. 9 Jan 1823 - Died Sat evening last in Stoughstown, Newton
  twp, Jacob Stough, sen., in his 71st year, soldier of rev war.

503. 16 Jan 1823
Married 31st ult by Rev B. Keller, James Clark, to Miss
  Margaretta Wartzbacher, of Dickinson twp.
- On 9th inst by same, John Bishop to Miss Esther Sollenberger,
  of Allen twp.
- On same day by same, Isaac Lefever, to Miss Elizabeth Rine, of
  Westpennsboro'.
Died suddenly on Tues 7th inst, Matthew Brown, for many years an
  inhabitant of this borough.
- On Sat night last in Perry co., Dennis Kerr.
- On Sun last near Landisburg, Perry Co., well advanced in year,
  James Davis, formerly a tavern keeper in this borough.
- On Fri morning last in the city of Lancaster, William Dickson,
  editor of the Intelligencer at an advanced age.

504. 23 Jan 1823 - Married Tues 15th inst by Rev Dr. Lochman,

Abraham Rupley, to Miss Elizabeth Keiteman, both of this co.

505. 6 Feb 1823
Married 24th ult by Rev B. Keller, Martin Rob, to Miss Ann Wildi,
  both of Hummelstown, Dauphin co.
- On 28th by same, Philip Cornman, to Miss Margaret Zeigler, both
  of N. Middleton.
- At the house of Dr. Thomas Cooper, Columbia, SC, Fri evening,
  Jan 10, 1823, by professor Henry, of the South Carolina
  College, George Walker, esq. of Lower Dublin twp, near
  Holmesburg, PA, to Miss Marianne Heming, formerly of the
  borough of Carlisle.
Whereas my wife Catharine Long has absconded from my bed and
  board... Samuel Long, Jr., Hopewell twp.

506. 20 Feb 1823
Married Thurs lat by Rev Dewitt, Henry Horr [Harr?] to Miss Mary
  Spire, both of Mechanicsburg.
Died Wed 12th inst, James Fleming, of North Middleton twp. Sat
  last of the consumption, at his late res near Newville,
  Richard Woods, aged about 63 years.
- Thurs last in East Pennsborough twp, Mrs. Catharine Redsecker,
  consort of Nicholas Redsecker, aged 75 years.

507. 26 Feb 27 1823
Married 15th inst in Allen twp, by P. Laverty, esq. Martin Lutz,
  to Mrs. Polly Martin, both of Cacalico twp, Lancaster Co.
Died Thurs evening last at an advanced age, Mrs. Jane Gibson,
  widow, of this borough.
- On Sun last, Mrs. Randolph, of North Middleton twp.
- Mon last at his residence near Landisburg, Perry Co., James
  Foster, aged about 30 years.

508. 13 Mar 1823
Married Thurs 27th ult by Rev Gray, William B. Mitchell, esq. of
  Juniata twp, Perry co, to Miss Rebecca Leyman, dau of Henry
  Leyman, esq. of Clark's Ferry, same co.
- Tues 4th inst by Rev W. R. De Witt, Samuel M'Kinsey, of
  Petersburg, Perry co., to Miss Isabella Peacock, of
  Harrisburg.
Died 22d ult. at a very advanced age, George M'Milan, of Toboyne
  twp, Perry co.; also recently, in Rye twp, same co, Barnhart
  Slew(?).
- Suddenly on morning of Sun 2d inst, Mrs. Margaret Carson,
  relict of the late John Carson, esq., decd, late of Dauphin
  co. in 63d year.
Lawrenceburg, IN, Feb 20 - Drowned on 6 Jan, George M'Kaa(?),
  not long since from Shippenburg, PA. He got into Taylor's
  creek, Boone co, KY, nearly opposite Lawrenceburg. The
  deceased has a brother and sister near Louisville, KY. His
  clothes and effects are at Samuel Liff's, Boone Co, KY -
  Oracle.

509. 24 Apr 1823
Married Thurs evening last, by Rev Benjamin Keller, Samuel Gould,
    to Miss Mary W. Gregg, both of this borough.
- On 12th inst, William Thompson, distiller, of Bedford co, put a
    period ot his existence by shooting himself.

510. 2 Feb 1826
Died Tues morning last, at an advanced age, Mrs. Mary Line, widow
    of William Line, late of Dickinson twp, decd.
- Fri last after a long and painful sickness, Mrs. Catharine
    Potto, aged about 68 years, of this borough. [See item #257]

511. 9 Feb 1826
Died at Springfield Fri last, after a severe lingering illness,
    Captain Robert M'Bride, soldier of the late war, for several
    years one of the Commissioners of Cumberland co - in his 36th
    year of his age.
Mon last, Margaret, only dau of Mrs. Sarah Porter, of this
    borough. [See item #258]
Tues 31st ult, William Leyburn, aged 30, of Harrisburg.

512. 2 Mar 1826
Married Thurs last by Rev Moody, Thomas Sterrett, of Mifflin twp,
    to Miss Jane Clarke, dau of George Clarke of this co.
- On 21 Feb by Rev Alexander Sharp, captain William F. Junkin, of
    Neshanock Mills, Mercer co., to Miss Eliza Adams of East
    Pennsborough twp, Cumberland co.

513. 30 Mar 1826
Married Thurs 16th inst by Rev Alexander Sharp, Andrew Harper, of
    Mifflin Mills, Mifflin twp, to Miss Elizabeth dau of William
    M'Culloch, decd, late of West Pennsborough twp.
Died Mon morning last, Mrs. Mary Ramsey, wife of William Ramsey,
    esq. of this borough. [After a severe illness - Dem. Rep.]
- In Harrisburg on Tues 21 inst. Robert E. Hobart, Esq. one of
    the representatives from Montgomery co, at an advanced age.

514. 5 Apr 1826 - Died Mon evening 27th Mar of a lingering
    illness, Mrs. Elizabeth Quigley, consort of col. James
    Quigley, of East Pennsborough twp, aged 36 years.

515. 13 Apr 1826
Married Tues 14 Mar 1826 by Rev H. Habliston, Jonathan Keffer, to
    Miss Mary Jacoby, of Southampton twp, Franklin co.
- By same Thurs 23d March, Samuel Karmeny, to Miss Susannah, dau
    of Jacob Fetter, senr. late of Carlisle, but now of
    Southampton twp, Franklin co.
- By same Thurs 30th ult, Jacob Snider, to Miss Elizabeth
    Flinder, both of Chambersburg.
- Same day by same, Jacob Sells, of Carlisle, to Miss Mary
    M'Ilroy, of Shippensburg.
Communicated - Died suddenly Tues night last, Capt. Dominick
    Cornyn, late of the U.S. army, for many years an active
    politician of this co - native of the county Leitrim, Ireland.

516. 20 Apr 1826
Married Thurs evening last by Rev George Duffield, Major James
     Williamson, to Miss Mary Urie, dau of Thomas Urie, Esq. all of
     North Middleton twp.
Died suddenly on Sat last in the city of Phila, whither he went,
     some months since, to improve himself in his profession,
     William Hendel, son of capt. George Hendel, of this borough;
     he was in his 19th year.

517. 27 Apr 1826
Married by Rev George Duffield, on 25th inst, Flemming Nesbitt,
     of Union co, PA, to Miss Ann W. dau of Paul Randolph, of North
     Middleton twp.
- On 21st inst by Rev Benjamin Keller, Dr. Jacob Bossler [Bassler
     - Dem. Rep.], to Miss Ann D. Herrman, both of Silver Spring
     twp.

518. 4 May 1826
Married Mon evening 22d ult by Rev Williams at Walton Farm,
     Cumberland co., William Audenried, Esq. member of the senate
     of Penn. to Miss Jane Maria, dau of Alexander Wills, Esq.
- At Huntingdon Wed evening, 2-th ult by Rev Minshall, John W.
     Stugert, Junior editor of the Republican Advocate, to Miss
     Catharine M'Cabe, both of that borough.
Died Thurs last in this borough at the residence of John D.
     Mahon, esq. her nephew, Miss Mary Duncan.
- On Tues 25 Apr in East Pennsborough twp, Mrs. Ann Maria
     Livingston, consort of Major John Livingston, after a
     lingering illness, aged 28 years.

519. 11 May 1826
Married in Phila 2d inst by Rev. W. H. Furness, John Wyeth, of
     Harrisburg, to Miss Lydia Allen, dau of late Thomas Allen,
     esq. of the former place.
- On Sun last in this borough, Monsieur Augee, professor of
     instrumental music, considerably advanced in years. [See item
     #268]

520. 18 May 1826
Married at Carlisle on 4th inst, Henry Miller, of Harrisburg, to
     Miss Elizabeth Rine, of Carlisle.
- At Harrisburg, same day, Allison Pinney, to Miss Catharine
     Diffendaffer, of Cumberland co.
- At Chambersburg, on 6th inst, Archibald M'Alister, esq. to Mrs.
     Sarahbella Dunlop, of Chambersburg.
- On Thurs last by Rev Geo. Duffield, William Shrom, merchant, to
     Misss Harriet Wilson, dau of John Wilson, merchant, all of
     Carlisle.
- By Rev J. S. Ebaugh, Sun last in Carlisle, Samuel Fager, to
     Miss Catharine Bell, both of Harrisburg.
Died 28 Apr at the Big Spring in this co, Alexander Scroggs, in
     his 77th year.
From York Recorder - Died Fri morning from a wound, Lieut. John
     Koontz, officer of the company of Penn. Volunteers, aged 35

years. He was stabbed with a bayonet in arresting John
Odenwalt during a riot in which George Odenwalt, brother of
John Odenwalt, made violent efforts to rescue his brother. To
prevent the rescue James Morris, lowered his musket and
directed the bayonet towards George Odenwalt who caught it in
his hand and caused it to thrust forward deeply into the groin
of Lieut. Koontz. Lieut Koontz was a member of the company of
York Volunteers which marched to Baltimore in 1814, and one of
its non-commissioned offiers.

521. 25 May 1826
Died Sun morning last, Mrs. Margaret Johnson, consort of James
Johnson, of Toboyne twp, Perry co, aged about 60.
- On Sun evening 30th ult, Miss Jane Linn, young lady of Saville
twp, Perry Co. - whilst on her way to church on horse back,
she received a kick from a horse in company, which fractured
one of her legs ... Forester.

522. 1 Jun 1826
Married at New York, lately, Henry Doty, to Mrs. Elizabeth
Stockdale, both formerly of this borough.
- At New Cumberland, by Rev Augustus H. Lochman, Samuel Gray, to
Miss Jane Willet.

523. 8 Jun 1826 - James Queen, living near Lebanon, murdered his
wife Sat 27 ult with a spade. He is now in the jail at
Lebanon. Har. Chronicle.

524. 13 Jul 1826 - Died suddenly Sat last, in South Middleton
twp, Anthony Glenn, considerably advanced in life.

525. 28 Sep 1826
Died in Landisburg Sun last after a lingering illness, Richard P.
Creigh, Esq. son of Dr. John Creigh, of this borough.
- At his residence in Milford twp, Mifflin co on Mon evening 18th
inst, of the bilious fever, William Sillheimer, paper maker.

526. 5 Jul 1827 - Married Tues 19th ult by Rev J. Shull, George
Swarner, to Miss Barbara Kennedy, all of Tyrone twp, Perry co
Carlisle Republican, And Farmer's and Mechanics' Gazette

527. 28 Jan 1830
Married 21st inst by Rev Emanuel Keller, Samuel Basehower to Miss
Barbary Moltz.
- On same day by same, David Coble to Miss Ann Eberly, all of
this co.
Whereas my wife Sally has left me ... She robbed me of a
considerable sum of money which was deposited in my bible,
together with a considerable quantity of household goods.
Simon Smith.

528. 11 Feb 1830
Married Wed 13th ult by Rev John S. Ebaugh, John Burns to Miss
Ann Maria Wundery.

- On same day by same, Jacob Wisler, to Miss Elizabeth Black.
- On Tues 26th by same, Christian Hast, to Miss Catharine Spahr.
- On Thurs 4th inst by same, Joseph Ingraim, to Miss Mary Ann Blaik, all of Cumberland Co.
Died Tues 19 Jan last of consumption, Mrs. Catharine Miller wife of Philip Miller of Mnroe twp, in her 43d year.

529. 18 Feb 1830
Married Thurs 11th inst by Rev John S. Ebaugh, Mode Griffith of York co., to Miss Eliza Faufman, of Cumberland co.
- On Wed 3d inst by Rev Williams, George M. Graham to Miss Eliza Alter, both of Westpennsborough twp.

530. 4 Mar 1830
Married Thurs 25th ult at Lisburn by Rev George F. Cain, Samuel Shipley of Lancaster Co, to Miss Sarah Atkinson, of Lisburn, Cumberland co.
- On same day by Rev F. Heyer, Adam Cocklin to Miss Barbara Gasta, all of this co.
- On evening of same day by same, David Krider to Miss Elisabeth Rugh (?) all of this borough.
Woodstock, VA, Feb 11. On Thurs evening last by Rev Jacob Medtart, Rev Lewis Eichelberger, Pastor of the German Lutheran Church in Winchester, to Miss Mary Ann, dau of John Miller, merchant of the firm of John and Abraham Miller of that place.
- On Mon evening last at the same place in the store of John and Abraham Miller, by Rev Riddle, Rev Kurtz, pastor of the Lutheran Church in Hagerstown to Miss Catharine dau of Henry W. Baker, mercahnt of the firm of Henry W. Baker and son.

531. 11 Mar 1830
Married Tues last in Harrisburg by Rev Augustus Lochman, James Mullin to Miss Rachael Barber, both of South Middleton twp.
- On 1st ult in Phila, by Rev Potts, Abraham De Rush, printer, to Miss Sarah Harkness, both formerly of this place.

532. 18 Mar 1830
Died Sat morning last in 29th year, Mrs. Hannah Beetem, wife of George Beetem of this borough, leaving husband and 7 small children.
- In Harrisburgh on 11th inst, after a lingering illness, Edmon F. Cryder, one of the editors of the Chronicle, aged 24 years.
- Yesterday morning, Mrs. Ann Irvin, in her 89th year.
Married Thurs last by Rev F. Heyer, Thomas Paxton, to Miss Maria, dau of Samuel Galbreath, all of Dickinson twp.
- On 4th inst by Rev Emanuel Keller, Christian Lewer, to Miss Fanny Cocklin.
- On same day by same, Jacob Kraut to Miss Mary Coover, all of Cumberland co.
- Tues evening 2d inst by Rev Henry Haverstick, Samuel Charles, editor of the Civillian, to Miss Margaret Wineour, dau of Henry Wineour, all of Cumberland, Md.
- On Thurs last in Chambersburgh, by Rev Rahauser, Wm. L. Smith, merchant, of Mechanicsburg, to Miss Mary Ann Bigler, of

Strasburg, Franklin co.

533. 25 Mar 1830
Married Thurs morning, March 4th, by Rev Heyer, John Lutz, to Miss Catharine Miller.
- On Tues March 9th, by same, William Tritt, to Miss Catharine Black.
- On Tues evening, March 16th, by same, George Hughes, to Miss Hannah Douglass.
- By same on Thurs March 18th John Watson, to Miss Hannah Meyer, all of this borough and vicinity.
Died some time last week, George Sanderson, of North Middleton twp.
- On Sun last in her 70th year, Mrs. Mary Franks, relict of Jacob Franks, decd, of this borough.

534. 1 Apr 1830
Died Sat last, Mrs. Hackett, relict of Plunket Hackett.
Married Thurs morning last in Harrisburg by Rev Annon, E. L. Dunbar, Esq. of Lewistown to Miss Mary Kyle, dau of Crawford Kyle, of Armagh twp, Mifflin co.
- On Tues evening, March 23d, by Rev Heyer, Edmund R. Davis, to Miss Jane Spottswood, both of this borough.
- On Thurs evening, March 25th, by same, John Robison, to Miss Isabella Stewart, both of this borough.

535. 8 Apr 1830
Died in Phila on Wed, 31st ult of consumption, Joseph W. O'Brien, in his 19th year, son of Com. Richard O'Brien, decd, formerly of this place.
- On Thurs morning last in her 48th year, Mrs. Catharine Trough, wife of John Trough, Innkeeper, of this borough.
- In Perry co., Sat morning last, Mrs. Catharine Sholl, consort of the Rev. Sholl, and dau of Leonard Keller, of this borough, in her 37th year.

536. 15 Apr 1830 - Married Thurs last by Rev Pringle, Adam Uhler, to Miss Catharine Reath, both of this co.

537. 22 Apr 1830
Married Thurs 8th inst by Rev George Duffield, Abraham Lamberton to Miss Margaret E. Clark, both of North Middleton.
- In the borough of Newville, on Thurs 8th inst, by Rev J. Williams, Jacob Kinsley to Miss Charlotte, dau of capt. John Roberts deceased.
- On Tues evening last by Rev A. Lochman, Dr. John H. Fagar, to Miss Eliza Jones, all of Harrisburg.

538. 29 Apr 1830 - Married on 27th inst by Rev F. Pringle, Samuel Bellshoover, to Miss Susan Rherer, both of S. Middleton, Cumberland co.

539. 20 May 1830 - Married 12th inst by Rev Augustus H. Lochman, Charles Bioren to Miss Harriet, dau of Gabriel Heister, Esq.

last surveyor General of this State.

540. 10 Jun 1830
Married Thurs 27th ult by Rev Helfenstine, Henry Bitner, of this
co., to Miss Sarah Moore, of York co.
- On Mon 31st ult by rev Samuel Brison, James Spottswood, to Miss
Margaret Kants, both of this borough.

541. 17 Jun 1830
Married Mon evening last by Rev Heyer, John Wallace, to Miss Jane
Beaty, both of this place.
- On Sun 6th Jun inst at Mechanicsburg, by Rev Williamson,
Captain George Donehower, of Phila, to Miss Hannah Hodge, of
Carlisle, PA.
Died in this place Mon last of quinsy, Miss Catherine
Helfenstein, dau of Rev. Albert Helfenstein of Baltimore, aged
about 13 years.

542. 24 Jun 1830
Died yesterday morning, Mrs. Margaret Weakly, relict of Daniel
Weakley, in her 29th year.
- On Mon morning last of pulmonary consumption, George Smith,
sen., aged about 40 years.

543. 29 Jul 1830
Died Sat last, Mrs. Rebecca McPherson aged about 40 years,
consort of Robert McPherson, of this borough.
- In Harrisburg on Mon, 19th inst, of consumption, Henry
Minshall, printer, aged 33 years.

544. 12 Aug 1830
Died Sat 31st Jul, Owen Evans of Dickinson twp, in his 54th year,
leaving wife and 9 children.
- On 30th May last at Rocky Mount, near Washington, Autauga co,
AL, John Baughman, formerly of this place, in his 32d year.
545. 19 Aug 1830
Died Mon 26th ult, Matthew Woodburn, of Newton twp.
- On 11th inst in this town, Rev. John Noblock, pastor of the
several congregations in the vicinity of this place, aged
about 32 years. About 3 weeks since the deceased was severely
attacked with dysentary. Perry Forester.

546. 26 Aug 1830 - Died Thurs last after a short sickness, Mrs.
Mary McMurrey, aged about 58 years, wife of Thomas McMurrey,
of this place.

547. 2 Sep 1830
Married 8th ult by Rev E. Keller, Benjamin McCord, to Miss Mary
Titler.
- On 10th ult, Christian Dashour(?) to Miss Elizabeth Kepfert.
- On 19th ult, Daniel Wolf, to Miss Ellen Wareheim, all of this
co.

548. 23 Sep 1830 - Married Thurs 16th inst by Rev John S.

Ebaugh, John Main, to Miss Elizabeth Rheem, all of this
borough.

549. 30 Sep 1830
Married 2d inst by Rev E. Keller, Martin Cocklin, to Miss Mary
  Gossler.
- On 16th inst. by same, Christian Stener, to Miss Catharine
  Stener.
- On 23d inst, Henry Herch, to Miss Elizabeth Snell, all of this
  co.
Died Sat evening last, Mrs. Anna Gertrude Chritzman, of
  Gettysburg, aged 67 years.

550. 14 Oct 1830 - Died on Sat evening last, Nicholas Harting,
  in his 51st year.

551. 21 Oct 1830
Married 7th inst by Rev J. S. Ebaugh, Andrew Holmes, to Miss
  Nancy Low, both of this place.
- On 12th by same, Wm. Sigler, to Miss Susan Roads, of Newville.
- On the 19th by same, John Palm, to Miss Susan Klink, of
  Stoughs town.
- On Tues last by Rev Wilson, Gen. Robert T. Stewart of Pitts-
  urg, to Mrs. Mary Hamilton, of Middlesex, Cumberland co.
Died Sun evening last, Mrs. Peffer, aged 77 years. and on Mon
  morning, Philip Peffer, aged 83 years, both of Dickenson twp.
- In this place Mon evening last, Alfred Cole, of New York about
40 years of age.

552. 11 Nov 1830
Died at New York on 3d inst, Mrs. Elizabeth O'Brien, consort of
  Lieut. Gabrial A. O'Brien, of the U.S. Cutter, Alert, and dau
  of the late Henry Watkinson of that city, aged 26 years.
- On Sat last, 6th inst, Matilda, infant dau of capt. John
  M'Cartney, aged about 4 years.

553. 23 Dec 1830
Married on evening of the same day by same, Jesse Zeigler, of
  North Middleton, to Miss Mary Ann Peffer, of this place.
- On Wed evening last by Rev Williamson, John M. Woodburn, of
  Carlisle, to Miss Ann D. Ege, dau of Peter Ege, of Pinegrove
  Furnace.
- On 11th ult by Rev John S. Ebaugh, John Slonecker to Miss
  Elizabeth Philips. - On 18th ult by same, John Fahrenbaugh to
  Miss Elizabeth Brandt. - On same day by same, Thomas Harris to
  Miss Elizabeth Selcil(?). - On 7th inst by same, Solomon
  Smirey to Miss Rachel Shur. All of Carlisle and its vicinity.

554. 30 Dec 1830
Married Thurs last by Rev G. Duffield, Smith Woodburn, to Miss
  Margaret, dau of Tho's Craighead, of South Middleton twp.
- On same evening, at the house of Abraham Williams, in Allen
  twp, by Rev Luey(?), Alexander Cathcart, merchant, of
  Dillsburg, to Miss Elmira Jane King.

CARLISLE GAZETTE

(Issues held by Cumberland County Historical Society
And The Hamilton Library Association)

555. 1 Apr 1829
Died Thurs last, aged 80 years, Mrs. Elizabeth Bentz, of this
   borough.
- On Sat last, John Sheffer, of N. Middleton twp.
- On Sun last at an advanced age, Mrs. Betsy Cain, of this
   borough.
556. 6 Jan 1830 - Married on 24th ult in Phila by Rev Engles,
   William Martin Crouce, formerly of this place, to Miss Rachael
   Campbell, of that city.

- - - - -

557. From *The Pennsylvania Genealogical Magazine*, Vol. XI
   (1930), 88-89.
Allen Township, Cumberland Co., PA.
Marriages 1828 - 1830. Taken from a Tax duplicate book of that
   place as entered by John B. Coover, Justice of the Peace,
   Director of Harrisburg Bank; brother-in-law of J. D. Rupp the
   historian, and a man of considerable wealth.

1828, The names of those persons that have been married in Allen
   Township, viz:
Nov 13, Daniel Krysher to Casiah Bowman. By Mr. Lochman.
Nov 27, Levi Murke to Susana Martin. By Mr. Dewit.
Dec 2, John Young to Elizabeth Hilt.
Dec 4, Daniel Grumbine of Hanover to Christiana Hollocher, near
   Berlin.
Dec 18, John Hollocher, to Eliza Shelly, by Mr. Lochman.
Dec 18, Mr. Hays to Miss Mary Ann Coover, by Mr. Williamson
Dec 25, Ira Long to Miss Elizabeth Forry, by Rev. Keller.

1829, Feb 26, Jonas Rupp to Sarah Heck. By Rev. J. Winebrenner.
Mar 2, Mr. Bearch to Jane Small. By Mr. Trisebauch.
Mar 5, George Chapman to Martha Eckels. By Mr. Williamson.
Mar 5, Mr. Greenewalt to Polly Alick.
Apr 16, David Miller to Miss Resser of York Co.
Apr 16, James Horner to K. Crouse; Mr. Humer to Miss McClair.
Apr 23, Jacob Bulmer to Catherine Hartman.
Sep 10, John Renniker to Miss Ann Hursh, by Mr. Heller; Mr. Sidle
   to Miss Bishop; Sml. Miller to Miss Hannah Philips.

Marriage proposals made 30 Mar 1829, accepted Apr 9, 1829: John
   B. Coover married 10 Sep 1829 to Miss Elizabeth Rupp, by Rev.
   Winebrenner (in Harrisburg at Mrs. Friedley's tavern). Took
   dinner there and then went up to river to Hallifax and lodged
   at Mr. Gigers and the next day we returned to Mr. George
   Rupp's, and the next day following we went to my father's.
1829, Sep 17, Mr. Lindle to Miss Eleanor Gregary.
Oct 24, William Wise to Margaret Mateer.

Nov 12, Jesse Houck to Miss Long.
Dec 10, Abraham Hartzler to Miss Nancy Eberly.
Dec 22, Dnl. Browley to Miss E. Ford.
Dec 12, Joseph Strock to Miss Margaret Negeley.

1820, Jan 21, Samuel Basehorn to Barbliana Mull.
Jan 21, David Coble to Mrs. Eberly.
Jan 28, Henry Bowman to Martha Musser of Lancaster.
Mar 4, Abraham Basler to Miss E. Harman.
Jun 10, John Snyder to Miss Mary Rupp.
          - Contributed by Miss Jessica C. Ferguson of Harrisburg.

- - - - -

559. From *The Pennsylvania Genealogical Magazine*, XII (1935).
Inscriptions from Old Graveyard, Allen, (locally known as
Churchtown, about 7 miles from Carlisle. Before the graveyard
was cleared in 1910 a copy of the inscriptions was made from
which this is taken.
Adam Leidich, born 6 Oct 1758; died 16 Jul 1829.
Joseph Bricker, born 26 Jun 1794; died 29 Aug 1822.
Russell Young, born 29 Apr 1763; died 1 Sep 1823.
Chasper (?) Diller, born 28 Feb 1768; died 16 Sep 1825.
Jacob Wolfe, born 21 Sep 1766; died 23 Sep 1823.
Hartman Morit, born 8 Nov 1734; died 30 Nov 1822.
John Leib, born 28 Jan 1782; died 13 Apr 1829.
Daniel McNeal, born 16 Dec 1796; died 16 Jan 1826.
                    Mrs. Lenora E. Flower.

- - - - -

560. From Inscriptions of those originally interred in the First
    Lutheran burying Ground of Carlisle, Pennsylvania, on the
    Northeast Corner of Hanover Street and Chestnut aveune, by
    Mrs. Guiles Flower. *The Pennsylvania Genealogical Magazine*,
    Vol. XII (1933) 88-91.
Elizabeth, wife of Conrad Eckert, died 31 Aug 1823, aged 34
    years, 9 mos, 1 day.
George Rutz son of Dewalt and Elizabeth Rutz, died 18 Mar 1825.
Ann Margaretta Rutkuhns, died 2 Sep 1823, aged 52 years, 5 mos,
    21 days.
Abraham Rupley died 30 Jan 1826.
John Dietrich Wunderlich born 11 Nov 1757; died 10 Dec 1829.
His wife Anna Margaret Yetter, born 19 Jul 1766; died 11 May
    1840.
Christopher Wunderlich born 11 Apr 1767; died 17 Feb 1823.
His wife Eleanore Imboden.
Daniel Wunderlich born 27 Aug 1737; died 1 Feb 1799.
His wife Eva Barbara Siechele born 28 Oct 1744; died 27 Apr 1821.
Sarah, wife of Samuel Nidy Neidigh], and dau of Mark and Sabinah
    Zegler, died 20 May 1830, aged 33 years, 4 mos and 12 days.
Philip Pepper, died 18 Oct 1830, aged 83 years.
Mary wife of Philip Pepper died 17 Oct 1830, aged 77 years.
Jacob Crevier, Esq. died 22 Oct 1822, in his 72nd year.
Andrew Zeigler born 25 Jun 1752; died 5 Jun 1827.

David Smith, Esq. born in Washington Co., MD, 7 Sep 1783; died
    Sep 1825, aged 42 years, 1 day.
Keziah S., wife of Daniel F. Lehman born 11 Jun 1827; died 4 Oct
    1849, aged 22 years, 3 mos, 23 days.
Mary, wife of Jacob Musselman died Sep 1826, in her 74th year.
M. A. Kinsily, died 14 Feb 1825, aged 10 years, 8 mos, 7 days.
Magdalen Low died 1 Feb 1826, in her 75th year.
Elizabeth Kutz, born 29 Oct 1814; died 10 Nov 1828.
Frederick Emanuel son of Rev. B. and Eliza Keller died 27 Mar
    1827, aged 5 mos, 23 days.

- - - - -

561. Allison United Meth Carlisle 1823-1833 [Records held by the
    Cumberland County Historical Society And the Hamilton Library
    Association]
Marriages by John Bear
1823 - Oct 30 Robert Sunsbury to Eleanor Bell (coloured) married
    by Robert Vinton
April 29 1824 John Quigley to Ann Catherine Dipple
Jul 1st John G. Fllod to Jane Holms
Jul 22 Frederick Hoke to Nancy Bricker
Aug 12 Jacob Spangler to Elizabeth Ellenor Waterberry
Sep 23 Elijah Williams to Margaret Musken (coloured)

Marriages by A. Griffith
1826 May 23 Wm. Crop(?) to Rachel Detterinan(?)
            Robert Quigly to Ann Croney
Oct 14 Wm. Musselman to Catherine Shewalter
Dec 21 mathew Leaton to Loray M. Bradley
1827 March 20 Thos. Brown to Margaret Philips
March 27 Philip Quigly to Catharine Weaver

1827 Marriages celebrated by Henry Slicer
Jun 14 Samuel Bear to Elizabeth Angnay
1828 Jun 19 Thursday Samuel Crop to Mary Mathews by C. A. Davis
    July 22 Tuesday, Henry Swisher to Maria Bugler, both of
    Harrisburg, by C. A. Davis.
Jul 22 Tuesday, Mores McCoy to Mary A. Ferris, both of Carlisle,
    by C. A. Davis.

Oct 3 Thursday, George Spansler to Mary McManus, both of
    Cumberland co, C. A. Davis.
Nov 27 Thursday in Washington City, D. Col., License dated same
    day.
Nathaniel B. Keene to Susan E. Davis, both of Wash. City by C. A.
    Davis.

1829 All by C. A. Davis
Jan 13 Tuesday, Henry Miller to Elizabeth Thompson both of
    Cumberland Co., PA, by C.A. Davis.
Jan 27 Tuesday, Frederick Sanns(?) to Mrs. Ann Natcher both of
    Cumberland co. by C. A. Davis.
Apr 2 Jacob Hoffer to Mary Ann Mayer, both of Cumberland Co, by

C. A. Davis.
Apr 7 Tuesday, Rev Jacob F. Kauber to Mary Ann Smith, both of Cumberland co.
Apr 9 Thuresday Robert Moore to Ann M. Kinney, both of Cumberland Co.
Apr 30, Thursday, Andrew Keiser to Mary Butler, both of PA.
May 5 Tues, John Sadler to Rachel Deitrick both of Adams Co.
May 14, Thurs, Joseph Crawford to Dolly Moore (colored) both of Cumberland Co.
May 18, Mon, John Earnest to Margaret Bradley, both of Cumberland Co.
May 28, Thurs, Daniel Seit, to Matilda Patton, both of Cumberland Co.
Jul 9 Thurs, William Keith to Mrs. Margaret Eckard, both of Cumberland co.
Sep 17 Thurs, Jefferson Worthington to Ann Kernan, both of Cumberland Co.
Dec 17, Thurs, Jesse Waters to Elizabeth Lynch, both of Cumberland Co.
Dec 17, Jacob Bretz of Adams Co to Mary Dipple of Cumberland Co.
Dec 22 Tues, John Reed to Mary Manly both of Cumberland co.
Dec 24 Thurs Willm. R. Rank to Elizabeth Franklin both of Cumberland Co.,

1830 Jan 17 Sabbath, George Yengst to Eliza Ramsey, both of Cumberland co.
Jan 21 Thurs, Daniel Hershman to Eliza Wyncoop, both of Cumberland Co.
Jan 28 Thurs, Daniel McCarty to Mrs. Sarah Degal, both of Cumberland Co.
May 31 1830 Mon, James Spottswood to Margreet Kants by Samuel Brison.
Nov 30 1830 Tues Jonathan Bierbown(?) to Lucetta Cary.
Samuel Brison.

First Evangelical Lutheran Church in Carlisle. Records have been deposited in the Lutheran Theological Seiminary, Gettysburg, PA. The translation is partly based on the work of Mrs. Pearl Reddig Fleck which was revised and corrected.
George Boyer and Elisabeth Strayer 4 Jan 1821.
Michael Hoover and Gosweiler [sic] 18 Jan 1821.
Ludiwg Noss and Catharine Foulk 25 Jan 1821
Robert Lion and Ann Lynch 25 Jan 1821
William Adams and Elisabeth Ball 1 Feb 1821
John Nagle and Margret Peffer 8 Feb 1821
John Bassler and Susan Keller 15 Feb 1821
Simon Spang and Miss Shade 8 Mar 1821
Samuel Bear and Maria Musselman 15 Mar 1821
John All and Maria M. Claudy 20 Mar 1821
Jacob Smith and Anna Maria Wolf 27 Mar 1821
Daniel Brenner and Elisabeth Strein 29 Mar 1821
George Richter and An Catharine Leib 29 Mar 1821
John Brenizen and Catharine Kneisely 5 Apr 1821
John Allbrecht and Miss Ruby 8 Apr 1821
Joshua Gohin and Ann Pee 3 May 1821

Philip Kohler and Chritina Kapp 3 May 1821
George Crall and Sarah Conner 3 May 1821
John Claus and Barbara Shoff 20 May 1821
Martin Reisinger and Elisabeth Weaver 27 May 1821
Solomon Bauman and Catharine Egolf 29 May 1821
John Ziegler and Barbara Bob 29 May 1821
Henry Buck and Ann Elisabeth Wattson 5 Jun 1821
George Jacob and Susan Hummer 7 Jun 1821
Charles S. Walters and Jane McDonald 7 Jun 1821
John Mitchely and Louisa Pfand 28 Jun 1821
James Louden and Maria Mayloney 12 Jul 1821
Mr. Diller and B. Wolf 31 Jul 1821
Jesse Spahr and Margret Peterman 5 Aug 1821
Daniel Smith and Elonor Shrom 30 Aug 1821
John Mitchelyy and Henricka Kopp 30 Aug 1821
Philip Swartz and Beata Deininger 4 Sep 1821
Alexander Liged and Rebecca Doey 6 Sep 1821
George M. Bear and Elisabeth Richter 11 Sep 1821
William Brenizer and Susan Kritzer 13 Sep 1821
James Eagens and Mary Zerman 13 Sep 1821
William Sponsler and Martha Varrens 24 Sep 1821
Henry Webbert and Elisabeth Brindel 4 Oct 1821
John Donley and Margret Liged 11 Oct 1821
John P. Jenner and Louisa Kake 11 Oct 1821
John Kimmel and Miss Messinger 23 Oct 1821
John Kimmel and Catharine Bishop 27 Oct 1821
Samuel Ruby and Elisabeth Rupp 1 Nov 1821
John Snyder and Christina Vannasdall 8 Nov 1821
John Sollender and Cathairne Ziegler 8 Nov 1821
Richard Waugh and Margret Holmes 8 Nov 1821
Christian Bauermaster and Jane Miller 13 Nov 1821
Andrew Heikes and Margret Hauerstein 29 Nov 1821
Christian Speidle and Elisabeth Smith 13 Dec 1821
John Meyer and Margret Clark 13 Dec 1821
George Kern and Catharine Ruch 20 Dec 1821
Andrew Gold and Ann Graham 20 Dec 1821
Hamilton Golding and Margret Gaudy 1 Jan 1822
James Torbet and Margret Carr 7 Jan 1822
John Berke and Hannah Carr 8 Jan 1822
Adam Gebhart and Elisabeth Pfund 15 Jan 1822
David Gehr and Sarah Dyson 24 Jan 1822
Benjamin Shyrer and Issabella Moreheart 7 Feb 1822
Samuel Andrew and Maria Miller 7 Feb 1822
John Keefer and Catharine Bretz 14 Feb 1822
John Hummer and Lydia Miller 19 Feb 1822
Samuel Mumma and Barbara Hertzler 21 Feb 1822
Andrew Krytzer and Sarah Kassel 21 Feb 1822
John Braucher and Sarah Speck 21 Feb 1822
Joseph Karch and Catharine List 24 Feb 1822
Gilbert Seewright and Sarah Carr 28 Feb 1822
Jacob Hummer and Catharine Brenner 26 Mar 1822
Jacob Herrman and Christina Young 26 Mar 1822
Samuel Holman and Sarah Hertz 4 Apr 1822
John N. Miltimore and Sarah Heiss 4 Apr 1822

David Fireobet and Maria Weibley 9 Apr 1822
John Adams and Mary Stewart 11 Apr 1822
David Schwanger and Maria Kuhn 11 Apr 1822
George Zinn and Maria Black 25 Apr 1822
Patrick McCauly and Elisabeth Engel 2 May 1822
Henry Ackerman and Catharine Eberley 2 May 1822
Henry Reinberger and Mary Ann Dyson 27 Jun 1822
Daniel Walter and Margreta Weibley 27 Jun 1822
Jacob Glime and Catharine Molen 19 Jul 1822
John Slehman and Susan Gross 25 Jul 1822
Adam Knower and Magret Bernhart 15 Aug 1822
Henry Schweigert and Susan Horning 27 Aug 1822
Jacob Gross and Catharine Bernhart 29 Aug 1822
John Hemphill and Anna Longsdorff 26 Sep 1822
Henry Peterman and Maria Shade 3 Oct 1822
William Thompson and Susan Kutz 10 Oct 1822
John Suesholtz and Maria Harriet 31 Oct 1822
Andrew Sherff and Catharine Fair 31 Oct 1822
Jacob Brown and Sarah Kampfer 3 Nov 1822
Samuel Smith and Sarah Kopf 7 Nov 1822
John McLaughlin and Jane Steward 7 Nov 1822
George Harter and Maria Baker 21 Nov 1822
Adam Smith and Susan Mader 28 Nov 1822
Joseph Bishop and Elisabeth Weaver 5 Dec 1822
Dr. Jacob A. Nice and Margret Sweitzer 5 Dec 1822
Peter Swords and Issabella Adams 24 Dec 1822
Henry Neil and Marisa Bretz 26 Dec 1822
James Clark and Margret Wartzabacher 31 Dec 1822
John Bishop and Ester Sollenberger 9 Jan 1823
Mr. Lefavre and Catharine Rine 9 Jan 1823
Martin Bob and Ana Wildy 24 Jan 1823
Philip Cornman and Margret Ziegler 28 Jan 1823
Christian Ebersole and Barbara Menig 4 Feb 1823
John Shoemaker and Christian Fogle 24 Feb 1823
William Lechler and Margret Wolf 25 Feb 1823
Henry Dumma and Catharine Snyder 27 Feb 1823
Emanuel Neuschwonger and Barb. Martin 11 Mar 1823
Jacob Landis and Margret Mohler 13 Mar 1823
David Kinkaid and Issabella Miller 13 Mar 1823
George Kiehl and Ana Maria Handshoe 13 Mar 1823
William Boileau and Maria Banker 8 Apr 1823
Herrman Underwood and Elisabeth Hoffman 10 Apr 1823
John Bosler and Ana Webbert 17 Apr 1823
Samuel Gold and Mary W. Craig 17 Apr 1823
Jacob Brumbaugh and Sarah Shoemaker 22 Apr 1823
Adam Longsdorff and Maria Sensaman 27 Apr 1823
Daniel Fisher and Susan Armor 29 May 1823
Rev. Ch. F. Cruse and A. V. W. Gallandet 5 Jun 1823
John Egolf and Barbara Leib 26 Jun 1823
Andrew Scott and Miss Greer 3 Jul 1823
Jacob Swiler and Ann Baker 24 Jul 1823
David Cockley and Lydia Hammer 14 Aug 1823
John Killhaffer and Eva Gramlich 21 Aug 1823
George Meder and Elisabeth Kinder 21 Aug 1823
David Wild and Sarah Fessler 25 Sep 1823

Andrew Heikes and Mary Cryder 9 Oct 1823
Jacob Steigleman and Eleanora Bell 13 Oct 1823
John Wolf and Ann Hertzler 16 Oct 1823
Abraham Goodjahr and Catharine Seip 16 Oct 1823
John Cook and Jane Crofford 19 Oct 1823
Dr. Julius Deppe and Jane Stewart 23 Oct 1823
Isaac Brant and Susan Plyler 23 Oct 1823
Abraham Ebersole and Susan Bretz 30 Oct 1823
David Webbert and Maria Wisler 6 Nov 1823
Jacob Shopwell and Catharine Smith 6 Nov 1823
George Mathews and An Cairns 14 Nov 1823
George Kolb and Margret McCalister 20 Nov 1823
Alexander C. Wilson and Catharine Stein 29 Nov 1823
Jacob Billman and Maria Weaber 4 Dec 1823
Anthony Aker and Mary Warm (Warns?) 16 Dec 1823
Jacob Jacobs and Elisabeth Duey 18 Dec 1823
Abraham Mickey and Elisabeth Kelly 18 Dec 1823
Joseph Cornbrobst and Sarah Cockley 26 Dec 1823
James Beaty and Elonor Brown 1 Jan 1824
Michael Miller and Susan Hower 8 Jan 1824
Hosea Summers and Elisabeth Nagle 15 Jan 1824
Samuel Showers and Sarah Spangler 22 Jan 1824
Peter McCavit and Sarah Sowers 22 Jan 1824
Samuel Hemminger and Elisabeth Spahr 5 Feb 1824
Peter Brendle and Margret Zug 12 Feb 1824
William Gillelen and Cath. Cavennaugh 19 Feb 1824
A. Skinner and Margret Pearson 1 Mar 1824
Andrew M. Smith and Susan Emminger 2 Mar 1824
Jesse Hower and Margret Kiehl 11 Mar 1824
Ths. Williamson Barber and Cath. Nagle 11 Mar 1824
Jacob Henkle and Elisabeth Spidle 16 Mar 1824
Abraham Acker and Mary Plyler 25 Mar 1824
Henry Bower and Sarah Mell 28 Mar 1824
Simon Eby and Catharine Herrman 15 Apr 1824
Samuel Minnig and Catharine Kolb 22 Apr 1824
Adam Stuckey and Maria Clauser 29 Apr 1824
Betholomy Yost and Jane Meclene 20 May 1824
William Smith and Elisabeth Reusenberger 24 Jun 1824
George Kampf and Susan Scarlet 15 Jul 1824
George Weibley and Sarah Billow 25 Jul 1824
John P. Lyne and Susan Wittich 21 Sep 1824
John Wunderlich and Elisabeth Gramlich 23 Sep 1824
Jacob Beltzhuber and Rebecca Leidig 28 Sep 1824
Archabald Garrel and Nancy Seplinger 30 Sep 1824
David Musselman and Sophia Feily 5 Oct 1824
John Harting and Cath. Lebenstein 7 Oct 1824
George Weise and Elonor Wunderlich 7 Oct 1824
John Allen and Catharine East 25 Nov 1824
Henry Susholtz and Lydia Billow 28 Nov 1824
John Ihrig and Elizabeth Lantz 28 Nov 1824
William Hannah and Sarah Coler 9 Dec 1824
William Sollenberger and An Baker 23 Dec 1824
Samuel Fetter and Mary Weise 23 Dec 1824
Thomas Street and Elizabeth Harris 10 Jan 1825

Henry Martin and F. Horst 18 Jan 1825
John Sugars and Fanny Steigleman 20 Jan 1825
Philip Baker and Catharine Hettrich 24 Jan 1825
Joseph Wolf and Aster Fress 24 Jan 1825
Adam Peffer and Mary Carr 24 Jan 1825
Moses Brownsberger and Mary Spangler 4 Mar 1825
James Dunbar and Mary Rollings 15 Mar 1825
John Ziegler and Maria Weise 22 Mar 1825
Michael Kuntz and Mary Hagers 24 Mar 1825
George Sudberry and An Sowers 24 Mar 1825
David Arris and Susan Eigleberger 28 Apr 1825
David Gehman and Margret Sauders 28 Apr 1825
Joseph Frost and Rachel Baeter 10 May 1825
William Scott and Sarah Wenrich 12 May 1825
John Pickart and Mary An Sholly 19 May 1825
Stephen Lash and Catharine An Cockley 19 May 1825
William Dunley and A. M. Brownewell 24 May 1825
Joseph Zimmerman and Eve Witcomb 26 May 1825
Philip Etter and Sarah Beaty 5 Jul 1825
James R. Boyd and Eliza Keller 26 Jul 1825
Ebenezer Miltimore and Susan Stineman 26 Jul 1825
John Hatten and Elizabeth Sipplinger 4 Aug 1825
John Saltzgeber and Catharine Dyse 4 Aug 1825
John Mell and Elizabeth Hammer 11 Aug 1825
Adam Wert and Sarah Ulrich 31 Aug 1825
Jacob Rupp and Catharine Eberly 20 Sep 1825
John Hartman and Susan Messinger 22 Sep 1825
Samuel Meyers and Rebecca Deerdorff 6 Oct 1825
Samuel Miller and Elisabeth Smyser 20 Oct 1825
John Brownewell and Ann Krill 20 Oct 1825
John Rausch and Catharine Koser 26 Oct 1825
Peter Moers and Maria Rudesill 27 Oct 1825
John Fenegle and Cathairne Balen 3 Nov 1825
George Longsdorff and Eliza Hacket 3 Nov 1825
George Werts and Maria Lau 3 Nov 1825
John Miller and Margret Epply 15 Nov 1825
David Rudy and Cathairne Wolf [no date given]
Abraham Miller and Elisabeth Spang 17 Nov 1825
George Ziegler and Sarah Sowers 17 Nov 1825
Vincent Williams and Issabella Boney 23 Feb 1826
John Gramlich and Catharine Lau 9 Mar 1826
William Gill and Sarah Musselman 9 Mar 1826
Daniel Mauntz and Ann Lippert 23 Mar 1826
M. Griest and Martha Powling 5 Apr 1826
John Dunbar and Jane E. Bell 11 Apr 1826
Jacob Ward and Mary Fister 13 Apr 1826
Dr. Jacob Bossler and An Doratha Herrman 20 Apr 1826
Henry Miller and Elisabeth Rine 4 May 1826
John Wolf and Magdelene Handshoe 16 May 1826
Fredrick Swolly and Sarah Frees 18 May 1826
William Morison and Catharine Weise 18 May 1826
Michael Spangler and Issabella Carr 25 May 1826
Christian Crall and Elisabeth Handshoe 25 May 1826
Samuel Morret and Mary Grabill 30 May 1826
Michael Livingston and Susan Stauffer 1 Jun 1826

Henry M. Brown and Sarah German 1 June 1826.
Fredrick Klug and Christina Sherer 8 Jun 1826
John Shade and Susan Allsbach 22 Jun 1826
Andrew Hecker and Charlotte Wahl 22 Jun 1826
Joseph Kneisely and Susan Smith 11 Jul 1826
Levi Miller and Mary Groop 25 Jul 1826
Jacob Hershe and Elisabeth Klepper 3 Aug 1826
Nehemia Underwood Reed and Julian Fair 3 Aug 1826
Elias Berlin and Hannah Braucher 10 Aug 1826
Christian Klink and Maria Fehler 17 Aug 1826
Andrew Brumbach and Rosana Kauffman 24 Aug 1826
Jacob Kutz and Sarah Fought 3 Sep 1826
Mr. Keefer and Miss Smith 19 Sep 1826
Jacob Hower and Hannah Kimmel 5 Oct 1826
David Eby and Elisabeth Shaffer 10 Oct 1826
Eli Miller and Eliza Frazer 19 Oct 1826
John Anthony and Margret Potts 19 Oct 1826
Jacob Weise and Sarah Fenegel 19 Oct 1826
Michel Wänger and Sophia Webber 2 Nov 1826
Lewis Kline and Barbara Glime 11 Jan 1827
George Groop and Lehna Maurer 11 Jan 1827
George Beltzhuber and An Maria Gross 18 Jan 1827
Henry Kryder and Elisabeth Havenstein 25 Jan 1827
Christian Fehler and Margret Stoneberger 23 Jan 1827
John Law and Maria Leonard 1 Feb 1827
Joseph Allison and Isabella Richers 15 Feb 1827
Robert Rupply and Margret Fought 17 Feb 1827
Jacob Musselman and Sarah Tobias 1 Mar 1827
Christian Dumma and Hannah Coler 6 Mar 1827
Henry Learing and Elisabeth Eigleberger 8 Mar 1827
Rudolff Hess and Ann Maria Wild 13 Mar 1827
George Heckman and Catharine Stam 15 Mar 1827
Andrew McCartney and Cath. McFadden 15 Mar 1827
Adam Wiest and Agnus Barnet 20 Mar 1827
Joseph Brownewell and Fanny Brand 22 Mar 1827
Joseph Haar and Rachel Schmieg 29 Mar 1827
Gabriel Line and Mary Peffer 2 Apr 1827
Moses Mundorff and Cosia Copperstone 19 Apr 1827
Jacob Forney and Elisabeth Senseman 3 May 1827
Ephraim Colestock and Hannah Boon 8 May 1827
John Brown and Elisabeth Krysher 8 May 1827
John Bauman and Maria Schambach 8 May 1827
Thomas McGuoid and Margret Wall 31 May 1827
Jacob Bishop and Margret Switzer 31 May 1827
John Whealer and Anna Keeny 16 Jun 1827
John Cornman and June [Jane?] May 24 Jun 1827
John Noble and Julian C. Lechler 24 Jun 1827
Jacob Lau and Catharine Cornman 12 Jul 1827
J. Daniel Rupp and Caroline K. D'Aristede 19 Jul 1827
Richard Adams and Mary Adams 26 Jul 1827
Samuel Stein and Catharine Meyer 9 Aug 1827
Samuel Beistlein and Sarah Brownewell 30 Aug 1827
George Whealer and Mary Sherer 5 Sep 1827
Samuel Miller and Hetty Sloneaker 6 Sep 1827

Mathew Bags and Elisabeth Hardy 6 Sep 1827
John Frohlick and Mary Coser 11 Sep 1827
John Bitner and Mary Fredrick 16 Sep 1827
Henry Stewart and Elisabeth Golden 27 Sep 1827
Rev. Nicholas S. G. Sharretts and Louisa H. Spottswood 9 Oct 1827
Jacob Spangler and Mary Klinedinch 16 Oct 1827
George Boyer and Fanny Engle 25 Oct 1827
George Bender and Mary Ann Snyder 8 Nov 1827
John Cockley and Susan Snyder 8 Nov 1827
Jacob Bosler and Margret Long 8 Nov 1827
John McDonnal and Susan Speidel 6 Dec 1827
John Eby and Elisabeth Schaeffer 27 Dec 1827
Jacob Frees and Mary Ann Baker 27 Dec 1827
Abraham Stevens and Nancy Scharlet 8 Jan 1828
Revd. Nicholas Stroh and Eliza Givler 16 Jan 1828
David Swonger and Rebecca Welch 22 Jan 1828
Soloman Brendel and Mary Ann Smith 24 Jan 1828
Henry Gosler and Mary Switzer 24 Jan 1828
James How and Mary Pennrose 24 Jan 1828
Jacob Martin and Catharine Forry 24 Jan 1828
Thomas Herron and Marg. Happel 31 Jul 1828
Jame Callien and Rebecca Guilasby 31 Jul 1828
Jacob Fanwell and Ann Elis. Schawley 5 Aug 1828
Jacob Uhler and Mary Whright 5 Aug 1828
Samuel Diller and Cath. Ritchwine 4 Sep 1828
John Fister and Agnes Weaver 2 Oct 1828
Jacob Weir and Sarah Scholl 11 Dec 1828
Isaac Shaefer and Henriette Sanno 18 Dec 1828

Married by F. Heyer:
Christian Frank and Sarah Minnig 22 Jan 1829
Martin Horst and Elisab. Hundsberger 10 Feb 1829
Conrad Westphal and Polly Frieze 19 Feb 1829
Henry Bohr and Mary Snyder 5 Mar 1829
Daniel Eckles and Martha Barbour 5 Mar 1829
David Rine and Anna Gevler 10 Mar 1829
Michael Watson and Mary Grier 19 Mar 1829
Rev. John Crawford and Maria Spotwood 19 Mar 1829
John Lippert and Elisabeth Watson 26 Mar 1829
Alexander F. Topley and Susan Zieger 26 Mar 1829
Isaac Curl and Maria Ward 2 Apr 1829
Jacob Stickle and Catharine Witcam 23 Apr 1829
George Sweigert and Margaret Cornman 23 Apr 1829
Leonard Diller and Sarah Smith 30 Apr 1829
Solomon Wolf and Elisabeth Hoppel 4 Jun 1829
Abraham Miller and Elisabeth Schub 11 Jun 1829
Samuel Gaudi and Elisa Savage Jun 11, 1829
Eli Egner and Dorcas Sowerbeck 12 Jun 1829
John Weiser and Susann Finnacle 23 Jun 1829
John Fehler and Anna Lorish 25 Jun 1829
John Swisser and Maria King 16 Jul 1829
John McFate and Mary Gold 6 Aug 1829
Jonathan Trough and Mary Humes 11 Aug 1829
Michael Low and Susanna Hartmann 10 Sep 1829
Rudolph Shaefer and Elisabeth Bresbon 23 Sep 1829

Joseph Shrom and Rebecca Kenower 3 Nov 1829
Benjamin Reuber and Sarah Low 19 Nov 1829
George Stenhower and Susanna Seip 26 Nov 1829
Adam Humrich and Mary Ziegler 3 Dec 1829
John Frieze and Sarah Miller 8 Dec 1829
Abraham Hertzel and Nancy Eberle 10 Dec 1829
William Bair and Elisabeth Wunderlich 22 Dec 1829
George Wahl and Sarah Boyles 7 Jan 1830
William Leaman and Catharine Meyer 23 Feb 1830
Adam Cockln and Barbara Garta 25 Feb 1830
David Kreiter and Elisabeth Ruch 25 Feb 1830
John Lutz and Catharine Miller 4 Mar 1830
William K. Tritt and Catharine Black 9 Mar 1830
Thomas Paxton and Maria Galbreath 11 Mar 1830
George Hughes and Hannah Douglass 16 Mar 1830
Jehn [Jehu?, John?] Watson and Hannah Meyer 18 Mar 1830
Edmund R. Davies and Jane Spottswood 23 Mar 1830
John Robison and Isabella Stewart 25 Mar 1830
John Shanklin and Elisabeth Shafner 22 Apr 1830
Philip W. Seibert and Catharine Hummel 27 Apr 1830
William Yeager and Mary Haviser 4 May 1830
William R. Gregg and Eliza Bradley 20 May 1830
John Wallace and Jane Baity 13 Jun 1830

Married by Charles F. Schaeffer:
Frederick Williams and Susanna Rheem 21 Dec 1830
Jesse Ziegler and Mary Ann Pepper 21 Dec 1830

"In many cases it is impossible to ascertain the ages of
  individuals who are buried - even their names are sometimes
  not handed in to the pastor, and hence, with every exertion,
  and after repeated inquiries, he is frequently obliged to
  leave the record of deaths in an imperfect condition.
It is the custom here, to bury the corpse, after the lapse of 20
  or 30 hours. The body is scarcely cold, before it is hurried
  into the grave. It is an unusual thing to keep the body two
  nights - if a person died in the evening, he is in his grave
  before the next evening - a practise repulsive to the
  feelings, but quite common in these parts. On one occasion, a
  boy, (who however was supposed to have died of the Cholera,
  which requires a speedy inhumation) died about 11 o'clock A.
  M. and was buried about 4 o'clock P.M. - the interval between
  the death and the burial was not five hours."
Dorothy Pracht bur. 1830 Churchtown.
John King died 23 Dec 1830.
                    - - - - -

First Presbyterian Church, Carlisle. Original copy on microfilm,
  with transcriptions also available, at the Cumberland County
  Historical Society And The Hamilton Library Association.

Married by Dr. George Duffield.
1821
Apr 10 Jno. Colwell, Shippensburg, Martha King- Dickinson.

May 8 Charles Donnelly, Mary Turner, Dickinson.
July 10 James Moore, Margaret Grayson, Carlisle.
July 28, Joseph Barber, S. Middleton, Margaret McKinley, of
  Carlisle.
Nov 29 John Agnew, Margaret Brown, Carlisle.

1822
9 Feb Jno. Duncan, Margaret Sterrett, Carlisle.
26 Feb Alexander Gillie, Mary White, both of Perry Co.
23 Feb Jno. Huston, Elizabeth Weakley, Dickinson.
30 May Geo. McCormick, Shippensburg, Agnes King, Dickinson.
30 May Stephen Kerr, Eliza McKean, Carlisle.
27 June Wm. Hutchinson, Susan Dickey, South Middleton.
14 Nov Wm. Weakley, Dickinson, Martha W. Ege of Pine Grove.
--- Peter Eyler, Margaret Johnston, Carlisle.

1823
27 Feb Alex. E. Gregg, N. Middleton, Mary Miller, Carlisle.
8 May Doan[?] Underwood, Mary Ann Rutter, Carlisle.
--- George Flemming, Margaret Brant, Carlisle.

1824
22 Jan Wm. Henderson, Carlisle, Elizabeth Parker, Allen Township.
4 March Saml. Hays, Isabella Phillips, Carlisle.
18 Apr Jno. Dunbar, Perry Co., Ann Douglass, Frankford Township.
22 Apr Robt. Clark, N. Middleton, and Margaret Smiley, Perry Co.
27 Apr Alexander Simpson, Ohio, Susan Williamson, E. Pennsboro.
2 Aug James Martin and Ellen Morrow, Carlisle.
12 Aug Jno. Riggel and Catherine Helphenstein, Dickinson.
14 Sep Jno. McKimey and Ann Smiley, both of Perry Co.
4 Nov Jno. Jones and Margaret Cunningham, both of Perry Co.
11 Nov Andrew Carothers, Esq. and Isabella Alexander, Carlisle,
  Elder 1st Church.
24 Dec Thos. Curtis, Lancaster Co., and Sarah Brown, E.
  Pennsboro.
30 Dec David Cook and Hannah Reighter, N. Middleton.

1825
4 Jan Wm. Sponsler, Carlisle and Ann Deelman of Allen Tp.
6 Jan Zaccheus Findlay and Margaret McCord, Perry Co.
15 Mar Rev. Wm. R. DeWitt and Mary E. Wallace, Harrisburg.
22 Mar Saml. Davidson, E. Pennsboro, and Mary Gray, Carlisle.
26 Apr Dr. Thos. Simonston and Elizabeth Banta, Perry Co.
4 May Benj. McIntire, Esq., Landisburg, and Ann Thompson,
  Carlisle.
5 May Jno. Wallace, Harrisburg, and Ann Culbertson, Carlisle.
28 Jul Saml. Galbraith and Mary Kantz, York Co.
20 Sep Dr. Joseph Martin and Rebecca Hugh, Hagerstown, Md.
12 Oct Michael Shannon and Eliza Miller, Perry Co.
19 Oct Jos. Henry Kuhns, Greensburg, and Mary Elizabeth
  Alexander, Carlisle.
8 Dec Matthew Moore, S. Middleton, and Sarah Warner,
  Mechanicsburg.
22 Jan [1826?] Chas. Yocum and Sarah Ann Emerson, New Cumberland.

1826
13 Apr James Williamson and Mary Urie, Cumberland Co.
25 Apr Fleming Nisbet, Union Co., and Ann Randolph, N. Middleton.
11 May Wm. Shrom and Harriet Wilson, Carlisle.
15 Jun James Evers and Eve Foss, Allen Tp.
11 Aug Thos. Martin and Jane Kennedy, Carlisle.
11 Aug Andrew Comfort and Priscilla B. Murray, Carlisle.
31 Aug Chas. Hall of Balto. and Ann Galbraith, Carlisle.
7 Sep Wm. Speakman and Mary L. Burkholder, Carlisle.
12 Sep Peter B. Smith and Mary Scobey, Carlisle.
14 Sep Jno. Ridgers, Perry Co., and Mary Harman, Cumberland Co.
14 Sep Robt. Fleming and Elisabeth Henwood, Carlisle.
5 Oct Sam'l Kleinpeter and Mary Fowler, Perry Co.
12 Oct Thos. Trimble and Sarah Urie, Cumberland Co.
7 Nov Jno. Hay of Middleton and Jane Jackson, Carlisle.

1827
6 Feb Daniel B. Holmes and Mary Giffin, both of N. Middleton.
15 Mar Hugh Greenfield, Chambers, and Elisabeth Sibbets,
   Dickinson.
27 Mar Thos. Seacock, Dickinson, and Ann Thomton, Newville.
29 Mar Henry Chalfant of Pittsburgh and Isabella E. Weakley,
   Dickinson.
17 Apr Wm. Culbertson, Lewistown, and Catherine Urie, N.
   Middleton.
31 May John McCafferty and Amelia Murphy, Perry Co.
14 Jun Parker Simison and Maria Humrick, Carlisle.
20 Sep Geo. Dougherty, York Co., and Mary Ann Stallsmith, Adams
   Co.
15 Nov Sam'l Waugh and Sarah Davidson, Cumberland Co.
15 Nov Sam'l McKenyon and Elisa Jane Kincade, Dickinson.
2 Dec Wm. Alexander and Mary Aughinback, Carlisle.
31 Dec Jacob Weaver and Mary Fulton, Carlisle.

1828
18 Mar Amos Alexander and Amanda Duffield, Chester Co.
25 Mar Mark A. Hodgson and Sophia Duffield, Chester Co.
10 Apr Robt. Kenyon, Gettysburg, and Eliza W. Halbert, Carlisle.
1 May Jno. Davidson and Elisa Wilson, Cumberland Co.
9 Sep Robt. Snodgrass and Margaret Noble, Carlisle.
Dec Jno. Smith and Margaret Snyder, Frankford Co.[Township?]

1829
8 Jan Jno. Wynkoop and Margaret Agnew, Frankford Tp.
10 Feb Thos. Chambers, Chambersburg, and Catherine Duncan,
   Carlisle.
1[?] Apr Rev. Geo. A. Lyons, D. D., Erie Pa, and Margaret
   Sterrett, Carlisle.
Apr[?] Rev. J. W. McCullough and Mary Louisa Duncan, Carlisle.
Apr Geo. W. Sheaffer and Elisa Aughinburgh, Carlisle.
10 Jun James Rhea and Adelina Weaver, Newville.
19 Jun Rev. Daniel Zacharias, D. D., York, and Jane Hays,
   Carlisle. German Reformed.

29 Jun Jason W. Eby and Ann Scobey, Carlisle.
27 Oct Rev. Henry S. Baugher, D. D., Gettysburg, Clarissa Brooks.

1830
6 Jan Geo. S. Brandon, Adams Co., and Nancy Craighead.
4 Feb Thos. Loudon, Perry Co., and Sarah Irwine, Middlesex.
11 Mar Wm. Bell and Margaret Irwine, Middlesex.
1 Apr Nathan Grist and Mary Ann White.
1 Apr Pierce Howard and Elisabeth Quigley, N. Middleton.
8 Apr Rev. Jacob Differbaugher and Jane Officer. (Ger. Reformed minister).
8 Apr Abraham Lamberton and Margaret E. Clark, N. Middleton.
-- Dr. Charles Cooper and Mary Hays, Carlisle.
27 May Geo. Mulhollen and Sophia Dewey, S. Middleton.
27 May Jacob Mel and Margaret Brownwell, N. Middleton.
-- David Dunwoody, Frederick Co., Md., and Sarah Bolander, Carlisle.
22 Jun David Hoover and Sarah Weibley, N. Middleton.
15 Sep Henry Metz and Mary Ann Cahoon, Harrisburg.

- - - - -

St. John's Episcopal Church, Carlisle. Copied from the microfilm at Dickinson College, Rolls 283 and 283a by Merri Lou Scribner Schaumann. From copies held by Cumberland County Historical Society And The Hamilton Library Association.

Deaths
Armstrong, Mr. James, a native of Ireland died 13 Sep 1821, aged 75 years.
Duncan, Miss Martha Ann, dau of Rebecca and Calender Duncan, died 5 Oct 1821, aged 9 years.
Noble, Charles, son of James Noble died 19 Dec 1821, aged 3 mos.
Gibson, Banister, son of Sarah Gibson, died 7 Jan 1822, aged 18 mos.

Record of Rev. Joseph Spencer:
Marriages
George Lee and Wilhelmina Foster 17 Oct 1822.
Thurs Thompson Brown and Miss Agnes Givin, 1822.
(Gilbertson) Friad and Miss Ann Noble, 1824.

Deaths: Hamilton, Miss Emeline died 7 Aug 1823
Miller, General Henry, attended his funeral Tues, 6 Apr 1824.
Watson, child of Mr. Watson, from the country, funeral Sunday 2 May 1824.
Veey, Mrs. - attended funeral Sat, 4 Feb 1826.

- - - - -

Silver Spring Presbyterian Church Records
Compiled by Helen I. Harman, 1959.
Married by Rev. Henry B. Wilson.
Aug 14, 1823 Barber, David to Ann Mill. Wit: Elizabeth Wilson

and J. R. Wilson.
March 5, 1823 Dunlap, James to Margret Mateer. Wit: Martin
Dunlap and Robert Mateer.
May 3, 1821 Eccles, Wm. to Jane Starr. Wit: Nathl. Eccles and
Wm. Clendenin.
March 29, 1821 Feister, James to Jane Morrison. Wit: John
Miller and Stephen Foulke.
Dec 6, 1821. Fought, Saml. to Ann Irvin. Wit: David Coble and
Wm. Irvin.
Sep 12, 1822 Grier, Joseph to Betsey Cook. Wit: George Ewing and
Matthias Swiler.
Feb 21, 1822 Hamaker, Isaac to Sarah Wiley. Wit: Wm. Waugh and
Thomas Fisher.
March 1, 1821 Huddleston [sic] to Rebekah Dickey. Wit: Samuel
Ruby and J. Swiler.
March 25, 1823 Irwin, Moses to Elizabeth O'Hail. Wit: Hugh
O'Hail and Thomas Wilson.
May 17, 1821 Kelly, Samuel to Jane Flloyd. Wit: Robert Dryson and
A. E. McCue.
Dec 19, 1822 Mateer, James to Elizabeth Spangler. Wit: James
Mateer, Sen. and Robert Mateer.
Feb 15, 1821 Moored, James to Charlotte Campbell. Wit: Eliza
Haldeman and Thomas Hunter.
Jan 30, 1823 Monosmith, James to Sarah Martin. Wit: John
Monesmith and Peter Schaeffer.
March 27, 1821 McCartney, John to Mary Noss [Foss?]. Wit: John
Trimble and David Bell.
24 May 1821 Nelson, Robert to Mary Mc---. Wit: Jno. Bailey and
Wm. Nelson.
28 Feb 1822 Porter, Ross to Elizabeth Burns. Wit: James Porter
and H. R. Wilson.
20 Nov 1823 Reisinger, Geo. to Maria Mulhall. Wit: James Mulhall
and Samuel Johnston.
28 Nov 1822 Ross, John to Jane Polinger. Wit: B. Bailey and John
Seesholtz.
23 Mary 1822 Sample, Samuel to Nancy McGuire. Wit: John Junken
and Wm. Adams.
1 Mar 1821 Sands, Sam'l to Mary Tate. Wit: Elizab'th Wilson and
Jane H. Wilson.
6 Feb 1823 Shaeffer, Emanuel to Isabella Husto--. Wit: John
Glendenin and Wm. Eccles.
26 Dec 1822 Trimble, Thos. to Sarah Ball. Wit: Geo. Trimble,
Sen. and Wm. Trimble.
24 Sep 1822 Waugh, Samuel to Mary Carothers. Wit: John Carothers
and Samuel Waught, Jr.
23 Jul 1822 Wilson, James to Mary Brally. Wit: Samuel Heisley
and H. R. Wilson.
12 Nov 1822 White, Shartes to Ellen Kirkpatrick. Wit: John White
and Cornelius Longrine.
"Dec 24, 1823 Attest Henry R. Wilson, late Pastor.
13 Jan 1829 Adams, Isaac to Hetty Criswill. Wit: Thomas
Carothers and Wm. Adams.
2 Dec 1824 Armstrong, John to Eliza Martin. Wit: Eleanor
Montgomery and Ann Martin.

24 Apr 1826. Audenreid, Wm., Esq. to Jane H. Wills. Wit: J. Andrew Shulze and B. Bernard, Esq.

4 Nov 1829 Barton, Jno. to Catharine Umberger. Wit: Absalom Martin and -- Umberger.

17 Jan 1828 Bricker, Peter to Catherine Butdorff. Wit: Geo. Buttorff and -- Monosmith.

14 Oct 1830 Brinkerhoef, Geo. to Elizabeth Livingston. Wit: Andrew Chapman and Jas. Brinkerhoef

25 Feb 1830 Abraham Bosler to Eliza Harman. Wit: Dr. J. Bosler and Christopher Harman.

Jul 1826 Brown, Henry to Sarah Butler. Wit: John Campblee and Lucy Canfield.

7 Feb 1825 Bush, John to Rebecca Boileau. Wit: James Williamson.

11 Dec 1829 Butdorff, John to Catharine Lauk. Wit: Thos. Fisher and Henry Butdorff.

6 Jan 1825 Campbell, John to Fanny Miller. Wit: C. Bowermaster and J. Williamson.

5 Mar 1829 Chapman, Geo. to Martha Eccles. Wit: Samuel Eccles and Andrew Chapman.

23 Dec 1829 Clark, James to Margaret Nelson. Wit: James Williamson.

13 Jun 1826 Craig, Hugh to Rachel Boyd. Wit: Benj. Anderson and G. W. Eckhart.

15 May 1827 Cresler, John to Mary Jones. Wit: Peter Lightner and R. Snodgrass.

25 Oct 1827 Coover, David to Mary Eckels. Wit: Samuel Eckels and Wm. Harkness.

27 Feb 1824 Culbertson, John to Hannah Reed. Wit: James Williamson and Ann Dunlap.

20 Mar 1828 Culp, Simon to Ellen Solander. Wit: Valentine Solander and John Bender.

2 Dec 1828 Dean, Dr. A. T. to Adeline Junken. Wit: Dr. Joseph Crain and Ellen Crain.

26 Sep 1826 Defenback, Henry to Sarah Strohm. Wit: John Mason and I. Daniel Rupp.

1 Feb 1827 Derrick, Peter to Cath. Canfield. Wit: Jonathan Mitten and Lucy Canfield.

28 Jan 1830 Diller, --- to Sarah Louk. Wit: Thomas Fisher and Wm. Walker.

25 Mar 1830 Eckels, Wm. Jr. to Margaret Ruston. Wit: John Trimble and Wm. Ruston.

28 Mar 1826 Epley, Joseph to Mary McCann. Wit: Benj. Anderson and Dr. Goforth.

23 Oct 1827 Fahnestock, John to Cath. Bosler. Wit: Dr. Jos. Crain and John Bosler.

30 Jun 1825 Ferguson, David to Rachel Eliza. McKee. Wit: Hays Brooks and Alexander McKee.

29(?) Dec 1825 Fought, Peter to Margaret Armstrong. Wit: John Armstrong and Jonathan Bell.

16 Jan 1829 Fought, Daniel to Patty Irvin. Wit: Peter Fought and Matilda Armstrong.

7 Dec 1826 Ford, Daniel to Cath. Koch. Wit: David Williamson and Eliza Ford.

1 Sep 1825 Floyd, Allen to Barbara Berkey. Wit: Michael Cockley and David Williamson.

27 Feb 1827 Gregor, Jacob and Ann Campble. Wit: David Weise and
Samuel McKinley.
1 Sep 1825 Green, Wm. to Hester Johnston. Wit: David Williamson
and Ann Williamson.
15 Feb 1827 Gill, James to Fanny Hyde. Wit: George Rupp and John
Gill.
26 Jan 1826 Gould, Thomas to Mary Divinnie. Wit: Chas. Godfrey
and Wm. Divinnie.
23 Dec 1830 Hagey, Robert to Elizabeth Armstrong. Wit: John
Armstrong and Thomas Martin.
8 Mar 1826 Hall, Wm. McClay to Ellen M. Williams. Wit: G. W.
Harris, Esq. and Wm. Walker.
20 Oct 1829 Hepburn, Sam'l to Rebecca Williamson. Wit: Thos.
Fisher and Joseph Briggs.
30 Nov 1826 Huston, James to Mary Sexton. Wit: John Clendenin
and Wm. Huston.
21 Jan 1830 Huston, Samuel to Ann McKee. Wit: Wm. Huston and
Geo. McKee.
19 Apr 1825 Junkin, Dr. Jos. to Adaline Crain. Wit: Chas.
Godfrey and Ann E. McCue.
Mar 1827 Kauffman, Christopher to Eliza Kauffman. Wit: James
Martin and Isaac Kauffman.
27 Mary 1830 Klyne, Wm. to Abbe Wyeth. Wit: Dr. Adam Keagy and
Augustus Wyeth.
16 Nov 1826 Lamberton, Ross to Jane Waugh. Wit: John Elliott and
Samuel Waugh.
17 Apr 1817 Leboyd, Wm. to Amanda Anderson. Wm. Orr and Benj.
Anderson.
16 Aug 1825 Mateer, Robert to Mary Bailey. Wit: James Mateer and
James Dunlap.
30 Aug 1825 Wm. Mateer to Mary Ann Porter. Wit: Wm. Walker and
Dr. Theo. Myers.
12 Nov 1829 Morrison, James to Matilda Armstrong. Wit: John
Armstrong and Andrew Armstrong.
26 Jul 1825 Mussleman, Geo. to Mary Museleman. Wit: James
Williamson.
28 Apr 1825 Myers, Dr. Theo. to Sarah A. Irvin. Wit: Dr. Asa
Herring and Wm. Alexander.
6 Apr 1826 McHoe, George to Rebecca Trimble. Wit: John Clendenin
and Samuel Waugh.
29 Mar 1827 McKinley, Samuel to Eliza Evans. Wit: Lewis Talbot
and I. Daniel Rupp.
9 Feb 1826 Occum, Abram to Mary Nieman. Wit: J. Williamson.
10 Jan 1827 O'Hale, Hugh to Elisabeth Brinkerhoef. Wit: Alex.
McCurdy and Geo. Brinkerhoef.
31 Mar 1829 Oliver, Dr. James G. to Jane Carothers. Wit: Wm. Orr
and James Graham.
14 Oct 1830 Pellinger, Geo. to Matilda Etter. Wit: William
Addams and Agnes Sample.
1 Jun 1830 Ross, William to Elizabeth Robinette. Wit: James
Robinette and Azel Walker.
22 Nov 1827 Starr, Samuel to Elizabeth Moorehead. Wit: James
Starr ad M. P. Williamson.
22 Feb 1827 Swarner, John to Nancy Waugh. Wit: Samuel Waugh and

Ross Lamberton.
7 Apr 1825 Sipe, Christian to Jane Wise. Wit: John Wise and
George Sipe.
29 Sep 1829 Smith, Alex. to Cath. Whisler. Wit: John Whisley and
Eli Smith.
4 Jun 1829 String, John to Nancy McDonald. Wit: Thomas McDonald
and Eliza McDonald.
23 Jan 1827 Talbot, Lewis to Jane Huston. Wit: Daniel McKinley
and Wm. Huston.
5 May 1825 Walker, James to Elizabeth Tytler. Wit: Geo. Schwartz
and George Tytler.
27 Dec 1827 Williams, David to -- . James Williamson.
9 Mar 1830 Williamson, Rev. McKnight to Jane Woods. Wit: Thomas
Trimble and Richard Woods.
6 Mar 1828 Wolf, John to Jane Orr. Wm. Orr and James Given.
13 Jun 1830 Whitcomb, Martin to Mary Shoemaker. Wit: Ann
Thompson and Phebe M. Williamson.
16 Dec 1828 Wykoff, Leopold to Elizabeth Crain. Wit: Richard M.
Crain and Dr. A. T. Dean.

- - - - -

*Cemetery Records from Jere Zeamer Records Genealogical Section
State Library, Harrisburg, PA, by Helen I. Harman,
Pennsylvania State Chairman, Gen. Recods Committee, N.S.D.A.R.
1960.*

(1) Meeting House Springs Grave Yard, near Carlisle
Forbes, Jane, d. 3 Oct 1830, aged 77 yrs, 7 mos, 19 days.
Forbes, John, d. 8 Sep 1823, in his 78th year.
Forbes, John P., . 1 Sep 1829, in his 41st year.
Forbes, Richard, d. 30 Aug 1823, in his 33d yr.
Forbes, John, d. 8 Sep 1823, aged 78 years, 5 mos, 23 days.
Sanderson, Alexander of North Middleton Twp., d. 14 Jun 1823,
aged 28 yrs.

(2) Graveyard on the Heikes Farm, in West Pennsboro Twp. about 1
1/2 miles west of Plainfield and short distance north of the
State Road.
Baker, Jonathan, d. 25 Oct 1821, aged 29 years, 4 mos. Heigis,
Margaret, b. 10 Jul 1808, d. 6 Dec 1822 - German.
Heiges, Elizabeth, d. 15 Jul 1824, in her 63d year - red sand
head stone. German.
Hikes, Catharine, d. 13 Jan 1828, aged 41 yrs.

(3) Graveyard on Riggleman Farm, short distance north of
Kersville in West Pennsboro Twp.
Rossler, John, b. 9 Jul 1791, d. 13 Sep 1820.

(4) Graveyard on Seitz Farm, about 2 miles east of Newville, in
West Pennsboro Twp. 1905. Lefever, Lawrence, b. 15 Dec 1764,
d. 24 Feb 1830.

(5) Graveyard on "Old Shellenberger Farm," near Valley View Hill,
West Pennsboro Twp.

Snyder, Elizabeth, wife of David Snyder, d. 12 Feb 1826, aged 63
  yrs, 9 mos.
Sneider, Rev. David, b. 14 Sep 1761, d. 12 Feb 1819.

(6) Graveyard on the Bitner Farm, West Pennsboro Twp.
Myers, Abraham, "Preacher of the Gospel," d. 28 Oct 1826, aged 68
  yrs, 5 mos.
Myers, Christiana, wife of John Myers, d. Nov 1805, aged 72
  years.
(7) On Wm. A. Lindsey Farm, West Pennsboro Twp.
Abraham, John Enoch, b. 1820, d. 6 Jul 1828.

- - - - -

History of the Big Spring Presbyterian Church, Newville, PA.,
  1737 - 1898 by Gilbert Ernest Swope. Published in 1898 by
  Times Steam Printing House, Newville PA.

Marriages by Rev. Joshua Williams, D. D.
Armor, Samuel and Hannah Davis, 7 Aug 1821.
Alter, Benjamin and Nancy Lindsay, 20 Mar 1823
Brown, Joseph and Nancy Richie, 25 Jul 1821.
Benner, Joseph and Elizabeth Cook, 2 Oct 1823.
Brown, John and Mary Richie, 30 Mar 1824.
Barr, William and Sarah Geddes, 27 Jul 1825.
Carothers, Josiah and Mary McNair, 4 Oct 1821.
Cook, Thomas and Sarah Scroggs, 5 Mar 1822.
Crowell, James and Mary Leckey, 18 Mar 1824.
Carnahan, William and Margaret Cooper, 27 May 1825.
Carothers, James and Mary C. Carothers, 24 Apr 1827.
Carothers, Martin and Ellen Duffy, Oct 12, 1827.
Cope, Benjamin and Sarah McDowell, Apr 25, 1822.
Davidson, John and Margaret Walker, Dec 11, 1823.
Duncan, William and Nancy Fulton, 30 Mar 1824.
Duncan, Joseph and Jane McNickle, 30 Dec 1824.
Donaldson, Thomas and Eleanor Turner, 10 Feb 1825.
Davidson, John and Eleanor Thompson, 9 Jun 1825.
Duffy, John and Sarah Longwell, 2 Aug 1827.
Davidson, William and Ann Leckey, 1 May 1828.
Davidson, Samuel and Catharine Leckey, 19 Oct 1830.
Dickson, John and Jane McKnight, June 20, 1822.
Ege, Joseph and Jane Woodburn, 7 Oct 1829.
Farrier, David and Jane Ryan, 25 Mar 1824.
French, James and Jane Cowen, 5 Apr 1826.
Graham, Robert and Elizabeth McFarlane, 10 Feb 1824.
Graham, George and Elizabeth Alter, 3 Feb 1830.
Heagy, David and Mary A. Young, 9 Jul 1821.
Holms, John and Elizabeth Albert, 25 Mar 1824.
Huston, Samuel and Ann Fulton, 22 Dec 1825.
Irvine, Samuel and Rosanna Dunbar, 14 Apr 1829.
Jacob, David and Eleanor Davidson, 8 Mar 1821.
Johnston, John and Elizabeth Pollock, 8 Nov 1821.
Kerr, William and Eliza Sterrett, 15 Jun 1824.
Kennedy, James and Maria Barr, 3 May 1825.

Kilgore, Ezekiel and Elizabeth Graham, 9 Nov 1825.
Knettle, William and Lacy Lindsay, 3 Jan 1828.
Kilgore, Jesse and Nancy Sharp, 13 Aug 1828.
Kinsley, Jacob and Charlotte Roberts, 8 Apr 1830.
Lowery, Isaac and Hannah Martin, 25 Dec 1821.
Logan, James and Ann Laird, 23 Mr 1824.
Leckey, George and Nancy Davidson, 28 Jul 1825.
Leburn, Robert and Nancy Bell, 14 Feb 1826. (colored)
Lefevre, David Alter and Mary H. Wilt, 20 Mar 1827.
Logan, George and Nancy Huston, 4 Oct 1827.
McDonald, Daniel and Elizabeth Kennedy, 18 Oct 1821.
McClelland, John and Eleanor Morrow, 27 Mar 1821.
McNeil, Samuel and Ann Irwin, 7 Feb 1822.
McKeehan, John and Tabitha McBride, 7 May 1822.
McFarlane, James and Sarah Shannon, 12 Mar 1822.
Moore, John and Molly Wilson, 14 Mar 1822.
McKibben, Joseph and Tabitha McCulloch, 11 Apr 1822.
McCune, Thomas and Sarah Fulton, 7 Oct 1822.
Myers, Jacob and Nancy McBride, 27 Feb 1823.
McCandlish, John and Maria McCormick, 13 Mar 1823.
McClelland, William and Sarah Wilson, 27 Mar 1823.
McCulloch, Thomas and Isabella Blean, 3 Apr 1823.
Mitchel, William and Mary Stephenson, 3 Jul 1823.
McCune, Joseph and Mary Davidson, 27 Apr 1824.
McCullough, John and Elizabeth Cowen(?), 28 Sep 1824.
McCormick, Samuel and Susanna Alter, 3 Mar 1825.
McCaleb, J. and Sarah Uhler, 24 Mar 1825.
McCord, Robert and Margaret Woodburn, 25 Oct 1825.
McCormick, Thomas and Jane Harper, 13 Dec 1825.
McFarlane, Alexander and Rosanna McCanon, 7 Jul 1826.
McFarlane, Clemens and Lydia Miller, 8 Mar 1826.
Miller, Samuel and Rachel Thompson, 18 Jan 1827.
McKinstry, James and Margaret Hays, 3 Dec 1828.
McKee, James and Isabella Fulton, 8 Jan 1829.
Montgomery, James Ramsey and Nancy Kilgore, 25 Nov 1823.
Nisbit, Fisher and J. Adams, 4 Mar 1824.
Noble, Daniel and Rachel George, 16 Mar 1826.
Nickle, William and Catharine ---, 13 Mar 1827.
Patton, Morgan and Elizabeth Campbell, 21 Mar 1822.
Ralston, David and Leacy McAlister, 6 Mar 1821.
Roberts, Robert and Isabella Grimes, 31 May 1821.
Riley, John and Mary Duffy, Sep 1821.
Randolph, John and Mary Knettle, 3 Jan 1822.
Ripton, Peter and Louisa Ross, 22 Apr 1824.
Ray, William and Anne McDonald, 12 Aug 1824.
Ross, John and Esther McWilliams, 24 Jan 1825.
Roberts, Andrew and Catharine Crotzer, 16 Mar 1829.
Randolph, Paul and Betsy E. Leckey, 9 Jun 1829.
Sharp, William and Jane Wilson, 5 Jun 1821.
Skiles, Davis and Elizabeth Moor, 18 Oct 1821.
Skelly, David and Jane Dougherty, 28 Mar 1822.
Skelly, Robert and --- Wilson, 12 Dec 1822.
Sturm, David and Elizabeth Wolf, 10 Feb 1824.
Shannon, James and Martha Mathers, 10 Jun 1824.
Shaw, John and Hetty Wilt, 30 Mar 1826.

Smith, Joseph and Eliza McCormick, 28 Jun 1827.
Smith, William and Maria Dougherty, 31 Jan 1828.
Stough, Samuel and Mary Peeples, 15 Apr 1829.
Underwood, John and Priscilla Leacock, 18 Mar 1824.
Wigly, Joseph and Elizabeth --- 23 Aug 1821.
Woodburn, Skiles and Margaret McKeehan, 20 Dec 1821.
Wills, Dr. David and Elizabeth Peebles, 14 Feb 1822.
Workman, William and Elizabeth Carothers, 5 Dec 1822.
Wightman, William and Mary Dunfee, 19 Feb 1824.
Woodburn, William and Margaret Geddes, 22 Jan 1828.

Inscriptions from tombstones of persons born prior to 1800 and
    died 1821-1830.
Brown, James, b. 31 Dec 1778; d 11 Oct 1822.
Buchanan, Mary, b. 1763; d 16 Oct 1823.
Buchanan, Gen. Thomas, b. 1747; d 13 Oct 1823 (Soldier of the
    Rev. War.)
Carnahan, Mary, wife of William, b. 1793; d. 7 Sep 1823.
Conway, Mary, b. 1765; d 8 May 1823.
Davidson, Ann, wife of James, b. 1794; d. 8 Jun 1827.
Davidson, John, b. 1743; d. 1823.
Davidson, Elizabeth Young, wife of John, b. 1772; d. 14 Sep 1823.
Denning, William, b. 1737; d. 19 Dec 1830. (The maker of the
    first wrought-iron cannon of the Revolutionary War.)
Dunbar, Isabella, b. 1799; d. 25 Sep 1824.
Dunbar, Mary, b. 1772; d. 30 Jan 1830.
Dunbar, John, b. 1767; d. 18 Oct 1829.
Gailbraith, Sarah, wife of William, b. 4 Oct 1748; d. 22 Jan
    1827.
Gillespie, Nathaniel, b. 1744; d. 16 Aug 1824.
Gillespie, Ann, b. 1782; d. 16 Nov 1827.
Hanna, Samuel, b. 1792; d. 8 Feb 1825.
Hanna, John, b. 1765; d. 11 Oct 1823.
Harper, Andrew, born 1799, died Jan 19, 1827.
Harper, Elizabeth, b. Jul 1806; d. 10 Oct 1827.
Harper, William, b. 1761; d. 18 May 1824.
Harper, Esther, wife of Wm., b. 1762; d. 13 Apr 1827.
Huston, James, b. 1784; d. 17 Jun 1825.
Huston, James, b. 1782; d. 17 Jun 1823.
Kennedy, Margaret, wife of Thomas, b. 1759; d. 16 Jan 1826.
Kilgore, William, b. 1756; d. 11 Oct 1823.
Kilgore, Isabella, wife of William, b. Oct 1761; d. 18 Feb 1826.
Kilgore, Jesse, b. 13 Dec 1773; d. 19 Aug 1823.
Laughlin, Atcheson, b. 1756; d. 11 Jan 1825.
Laird, Thomas, b. 1794; d. 19 Apr 1830.
Lenney, William, b. 1782; d. 20 Oct 1823.
Leckey, Sarah B., b. 1 Sep 1789; d. 6 Oct 1823.
Logan, James, b. 1782; d. 26 Oct 1828.
McCormick, Margaret Young, wife of Thomas, b. 20 Jan 1766; d 20
    Feb 1824.
McCandlish, William, b. 1768; d. 9 Apr 1827.
McCandlish, Jane, wife of William, b. 1781; d. 4 Aug 1827.
McCandlish, Maria, wife of John, b. 1802; d. 1 Oct 1827.
McCulloch, James, son of John, b. 1761; d 13 Aug 1825.

McCulloch, William, b. 1778; d 8 Nov 1824.
McCrea, Margaret, wife of William, b. 1759; d. 1822.
McDannel, Daniel; son of Daniel, b. 23 Mar 1792; d. 13 Nov 1825.
McDowell, Samuel, b. 1764; d. 24 Apr 1830.
MCDowell, John, b. 1778; d. 9 Jan 1829.
McIntire, John, b. 1745; d. 16 Aug 1830.
McIntire, Margaret, wife of John, b. 1756; d. 17 Sep 1830.
McKeehan, Margaret, wife of Benjamin, b. 22 Feb 1758; d. 24 Apr 1829.
Mickey, Robert, b. 21 Dec 1746; d. 3 Dec 1827.
Mickey, Ezemiah, b. 1755; d. 8 Dec 1830.
Pierce, Jane, wife of Joseph, b. Dec 1768; d. 25 Feb 1827.
Patterson, Mary, wife of Andrew, b. 1734; d. 15 Mar 1827.
Patterson, Thomas, son of Andrew, b. 1773; d. 10 Dec 1822.
Peebles, Capt. Robert, b. 1776; d. 7 Jan 1830.
Reed, Hugh, b. 1783; d. 1823.
Richy, William, b. 1760; d. 3 Feb 1830.
Sharp, James, b. 27 Jan 1774; d. 28 Feb 1823.
Sterrett, David, b. Apr 1767; d. 26 Jul 1825.
Sterrett, Rachel, b. 1796; d. 28 Dec 1823.
Stevenson, Margaret, d. 1 Apr 1821.
Smith, Hugh, b. 1750; d. 17 Mar 1823.
Smith, Elizabeth McCormick, wife of Hugh, b. 1764; d. 22 May 1822.
Thompson, Matthew, b. 1754; d. 19 Oct 1823.
Trego, Rebecca, wife of Moses, b. 1762; d. 7 Oct 1823.
Wallace, Agnes, b. 1767, d. 28 May 1827.
Weakley, Samuel b. 1755; d. 10 Feb 1829.
Weakley, John, b. 1778; d. 22 Nov 1826.
Wilson, Matthew, b. 1746; d. 6 Jan 1824.
Williams, James C., son of Rev. Joshua, b. 1801; d. 1822.

- - - - -

History of the First United Presbyterian Church, Newville, PA, 1764 - 1978. Formerly The Seceder Church, The Associate Reformed Church and The United Presbyterian Church of Big Spring. Compiled by Georgeia P. Rife.
Marriages by Rev. A. Sharp. 1824 - 1829
John McCune and Mary Ann Wilson, Sep 23, 1824. Wit: William McCune and Samuel Irvin.
James Buchanon and Eleanor McCune, Sep 28, 1824. Wit: William Lusk and Dr. John Geddes.
Thomas Mathers and Polly Spear, Feb 1, 1825. Witnesses: James Elliott and Samuel McCormick.
Michael L. Kerley and Jane Hannah, March 22, 1825. Witnesses: James Reed and Alexander Cox.
George Oxer and Elizabeth Harlan, March 29, 1825. Witnesses: Andrew Sharpe and James Harland.
James Sharp and Mary Ann McCune, (no date). Witnesses: Robert McCune and Thomas Sharp.
Moses Lindsey and Eleanor McHamee(?) March 31, 1825. Witnesses: John Harper and David Lindsey.
Edward Phillips and Jane Adair, Dec 20, 1825. Witnesses: Samuel Irvine and William Dunlap.

William F. Junkin and Eliza Adams, Feb 21, 1826. Witnesses:
Robert Bryson and James Graham.
Andrew Harper and Elizabeth McCullough, March 23, 1826.
Witnesses: James McKeehan and John Harper.
Mathew Laird and Susan Middleton, April 20, 1826. Witnesses:
James Elliott and James Wallace.
James Armour and Eliza Dear Dorf, Aug 8, 1826. Witnesses: James
Thompson and Joseph Thompson.
James Elliott and Rachel Mitchell, (no date). Witnesses: Jessie
Kilgore and John Mitchell.
David Ewing and Mary Richie, Oct 3, 1826. Witnesses: Robert
Kilgore and William Meridith.
Samuel Aikman and Jane Martin, Oct 12, 1826. Witnesses: James
Boyd and Christopher Aua(?).
David Ralston and Margaret Sharp, March 19, 1827. Witnesses:
James Sharp and ( ) Work.
Samuel Magan and Betsy Gurl, March 29, 1827. Witnesses: Samuel
McElheney and Robert McGlaughlin.
John Dougherty and Lettitia Sharp, March 29, 1827. Witnesses:
Thomas Sharp and George Dougherty.
James Harland and Mary Ferguson, Dec 27, 1826. Witnesses: George
Harland and William Nichesan(?).
David Blean and Margaret Clark, (no date). Witnesses: Thomas
McCullough and Jesse Kilgore.
Capt. James McElhenny and Betsy Lusk, Aug 21, 1827. Witnesses:
Robert Lusk and Robert Patterson.
Elliot Robertson and Mary Gazzett, Aug 30, 1827. Witnesses: John
Sharp and William Harper (Mr. Robertson is from Perry Co).
John Graxler and Cassendanna Skelly, May 17, 1827. Witnesses:
John Graham and James McCaslem(?) (Mrs. Skelly widow of George
Skelly and daughter of ( ) Wilson).
James Hanery(?) and Eliza McNeal, Oct 11, 1827. Witnesses: Dr.
Hays and William Fulton.
Andrew Caill and Eliza McCullough, Nov 1, 1827. Witnesses:
Alexander McCahan and John McCullough (Mr. Caill is from Perry
Co).
William Brown and Jane McElwane, Dec 6, 1827. Witnesses: William
Hannah and Archibald Gribbel.
Thomas Heffelfinger and Nancy Watson, Dec 25, 1827. Witnesses:
Philip Hanere(?) and John Gribbel.
James Fulton and Grissella Blean, March 4, 1828. Witnesses: John
Blean and James McFarlene.
James Moore and Betsy McCabe, May 21, 1828. Witnesses: Hon.
Isaiah Graham and Jesse Kilgore.
Richard Devor and Leah Shriner, July 29, 1828. Witnesses: Jacob
Au and Samuel Aikman.
Benjamin Mickey and Eliza Wilson, Aug 7, 1828. Witnesses: John
McCune and William Pubbs(?).
Daniel Rutherford and Catherine Laird, Sept. 9, 1828. Witnesses:
Robert Carnahan and John Sharp.
(---) and Elizabeth Bighan, Sept. 18, 1828. Witnesses: David
Bighan.
William McCullough and Jane C. MaKee, Nov 26, 1828. Witnesses:
Alexander McCahan and Joseph MaKee.

William Myers and Polly or Sally Graxler, March 17, 1829.
Witnesses: Jacob Graxler and Betsy Penwill.
Dr. George H. Parker and Mrs.Mary Ann Smith, April 1829.
Witnesses: J. B. Blair and James P. Ramsey (in Phila).

TOMBSTONE INSCRIPTIONS FROM NEWVILLE CEMETERY
of persons who died 1821-1830.

Isabella Blean born 1745, died August 12, 1828/ Mary, wife of
Robert, born 1770, died April 10, 1833/ Robert, Sr, born 1770,
died July 23, 1848.
Elizabeth Dunlap, wife of William, born 1785, died May 30, 1839.
William born 1781, died October 20, 1826.
William Heannon, Sr, born 1766, died Oct 25, 1825, aged 59 years.
James Huston, son of William and Mary, born 1780, died January 5,
1824, in his 42nd year.
Mary Huston, born 1757, died May 4, 1822, aged 65.
William Huston, born 1753, died February 6, 1821, aged 68 years.
Sarah Lamb, born 1792, died January 21, 1827.
Jane Piper, born 1786, died 1823. Margaret Clelland, wife of
James, died near the same time.
Samuel Piper, born 1739, died 1822.
Alexander Sharp, born 1756, died December 8, 1824, aged 68 years.
Thomas Sharp died Jun 15, 1830, aged 29 yrs, 4 months, unmarried.
Alexander Scroggs, died 1826.

MIDDLE SPRING PRESBYTERIAN CHURCH, SHIPPENSBURG TOWNSHIP
(from microfilm of the original records)

Marriages
Jacob Thrush and Margaret Mathews Feb 8, 1821.
Robert Thompson and Susanna McMammony, March 29, 1821.
Francis Neir and Margaret Early, April 12, 1821.
James Stewart and Mary Hayes, April 24, 1821.
Robert Davies and Hannah Jamison, May 3, 1821.
David Spear and Jean White, May 15, 1821.
Alexander McCreight and Ann Culbertson, May 17, 1821.
Daniel Campbell and Margaret Woodburn, May 29, 1821.
John Wallace and Jean McLane, May 29, 1821.
John McCandless and Priscilla Forrest, June 19, 1821.
Elijah Ellis and Amanda Cox, Septem. 11, 1821.
Robert Hensthorn and Jean Spear, October 9, 1821.
John Ferguson and Jean Mitchel, December 13, 1821.
William Mitchel and Mary Hannah, Jan 8, 1822.
Daniel Dean and Betsy Brackenridge, Feb 14, 1822.
Thomas McAnurlin and Mary Ann Comb, March 7, 18922.
Joseph Kilgore and Rachel Sterrit, March 21, 1822.
William Kilgore and Eliza Duncan, March 21, 1822.
Alexander Kelso and Mary Clark, April 2, 1822.
John Clark and Jane Green, April 9, 1822.
Joseph McIlheny and Jean Shannon, August 22, 1822.
Adolphius Robinson and Sally Fochender, November 5, 1822.
George Keyner and Molly Shields, December 10, 1822.

John Anderson and Ruth Searfoss, December 17, 1822.
Joseph Snyder and Maria Croft, Feb 25, 1823.
John McLene(?) and Sally Ann Duncan, Feb 27, 1823.
William Kelso and Polly Bobbs (Botts?), March 4, 1823.
Isaac Ward and Mary Rodgers, April 1, 1823.
John Turnbaugh and Mary Green, April 10, 1823.
Jacob Roan and Mary Borman, April 11, 1823.
George Croft and Jane Clark, May 1, 1823.
David Krause and Peggy Dunmere, May 13, 1823.
Alexander McCune and Molly Caldwell, May 22, 1823.
William Jameson and Nancy Basels, Sep 16, 1823.
Christopher Millar and Mary Smith, December 9, 1823.
Thomas Gill and Mary Ritchey, December 25, 1823.
Joshua Peeling and Margaret Wilson, Jan 5, 1824.
Johnston Snody and Ann Reynolds, Jan 6, 1824.
George Dunbar and Martha Donaldson, Jan 8, 1824.
David Ritchie and Elizabeth Kelso, Jan 20, 1824.
Wm. Fleming and Rachel Moore, Jan 20, 1824.
John Beemer and Jean Junkins, Feb 12, 1824.
Solomon Brinkhart(?) and Polly Rundecker, Feb 13, 1824.
Alexander Lindsy and Elizbeth Patterson, March 18, 1824.
Jacob Whitmire and Rachel Fockender, March 23, 1824.
Capt. David Duncan and Ellenor Blake, March 30, 1824.
Samuel Sterrit and Betsy Ann Danforth, April 1, 1824.
Joseph Thrush and Katherine Peffer, April 29, 1824.
Jacob Pague and Sally Spear, April 29, 1824.
Alexander McKean and Polly Kesler, June 29, 1824.
Wm. Kallen and Polly Culbertson, July 6, 1824.
John Hendrics and --- Speer, July 29, 1824.
John Johnston - Colour and Cinthia Thompson, Septem. 14, 1824.
Jacob Bowers and Elizabeth Hickis, November 16, 1824.
John Buhart (Berhart) and Mary Ann Barkloe, Feb 1, 1825.
Noble Roberts and Elizabeth Sterit, Feb 3, 1825.
James Beaty and Issabella Clark, Feb 17, 1825.
Henry Nesbit and Sally Ann Hickman, Feb 24, 1825.
William Crisler and Susan Ritchey, March 3, 1825.
Andrew Stewart and Elizabeth Johnston, April 28, 1825.
George Doup and Elizabeth Nixon, May 31, 1825.
Daniel Wallager and Sally Oats, June 16, 1825.
Robert Elliot and Nancy Early, Sep 22, 1825.
Jacob Heck and Molly Meanes, November 23, 1825.
William Boyd and Sally Walker, December 1, 1825.
James Strain and Jane Fleming, December 29, 1825.
Saml. Zane and Betsy Canetis, colour, Jan 3, 1826.
Jesse Riffle and Sarah Brackinrige, Jan 5, 1826.
Thomas Carlisle and Sally Ann Bunn(?), Jan 31, 1826.
John Humes and Nancy McCalmon, Feb 2, 1826.
Thomas Sterrit and Jane Clark, Feb 23, 1826.
John Boyd and Elizabeth Walker, March 23, 1826.
Charles McIlfresh and Jane McFarland, April 27, 1826.
James Rodgers and Jane Linn, May 11, 1826.
--- Thompson and --- Spencer, April 20, 1826.
John Spencer and Katharine McManime, May 25, 1826.
Jacob Fassnaught and Mary Vanderbelt, June 6, 1826.

Jacob Darr and Eliza Linsey, June 6, 1826.
Henry Dewalt and Mary Prior, June 8, 1826.
Francis Loughead (Longhead?) and Phebe Cox, Octo. 24, 1826.
--- Vanderbelt and Sally Graham, Octo. 26, 1826.
Dr. Wm. Raum and Elizabeth Moodey, Jan 25, 1827.
John Foreman and Elizabeth McKinney, March 6, 1827.
Joseph Lyon and Elizabeth Bucher, March 13, 1827.
Hugh Young and Sally Smith, April 5, 1827.
Dr. Wm. R. Stewart and Dinah McKinney, April 5, 1827.
Charles Dixon and Nancy Grimes (Gormes, Goimes?), May 8, 1827.
John G. Martin and Rebecca Spangler, May 31, 1827.
John Smith and Ann Calvert, June 12, 1827.
Robert Cochran and Eliza Linn, June 14, 1827.
James Johnston and Margaret Clark, June 19, 1827.
John Kerr and Mary C. Williams, June 19, 1827.
Robt. Anderson and Credela Ferguson, August 16, 1827.
William Walker and Eliza Wiley, Octo. 4, 1827.
Alexander M. Hill and Polly Johnston, Octo. 18, 1827.
Alexander Steen and Rosanna Hunter, Octo. 30, 1827.
Jeremiah and Margaret Hall, colour, Jan 3, 1828.
Moses and Hannah, colour, March 18, 1828.
John Runk and Eliza Richardson, April 24, 1828.
Jonas Hoover and Mary Lordsbaugh, May 1, 1828.
Barnabas Thrush and Elizabeth Green, May 6, 1828.
George Atherton and Elizabeth Casey, May 8, 1828.
Adam Lemmon and Catharine Stoever (Storever), June 3, 1828.
Alexander Wilson and Agness Herron, June 11, 1828.
James Brown and Susan Snapper, July 8, 1828.
Jacob Fry (Foy?) and Rachel Fleek, August 7, 1828.
James Hemphill and Martha Strain, Sep 4, 1828.
Jacob Raum and Mary Bailey, Octo. 7, 1828.
Thomas Hastings and Rebeccah Pague, Octo. 21, 1828.
George Johnston, Esq. and Sarah Clark, Octo. 23, 1828.
John Gibbons and Hetty McDonnel, colour, Octo. 23, 1828.
Abram S. McKinny and Margaret Reynolds, Octo. 27, 1828.
James Wilson and Issabella McCoy, November 6, 1828.
James Louis and Elizabeth Trait, November 13, 1828.
John Wilson and Ellen Pritchard, December 4, 1828.
William Davis and Leah Schrebaugh, December 9, 1828.
Robert Smith and Nancy Walker, March 5, 1829.
Robert McGlaughlin and Hannah Morrow, March 26, 1829.
John Ocher and Margaret Gourd, March 26, 1829.
Robert McCune and Nancay Gibb, March 26, 1829.
Samuel Westheffer and Susan Smith, April 3, 1829.
John Reynolds and Sarah Cooper, May 14, 1829.
Wilson Morrow and Barbara Metz, May 21, 1829.
John Rankin and Elmina Kell, June 25, 1829.
Benjamin Frazure and Mary Ann Amos, June 30, 1829.
John Holtrec (Holtree?) and Eliza Roan, Sep 17, 1829.
John Swanger(?) and Sally Boyd, Octo. 1, 1829.
Alexander Spence and Jane Davenport, Octo. 22, 1829.
Saml. Trait and Ann Eliza Clark, November 3, 1829.
Joseph Black and Naomi Amos, November 3, 1829.
William Kulp and Eliza Wonderlich, December 15, 1829.
William Gallaher and --- Martin, December 17, 1829.

George Geir and Ellen McSurdy, March 11, 1830.
James Wills and Ruth Wilson, March 17, 1830.
Moses Hemphill and Marjery Clarke, March 25, 1830.
William Skelly (Shelly) and Mary Shreiner(?), March 30, 1830.
George Duncle and Margaret Boyd, April 1, 1830.
Samuel Laurins and Ann Amanda Shell, April 5, 1830.
David Witherspoon and Nancy Ann Carothers, May 18, 1830.
Joseph Hoch and Jane Clark, June 1, 1830.
George Rowan and Ann S. Esther Peck(Slothespeck?), July 1, 1830.
Wm. Spear and Jane Colhoun, November 4, 1830.
Samuel Beaty and Lucinda Allen, December 9, 1830.
Tom and Jenny, colour, married a number of years since, the time
    forgotten.

- - - - -

United Presbyterian Church, Shippensburg.
(From microfilm of the original)

John Means died Sep 1, 1823.
Mary Means died Augt. 19, 1826.
Mary McCoobry died Feb 25, 1825.
Marshal Means died Sep 5, 1830.
Margt. Reynolds died 1836.
Martha Johnston died 1823.
Andw. Thompson died 1823.
John Peale died July 15, 1828.
Elizh. Hendricks died May 24, 1828.
Isabella Griffin died Jany. 14, 1829.
Jane McCandless died June 25, 1829.
Wm. McLean died Sepr. 19, 1826.
James Peale died May 7, 1829.
Cathrine Carlyle died 1823.
Jane Means died July 14, 1828.
Mary Reynolds died July 11, 1824.
Margt. W. Henderson died Augt. 24, 1824.
Alexr. Stewart died Decr. 12, 1830.
Elizh. Pomroy died Sepr. 26, 1826.
Ruth Duncan died Sep 1823.
Agnes McKee died Sep 1823.
Dinah McKinney died 1823.
Daniel N. Pomroy died Feb 9, 1827.
Jane Pomroy died Mar 1, 1830.
John W. L. Hogue, received from Silverspring, died Apr 1828.
Zacchius Davis died Jany. 1, 1830.
Elizh. S. Herron died July 23, 1828 - "entirely deranged".
Jane Devor died Oct 8, 1826.
Agnes Stockton, recd. from Middlespring, died Nov 13, 1830.
Saml. Blythe died 1830.
Elizh. Brewster died July 26, 1830.
Margt. Nisbet of Abm. died March 26, 1829.
Mary Duncan died Dec 1, 1828.
Jane Ross died May 17, 1830.

Marriages

Jan 15, 1822 - Daniel Nevin Pomeroy to Jane Means.
April 30, 1822 - David Bigham to Griselda Means.
December 25, 1823 - Robert Cochman to Margaret W. Henderson.
March 25, 1824 - Thomas Sibbet to Catharine Ryan.
April 8, 1824 - John Waddle to Mary Reynolds.
July 1, 1824 - Thomas C. Knight to Elizabeth Matus.
July 1, 1824 - Dr. Alexander Stewart to Jane King.
August 12, 1824 - James Bay to Elizabeth Keel.
Sep 9, 1824 - Steel Matthews to Jane McCollum.
Sep 9, 1824 - Daniel Spitler to Elizabeth Reichart.
Sep 24, 18724 - Samuel Walker to Catharine Houser.
Sep 28, 1824 - Rev. Joseph McCanell to Jane B. Leeper.
Dec 28, 1824 - Richard Woods to Sarah Golden.
Dec 30, 1824 - James Blair to Sarah Shoaff.
Jan 4, 1825 - James Irvin to Eliza McClean.
Jan 6, 1825 - Walter Sloan to Eliza Greer.
Jan 11, 1825 - John Brookins to Margaret McClay.
Jan 25, 1825 - James Clark to Elizabeth Smith.
March 31, 1825 - Frederick Moony to Margaret Williams.
May 5, 1825 - Samuel Gilmor to Anne Lausman (Laupnan?).
May 19, 1825 - Robert Robinson to Elizab. Cummins.
May 31, 1825 - James Coffey to Molly Hilands.
Sep 20, 1825 - Henry Carlile to Nancy Griffen.
Oct 6, 1825 - John Thrush to Sarah Todd.
Nov 3, 1825 - Jacob Clippinger to Issab. Stewart.
Dec 22, 1825 - Joseph Weaver to Eliz. Hefflinger.
Feb 2, 1826 - Robert Barr to Nancy Laughlin.
Nov 22, 1825 - Rev. Jas. M. Olmstead to Nancy Mahon.
Feb 28, 1826 - John Reside to Elizabeth Caser (Coser?).
June 7, 1826 - Jacob Hocker to Eliza Lindsey.
June 13, 1826 - John McCoy to Margaret Weaver.
Sep 5, 1826 - John D. Creigh to Caroline Williamson.
Sep 14, 1826 - John Sinclair to Mary Dougherty.
Jany 11, 1827 - Geo. C. McCune to Molly Austin.
Mar 28, 1827 - Robert Bell to Elizabeth Smith.
Apr 19, 1827 - Thomas Kindel to Marg. Nisbet.
Aug 2, 1827 - John Eyler to Nancy Coffey.
Oct 9, 1827 - John Hilands to Susan Oberon.
Jan 31, 1828 - John Beidleman to Susan Peebles.
Feb 12, 1828 - Michael Mock to Peggy Ann Beidleman.
Feb 21, 1828 - Alfred Matthews to Peggy Doughenbaugh.
March 1, 1828 - Daniel Trimble to Jane Cook.
March 6, 1828 - George Hale to Maria Armstrong.
March 27, 1828 - George Nisbet to Mary Blackburn.
--- 1828 - Aaron Kaufman to Peggy Bennet.
April 10, 1828 - Samuel Morrow to Jane Snapper.
July 8, 1828 - James Willis to Elizabeth Moore.
July 29, 1828 - Dr. John Peale to Martha Sturgeon.
Aug 21, 1828 - William Harman to Louisa Fry.
Sep 16, 1828 - Rev. Sidney Weller to Eliza McCanell.
Oct 9, 1828 - Thomas Cummings to Issab. McConnell.
Oct 16, 1828 - William Carothers to Ann Line.
Oct 30, 1828 - Daniel Pressler to Freederica Lantz.
Dec 11, 1828 - John Herron to Jane Wilson.
Feb 19, 1829 - William M. Grier(Gres?) to Sarah Mahon.

Feb 24, 1829 - Jesse Carothers to Mary Ann Williamson.
March 3, 1829 - Robert Barnes to Sarah Ann McConnell.
March 3, 1828 - Dr. Wm. Rankin to Caroline Nevin.
March 26, 1829 - Thos. Sanderson to Maria Ambers.
Apr 28, 1829 - Robert Irvine to Mary Russell.
April 30, 1829- John Darr to Jane McBride.
May 14, 1829 - David Shields to Eliz. Williamson.
May 26, 1829 - Wm. Kingsborough to Hannah Murphy.
June 2, 1829 - William Peale to Anne Sturgeon.
Sep 29, 1829 - James Davidson to Jane McKee.
Oct 15, 1829 - Robert Hilands to Marg. McCandless.
Jan 19, 1830 - James Brackenridge to Martha Orr.
Feb 11, 1830 - James Bannington to Mary Ann Gutshaw.
Feb 11, 1830 - James Gutshaw to Eliza Bennet.
Oct 12, 1830 - Robt. T. Stewart, Esqr. to Mary Hamelton.
Nov 23, 1830 - Peter Orts to Catharine Ann Clippinger.

- - - - -

ST. STEPHEN EVANGELICAL LUTHERAN CHURCH,
New Kingston, Silver Spring Twp.

Buried 11 Nov 1825, Dorothea Herman, nee Borstin, born December
25, 1738, aged 86 years, 10 months and 16 days.
Buried 3 April 1826, Jacob Hummer, aged about 31 years, 10 months
and 26 days.
Buried 8 May 1827, Johan Adam Heidelman, born 1746, November 1,
died May 6, 1827, aged 80 years, 5 months, 5 days.

- - - - -

From William Henry Egle, *Notes and Queries, Historical,
Biographical and Genealogical*, 1897 vol. p. 180.

Maxwell, Margaret, b. 1798; d. Jan. 1, 1830.
Peebles, William, b. Oct. 2, 1791; d. Oct. 22, 1830.
Smith, Jacob, b. 1762; d. May 26, 1825.
Wherry, John, b. 1776; d. April 14, 1828.
Wherry, Samuel, b. 1746; d. Jan. 21, 1826.
G. E. Swope, Newville.

- - - - -

War of 1812 Veterans
Compiled for the Cumberland Valley Chapter, Daughters of 1812.
(Book # Cr/VET)

Abraham Funk U.S. Infantry, 51st Reg. 6th Co., Private, died
1825, age 74, born 1751, buried Camp Hill Borough. Among
those transferred from Oyster Point to Camp Hill. Ref: Series
6, Vol. 7, page 115. Pa. Archives.
Joseph Gibson, PA Vol. Infantry, 2 Co. 1st Brig. born Feb 2,
1790, died Jan 14, 1827, buried St. John's Cemtery, Hamden
Twp. Ref: Series 6, Vol. 9, page 37. Pa. Archives.
Joseph Halbert, U.S. Infantry, 2nd Regt., 7th Div. Captain, born
1776, died 1825, buried Old Graveyard, Carlisle, PA. PA

Archives, Series 6, Vols. 7 and 9.

Michael Humer, U.S. Infantry, born Feb 22, 1754, died Feb 12, 1830, buried Trindle Spring Cemetery, Silver Spring Twp. Ref: Pa. Archives, Series 6, Vol. 8, page 1337.

Thomas Jones, U.S. Infantry, born 1785, died 1829, 12th, 1st Division, Rank: Adjutant, buried Old Graveyard, Carlisle, PA. Pa. Archives, Series 6, Vol. 7, page 438.

John Leib, Army Militia, born Jan 28, 1782, died April 13, 1829, buried Old Graveyard, Churchtown, Sq. Monroe Twp., Pa. Archives, Series 6, Vol. 8, page 1401.

John Line, Army Militia, sergeant, born January 29, 1763, died Feb 8, 1827, buried Line # 1 burying ground, Dickinson Twp. Pa. Archives, Series 2, Vol. 12, page 82.

Edward Magauran, Army Infantry, rifle company, 1st Brigade, private, born 1750, died 1825, buried Old Graveyard, Carlisle, PA. Private in Capt. Roberts, Volunteer Rifle Company, Pa. Archives, Series 6, Vol. 7, page 429. Name mispelled in records as Morrorm.

Abraham Myer, private, Militia, Col. Woods' Company, born Feb 7, 1788, died Sep 21, 1828, bur. Trindle Springs Cemetery, Silver Springs Twp. Ref: Pa. Archives, Series 6, Vol. 5, page 275.

Robert Peebles, U.S. Infantry, 141st Reg. 16th Div., Captain, born 1776, died 1830, buried Big Springs Presbyterian, Corporation St., Newville, PA. Pa. Archives, Series 6, Vol. 7, page 797.

James Quigley, Cuberland County Militia, 1st Regt., Colonel, born 1768, died Oct, 28, 1827, buried Silver Springs Cemetery, Silver Spring Township, PA. Pa. Archives, Series 6, Vol. 5, page 170.

Samuel Sample, militia, Capt. McClean's company, private, born 1786, died 1828, buried Silver Spring Cemetery, Silver Spring Township, ref: Pa. Archives, Series 6, Vol. 8, pages 69, 74, 78.

John Simpson, U.S. Infantry, 3rd company, private, born 1762, died 1826, buried God's Acre Cemetery, King-Prince Streets, Shippensburg. Pa. Archives, Series 6, Vol. 7, page 72.

Jacob Wolfe, 6th Battalion, Captain Wm. Strain's company, born Sep 21, 1766, died Sep 23, 1823, buried Old Graveyard, Churchtown, Sq. Monroe, Twp. Pa. Archives, Series 5, Vol. 6, page 430.

BAXTER James 55
Rachel Ann 16
BAY James 121
BAYARD Juliet
Elizabeth 70
Rev. 70
Samuel 70
Walter A. 82
BEALL William Dent 36
BEALLE David 68
Thomas 78
BEAMS Ann 83
BEAR George M. 98
John 96
Michael 74
Samuel 96, 97
Susan 70
BEARBOWER Henry 68
BEARCH Mr. 94
BEATTY James 1
BEATTY Mrs. 1
BEATY James 3, 100,
118
Jane 92
Samuel 120
Sarah 101
BEAUCHAMP William 11
BECHLER John 74
BECKER Catharine 66
BEDFORD Gunning B. 52
Gunning 73
BEEGHLER Maria 26
BEELEN Francis 10, 74
Johana 10
Johana 74
BEELMAN Miss 12
BEEMER John 118
BEETEM George 40, 90
Hannah 40, 90
BEIDLEMAN John 121
Peggy Ann 121
BEISTLEIN Baltzer 37
Margaret 60
Samuel 102
BELL Catharine 88
David 108
Dr. E. H. 79
Eleanor 96
Eleanora 100
James 52
Jane Elizabeth 52
Jane E. 101
Jonathan 109
Nancy 113
Rachel 45
Robert 45, 121
Samuel 28
Thomas 73
Walter 24, 52
William 17, 107
BELLSHOOVER Samuel 91
BELSHOOVER George 48
Regina 48
Sarah 23
BELTSHOOVER Sarah 23
BELTZHOOVER George 56

BELTZHUBER George 102
Jacob 9, 100
BENDER Barbara 63
Catharine 84
George 103
John 109
BENJAMIN John 4, 76
Mrs. 4
BENNER Joseph 112
Philip 26
Ruth 26
BENNET Eliza 122
Jasper 74
Peggy 121
Rev.J. 46
BENTZ Elizabeth 94
BERGER George 72
BERHART John 118
BERKE John 98
BERKEY Barbara 109
BERLIN Elias 54, 102
BERNARD B. 109
BERNHART Catharine 99
Margret 99
BERRIAN Rev. Dr. 43
BERRIEN Rev. 23
BERRY Catharine 82
Thomas 82
BIDDLE Valeria F. 4
William M. 4
BIERBOWER Jonathan 47,
97
BIGGS Ann 7
BIGHAM David 121
Thomas A. 81
BIGHAN David 116
Elizabeth 116
BIGLER Catharine 42
John 42
Mary Ann 90
BILLMAN Jacob 3, 100
BILLOW Lydia 11, 100
Sarah 8, 100
BIOREN Charles 91
BISHOP Ann 64
Catharine 98
Christian 63
Jacob 58, 102
John 85, 99
Joseph 99
Mary 66
Miss 94
BITNER --- 112
Henry 92
John 103
BLACK Anthony 35
Catharine 40, 91, 104
Elizabeth 38, 90
John A. 25
Joseph 119
Maria 99
Mary Ann 39
Mary 35
Matthew 5
Peter 48
William 12

BLACKBURN Mary 121
BLACKFORD Benjamin 24
BLAIK Mary Ann 90
BLAINE R. 82
BLAIR J. B. 117
James 121
Mary 81
Sarah 58
William 58, 81
BLAKE Ellenor 118
BLEAN David 116
Grissella 23, 116
Isabella 113, 117
John 116
Mary 117
Robert 50, 117
BLOOM Daniel 14
BLYTHE Samuel 120
BOAL David 10
BOB Barbara 98
Martin 99
BOBBS Polly 118
BODEN Jane 27
John 27
BOHR Henry 64, 103
BOILEAU Rebecca 109
BOILIEU Rebecca 13
BOLANDER Sarah 41, 107
BOMBERGER Jacob 34
Old 34
BONEY Issabella 101
BONNER Thompson T. 22
BOOKS Elizabeth 34
BOON Hannah 57
Hannah 102
BOOR Henry 5
BORMAN Mary 118
BORSTIN Dorothea 122
BOSLER Abraham 109
Catherine 109
J. 109
Jacob 60, 103
John 99, 109
Samuel 35
BOSSLER Jacob 88, 101
BOTTS Polly 118
BOVARD Charles 58, 67
Maria 67
Rachel 58
BOVENMEYER Philip 10
BOWER Henry 100
Jesse 4
BOWERMASTER Anna Maria
16
C. 109
BOWERS Jacob 118
BOWMAN Casiah 94
Catharine 63
Henry 95
BOYD Adam 73
Eliza 61
Elizabeth 73
James R. 101
James 73, 116
John 73, 118
Margaret 120

79, 86
W. R. 21
William R. 84, 105
DICKERSON Alexander 42
  Joshua 42
DICKEY Rebekah 108
  Susan 105
DICKOVER Benjamin 34
DICKSON Andrew 15
  Ann Eliza 73
  John 112
  William 73, 85
DIEHL Samuel 50
DIERDORFF Samuel 23
DIFFENDAFFER Catharine
  88
DIFFERBAUGHER Jacob
  107
DILLER --- 98, 109
  Chasper(?) 95
  Leonard 103
  Samuel 63, 103
DIMMICK Dan 13
DINWIDDIE James 77
DIPPLE Ann C. 6
  Ann Catherine 96
  Joseph 11
  Mary 38, 97
  Michael 11, 38
DISH Christian 29
DIVEN Andrew 66
  Joseph 40
DIVINNIE Mary 110
  William 110
DIXON Charles 119
  James 4
DODDS Ann 85
DOEY Rebecca 98
DOLL Susanna 47
DOLTON Mr. 24
DONAHOE Barclay 27
DONAHU Maria 37
DONALDSON Martha 118
  Thomas 112
DONALLY Mrs. 69
DONAVIN Issabella 26
DONEHOWER George 92
DONLEY John 98
DONNELLY Charles 105
DORF Eliza Dear 116
DORNBAUGH Joseph 17
DORSHEIMER Philip 78
DORSHIMER Ann 3
DOTY Henry 89
DOUGHENBAUGH Peggy 121
DOUGHERTY George 106,
  116
  Jane 113
  John 116
  Maria 114
  Mary 121
DOUGLASS Ann 5, 105
  Hannah 91, 104
  William 5
DOUP George 118
DOYLE Ann 15

Elisha 15, 22
Nancy 15
DRAWRBACH Mary 38
DRENKLE Mrs. 73
DRYSON Robert 108
DUBOISE Rev. 71
DUCK Philip 44
DUEY Elisabeth
  (Elizabeth) 3, 100
  Jane 37
  John 24
  Miss Ra'l 46
  Samuel 65
DUFFIELD Amanda 24, 106
  George 3, 5, 8, 12,
    14, 15, 19, 24, 24,
    27, 29, 31, 32, 32,
    33, 33, 33, 37, 39,
    41, 41, 41, 49, 50,
    54, 56, 58, 58, 62,
    62, 67, 68, 71, 74,
    77, 80, 88, 88, 88,
    91, 104
  Rev. 6, 12, 31, 45,
    54
  Rev. G. 10, 16, 22,
    54, 79, 81, 93
  Sophia 24, 106
DUFFY Ellen 112
  John 66, 112
  Mary 113
  Rev. 63
DUM Thomas 55
DUMMA Christian 56, 102
  Henry 99
DUNAHU Barkley 28
DUNBAR E. L. 91
  George 118
  Isabella 73, 114
  James 101
  John 5, 48, 52, 73,
    101, 105, 114
  Mary 114
  Mr. 65
  Robert 55
  Rosanna 112
DUNCAN Calender 107
  Catharine 29, 106
  David 118
  Eliza 117
  Jesse 61
  John 80, 83, 105
  Joseph 112
  Martha Ann 107
  Mary Louisa 32
  Mary E. 76
  Mary Louisa 106
  Mary 88, 120
  Rebecca 107
  Ruth 120
  Sally Ann 118
  Samuel 39
  Stephen 25
  Thomas 21, 29, 70,
    76, 83
  William 5, 112

DUNCLE George 120
DUNFEE Mary 71, 114
DUNLAP Ann 109
  James 39, 108, 110
  Martin 108
  William 115
DUNLEY William 101
DUNLOP Sarahbella 88
DUNMERE Peggy 118
DUNOHOO Rev. 36
DUNWOODY David 107
DWEN Anistatia 26
  John 25
  Patrick 74
  Rev. 26, 32, 55, 62
  Rev. P. 43
DWENN Patrick 74
DWIN Patrick 10
DWINN Rev. 6
DYSE Catharine 48
DYSON Mary Ann 99
  Sarah 98

EAGEN James 78
EAGENS James 98
EARLY Elizabeth 49
  Margaret 117
  Nancy 118
EARNEST John 32, 97
EAST Catharine 11, 100
EATON Isaac 68
EBAUGH David K. 9
  John S. 23, 24, 26,
    23, 7, 40, 38, 44,
    30, 27, 44, 45, 44,
    31, 47, 46, 46, 30,
    37, 39, 38, 68, 72,
    65, 84, 93, 90, 93
  Rev. 12, 20, 24, 78,
    79, 81, 82, 85
  Rev. J. S. 8, 12, 13,
    14, 29, 32, 35, 39,
    48, 49, 51, 54, 59,
    60, 62, 63, 64, 66,
    67, 69
  Rev. John S. 89, 93,
    88
EBERLE Nancy 67, 104
EBERLEY Catharine 99
EBERLY Ann 89
  Catharine 101
  Elizabeth 46
  Joseph 3
  Mrs. 95
  Nancy 95
EBERSOLE Abraham 100
  Christian 99
EBEY Nancy 54
EBRIGHT John 45
EBY David 34, 102
  Elizabeth 34
  Jacson W. 107
  Jason W. 33
  John 60, 103
  Simon 6, 100
ECCLES Martha 109

857555655635566566

66556666555556666565656665656655

Nathaniel 108
Samuel 109
William 108
ECKARD Dr. 68
  Margaret 97
  Mrs. 68
ECKART Mr. 18
ECKELS Martha 94
  Mary 109
  Samuel 109
  William 109
ECKERT Abraham 5
  Conrad 95
  Elizabeth 95
  Margaret 33
ECKHART G. W. 109
ECKLES Daniel 64, 103
  Nancy 39
EDMISTON James 34
EDMUNSON James 34
EDWARDS Joseph 85
  Mary 62
EGE Ann D. 93
Ege Joseph Arthur 36
  Joseph 112
  Martha W. 105
  Michael 56
  Peter 36, 93
EGLE William Henry 122
EGNER Eli 66, 103
EGNLES Rev. 68
EGOLF Catharine 98
  John 99
EICHELBARGER Sarah 66
EICHELBERGER Catharine 1
  Frederick 79
  Lewis 90
EIGLEBERGER Elisabeth 102
  Elizabeth 56
  Susan 101
  Susanna 15
ELLIOT Jesse 19
  Robert 118
ELLIOTT David 11
  James 22, 65, 115, 116
  John 33, 110
  Rev. 32
ELLIS Elijah 117
EMERSON Sarah Ann 105
EMINGER John 84
EMMINGER Andrew 4
  Susan 100
  Susanna 4
ENDRESS Rev. Dr. 59, 60
ENGEL Elisabeth 99
  England 80
ENGLE Fanny 103
ENGLES Rev. 94
ENSMINGER Jonathan 19
EPLEY Joseph 109
EPPLY Margaret 49, 101
ERSKINE John 71

ETTER Matilda 110
  Philip 101
EVANS Eliza 110
  Owen 92
EVAUGH John S. 26
EVERS James 106
EVETTS --- 58
EWING David 116
  George 108
  George W. 44
EYLER John 121
  Mrs. 54
  Peter 54, 105

FAGAR John H. 91
FAGER Samuel 88
FAHNESTOCK G. 1
  Hanna 73
  John 31, 58, 109
  Mary B. 31
  Mr. G. 77
  Obed 73
FAHRENBAUGH John 93
FAILOR Maria 54
FAIR Catharine 99
  Julian 102
FAIRLAMB George A. 65
FAIRS Julian 53
FALLER John 43
FANWELL Jacob 26, 103
FARNEY Rebecca 74
FARRIER David 112
FASSNAUGHT Jacob 119
FAUFMAN Eliza 90
FAUST Jacob 55
  Joseph 62
FEARY John 73
FEASTER Sarah Ann 22
FEHLER Christian 56, 102
  John 66, 103
  Maria 102
FEIDEL Peter 66
FEILER Martha 66
FEILY Sohia 9, 100
FEISTER James 108
FENEGEL Sarah 102
FENEGLE John 101
FENGAL John 49
FENTON Elizabeth 4
FERGUSON Credela 119
  David 109
  Jessica C. 95
  John 117
  Mary 116
  William 23
FERIS James 72
  Mary A. 26
FERRIS James 73
  Mary A. 96
  Robert 73
FESSLER Sarah 99
FETTER Jacob 87
  Samuel 12, 100
  Susannah 87
FETTERMAN Rachel 52

FILEY John 58
FINDLAY John 11
  Nancy 8
  William 8
  Zaccheas 105
FINDLEY William 75
FINEGAL Sarah 55
FINNACLE Susan(n) 66, 103
FIREOBET David 99
FIRMAN Isabella 30
FISHBURN Peter 48
FISHER Daniel 61, 99
  Eliza 13
  George 72
  Joseph 35
  Mary 12, 101
  Samuel 41
  Thomas 79, 108, 109, 110
  Wilson 72
FISTER John 22, 63, 103
  Mary 52
  Sarah Ann 22
FITZIMONS Patrick 53
FLECK Pearl Reddig 97
FLEEGER Charles 38
FLEEK Rachel 119
FLEMING George 68
  James 86
  Jane 118
  Joseph 41
  Margaret 7
  Robert 43, 106
  William 3, 118
FLEMMING George 105
  James 72
  Mr. 54
FLINDER Elizabeth 87
FLLOD John 7
  John G. 96
FLLOYD Jane 108
FLOWER Guiles 95
  Lenora E. 95
FLOYD Allen 109
FOCHENDER Sally 117
FOCKENDER Rachel 118
FOGLE Christian 99
FOOSE John 2
FORBES Jane 111
  John 111
  John P. 35, 111
  Richard 68, 111
FORD Ann 18
  Daniel 109
  Eliza 109
  Henry 18
  John 28
  Miss E. 95
FORDREY Susan 44
FOREMAN John 119
FORNEY Jacob 57, 102
  Mary 19
FORREST Priscilla 117
  Thomas 14
FORREY Catharine 61

Elizabeth 114
Esther 114
Jane 113
John 115, 116
Kenton 73
Mr. 14
William 114, 116
HARR(?) Henry 86
HARRIET Maria 99
HARRIS Elizabeth 100
G. W. 110
Jacob 30
Thomas 46, 62, 93
HARRISON Elizabeth M.
    75
John 75
HARRY Mary 18
Mrs. 48
HARTER George 99
HARTING John 9, 100
Nicholas 93
HARTMAN Catherine 94
J. 54
John 101
Nicholas 20
Susannah 66
HARTMANN Susanna 103
HARTZELL Abraham 67
George 74
HARTZLER Abraham 95
HASLER John 66
HASSINGER David 35
Rev. 57
Rev. D. 48
HAST Christian 90
HASTINGS Thomas 119
HATTEN John 48, 101
HATZFIELD Adolph 37
HAUENSTEIN Maria 31
HAUENSTINE Elizabeth
    56
HAUERSTEIN Margret 98
Elisabeth 102
HAVERSTICK Henry 90
HAVERSTOCK Magdalene
    31
HAVISER Mary 42, 104
HAW Mrs. 54
HAY John 106
HAYES Mary 117
HAYS Adam 54
Ann 22
David S. 29
Dr. 116
Jane 3, 33, 70, 106
John 3, 70
John S. 22
Joseph 33, 42, 59
Margaret 113
Mary 42, 49, 107
Mr. 94
Nancy 59
Samuel 71, 105
Thomas 66
HEAGY Ann 63
David 112

John 60
Miss 63
HEANNON William 117
HEBEISEN Maria 42
Michael 42
HECK Jacob 118
Sarah 94
HECKER Andrew 53, 102
HECKMAN George 56, 102
John 14
HEFFELFINGER John 35
Joseph 37
Thomas 116
HEFFLINGER Elizabeth
    121
HEHL Jacob 13
HEIDELMAN Johan Adam
    122
HEIGES Elizabeth 111
HEIGIS Margaret 111
HEIKES --- 111
Andrew 1, 98, 100
HEISLEY Samuel 108
HEISS Sarah 98
HEISTER Gabriel 91
Harriet 91
HEITSHU Mary 54
Philip 54
HEKMAN Susanna 66
HELFENSTEIN Albert 92
Catherine 92
Jonathan 36
Rev. 34
Samuel 48
HELFENSTINE Albert 30
Rev. 92
HELLER Mr. 94
HELMUTH Rev. D. 77
Rev. Dr. 1
HELPHENSTEIN Catherine
    105
HEMING Marianne 86
HEMMINGER Mrs. 26
HEMMINGER Samuel 4, 26,
    100
HEMPHILL James 119
John 99
Moses 120
HENDEL George 88
Mary A. E. 27
Mary Ann Elizabeth 77
William 77, 88
William B. 38
HENDERSON Daniel 8
James 11, 13
John 62
Margaret 11
Margaret W. 120, 121
Thomas 13
William 105
William M. 3
HENDRICKS Elizabeth 120
John 2
Susanna 3
HENDRICS John 118
HENE Thomas 3

HENEMAN Abraham 38
HENEY Thomas 3
HENKLE Jacob 4, 100
HENLY Catharine 46
Joseph 46
HENRY Harriet 77
Judge 77
Mary 12
Nathaniel 79
Samuel 60
HENSTHORN Robert 117
HENWOOD Abraham 72
Elisabeth (Elizabeth)
    54, 106
William 24
HEPBURN Samuel 110
HEPPEHAMER David 12
HERBEST John 36
HERBST John 56
HERCH Henry 93
HERMAN Dorothea 122
Rev. 73
HERR John 37
HERRING Asa 110
HERRMAN An Doratha 101
Ann D. 88
Catharine 100
Jacob 98
HERRON Charles 79
Elizabeth S. 120
John 121
Thomas 103
HERSH George 9
HERSHE Jacob 53, 102
HERSHEY John 51
HERSHMAN Daniel 97
HERST Ann 66
HERTSLER Ann 1
HERTZ Sarah 98
HERTZEL Abraham 104
HERTZELL Catharine 17
Peter 17
HERTZLER Ann 100
Barbara 98
HESS Rudolff 102
Rudolph 56
HETICH Catharine 13
HETTRICH Catharine 101
HEYER F. 103
Rev. 29, 30, 33, 64,
    67, 91, 92
Rev. F. 26, 39, 40,
    42, 63, 64, 65, 66,
    67, 90
HICKIS Elizabeth 118
HICKMAN Sally Ann 118
HIESTAND John 13
HIESTER Elizabeth 17
Joseph 17
HIKES Catharine 23, 111
John 23
HILANDS John 121
Molly 121
Robert 122
HILL Alexander M. 119
Rev. 7

Sarah 107
JACK Charles J. 3, 70
JACKSON Jane 106
    Sarah 72
    Truston 33
JACOB David 112
    George 98
JACOBS Jacob 100
    Joseph 3
    John 75
JACOBY Mary 87
JAMES Thomas 81
JAMESON William 118
JAMISON Hannah 117
JENNER John P. 98
JENNINGS Rev. Dr. 11
JENNY 120
JOB Benjamin 44
JOHNSON Cynthia B. 42
    Eleanor 75
    Hugh 75
    James 6, 89
    John V. 36
    Margaret 89
JOHNSTON Elenor 41
    Elizabeth 118
    George 119
    Hester 110
    Hugh 51
    James 10, 74, 119
    John 7, 112, 118
    Margaret 105
    Martha 120
    Mrs. 7, 42
    Polly 119
    Samuel 108
    William 74
JONES Eliza 91
    Elizabeth 62
    Hannah Ann 16
    John 105
    Mary 58, 109
    Mr. B. M. 75
    Rev. A. 40
    Samuel 9
    Thomas 31, 123
JOURDON Mrs. 50
JUMPER Conrad 82
    Eve 82
    Henry 12
JUNKEN Adeline 109
    John 108
JUNKIN Adeline C. 28
    Ann 23
    Joseph 15, 22, 110
    William F. 87, 116
JUNKINS Jean 118

KAKE Louisa 98
KALLEN William 118
KAMPF George 100
KAMPFER Sarah 99
KANTS Marg(a)ret 42,
    92, 97
KANTZ Mary 105

KAPP Chritina 98
KARCH Joseph 98
KARMENY Samuel 87
KASSEL Sarah 98
KAST Jacob 45
KAUBER Jacob F. 97
KAUFFMAN Christopher
    110
    Eliza 110
    Isaac 110
    Jacob 17
    Rosa(n)na 54, 102
KAUFMAN Aaron 121
    Ann Eliza 51
KEAGY Adam 110
KEEFER --- 102
    John 98
KEEL Elizabeth 121
KEENE Nathaniel B. 96
KEENY Anna 102
KEFFER Joanthan 87
KEIGLEY Jacob 53
KEISER Andrew 31, 97
KEITEMAN Elizabeth 86
KEITH John 79
    Sarah 22
    William 22, 33, 97
KELL Elmina 119
KELLER Andrew 77
    Ann Catharine 46
    Barbary Ann 61
    Benjamin 3, 8, 21,
        55, 57, 60, 78, 80,
        87, 88
    Catharine 81
    Daniel R. 54
    Eliza 96, 101
    Elizabeth 7
    Emanuel 89, 90
    Frederick Emanuel 57
    , 96
    Henry 7
    John George 14
    Leonard 40, 46, 77,
        81, 91
    Peter 61
    Rev. 28, 94
    Rev. B. 1, 2, 3, 4,
        5, 6, 9, 11, 12, 13,
        14, 15, 16, 19, 22,
        25, 48, 49, 51, 52,
        53, 54, 55, 56, 57,
        58, 59, 60, 61, 62,
        63, 64, 65, 66, 79,
        85, 86, 92, 96
    Rev. Benjamin 85
    Rev. E. 93
    Susan 97
KELLEY E. S. 30
    Eben S. 64
    Robert 53
KELLY Elisabeth 100
    Elizabeth 3
    Samuel 108
KELSO Alexander 117
    Elizabeth 71, 118

William 16, 118
KEMP Right Rev. Bishop
    58
KENNEDY Barbara 89
    Elizabeth 113
    George 44
    James 15, 112
    Jane 106
    John 45
    Margaret 114
    Mary 45
    Mr. B. 45
    Thomas 114
KENNER Charles F. 50
KENNY Ann 58
KENOWER Rebecca 67, 104
Kentucky, Boone County
    86
KENYON Robert 62, 106
KEPFERT Elizabeth 92
KER John 76
    Sarah 76
    William 7
KERLEY Michael L. 115
KERMAN Catharine 6
KERN George 98
KERNAN Ann 35, 97
    Furgus R. 49
    Mrs. 51
    Thomas 35
KERR Andrew 7, 24, 80
    Col. 69
    Debra 39
    Dennis 85
    Isabella 52
    Jacob 39
    John 69, 119
    Mary 13
    Sarah 80
    Stephen 51, 81, 105
    William 51, 72, 112
    William J. 73
KESLER Polly 118
    Rev. 72
KETTERING Catharine 72
    Valentine 59, 72
KEYNER George 117, 118
KID Nancy 47
KIEHL Catharine 45
    George 99
    Marg(a)ret 4, 100
    Mary 37
KIERNAN James 26
KILGORE Ezekiel 113
    Isabella 114
    Jesse 113, 114, 116
    Jessie 116
    Joseph 117
    Nancy 113
    Robert 116
    William 1, 114, 117
KILHEFFER Henry 44
KILLHAFFER John 99
KIMMEL Hannah 102
    John 98
KINCADE Elisa Jane 106

Daniel F. 96
Keziah S. 96
William 30
LEHMER Christian 62
LEIB An Catharine 97
Barbara 99
Christian 57
John 95, 123
Michael 85
Peter 13
LEIDICH Adam 95
LEIDIG Jacob 31
Polly 49
Rebecca 9, 100
LEIPER Thomas 17
LEMMON Adam 119
LEMONS Isaac 39
LENHART Henry 60
LENNEY William 114
LEONARD Christian 17, 48
Daniel 68
Eliza 34
Maria 102
LEVINGSTON Hugh 70
LEVIS William 58
LEVISTON Hugh 3
LEWER Christian 90
LEWIS Eli 74
James 63
LEYBURN Elizabeth 22
Robert 11, 22
William 87
LEYMAN Henry 86
Rebecca 86
LIFF Samuel 86
LIGED Alexander 98
LIGED Margret 98
LIGHTCAP Joseph 27
Mary 49
LIGHTNER Henry 37
Nancy 28, 37
Peter 109
LINDLE Mr. 94
LINDSAY Ann 75
Lacy 113
Nancy 112
Thomas 75
LINDSEY David 115
Eliza 121
Moses 115
William A. 112
LINDSY Alexander 118
LINE Abraham 3
Ann 27, 121
Catharine 84
Emanuel 67
Gabrial, Gabriel 57, 102
George L. 67
John 56, 123
Maria 67
Mary 87
Mrs. 51
Rebecca 57
William 45, 51, 82,

87
LINN Eliza 119
James 36
Jane 89, 118
LINSEY Eliza 119
LION Robert 97
LIPPERT Ann 101
John 64, 103
LIST Catharine 98
LITTLEJOHN Elizabeth 10
Isabella 23
Samuel H. 10, 75
William 69
LIVINGER Catharine 6
LIVINGSTON Ann Maria 88
Elizabeth 109
John 88
Michael 52, 101
Rev. 38
LIVINSTON Eliza Matilda 71
P. W. 71
LOCHMAN Augustus 90
Augustus H. 19, 42, 48, 49, 73, 89, 91
George 49, 53
Mr. 94
Rev. 6, 38, 53, 61, 68, 84
Rev. A. 91
Rev. A. H. 44, 55, 59
Rev. D. 47
Rev. Dr. 1, 3, 5, 8, 10, 12, 13, 14, 15, 18, 69, 73, 74, 78, 79, 83, 85
LOCKERMAN John R. 56
LOCKMAN Augustus H. 19
LOGAN Eleanor 76
Elizabeth 13
George 113
Henry 13
James 28, 113, 114
LOGUE George 21
Joseph 85
LONG Catharine 86
Ira 94
Marg(a)ret 60, 103
Miss 95
Samuel 86
LONGANECHER Maria 55
LONGENECKER Cathrine 82

LONGRINE Cornelius 108
LONGSDORF George 49
LONGSDORFF Adam 99
Anna 99
George 101
LONGWELL Sarah 112
LORDSBAUGH Mary 119
LORISH Anna 66, 103
LOSH Stephen 16
LOUDEN James 98
LOUDON Archibald 84
Hennah 84
Thomas 39, 107

LOUGHEAD Francis 119
LOUGHRIDGE Abraham 80
LOUIS James 119
Louisiana, New Orleans 16, 17, 20
LOUK Sarah 109
LOW Magdalen 96
Michael 66, 103
Nancy 46, 93
Sarah 67, 104
LOWERY Isaac 113
LOWRY Edward J. 42
LUEY(?) Rev. 93
LUKENS Jacob 28
LUSK Betsy 116
Robert 116
William 115
LUTS Adam 55
LUTZ Baltzer 54
John 40, 91, 104
Martin 18, 86
Mr. 48
LYNCH Ann 97
Elizabeth 97
Maria 55
LYNE John P. 9, 100
LYON George A. 31
Joseph 119
LYONS George A. 106

M'ALISTER Archibald 88
Miss 2
M'ALLISTER Archibald 80
Elizabeth 80
M'BRAERTY James 70
M'BRIDE Robert 87
M'CABE Catharine 88
M'CANDISH Maria 21
M'CARMICK George 81
M'CARTNEY John 27, 93
Maria 27
Matilda 93
M'CARTY Bartholomew 21
M'CAVITT Peter 4
M'CLAN Robert 30
M'CLELLAND Jane 50
Nancy 34
Rev. 23
Rev. A. 49
M'CLUNE James 65
M'CLURE Alexander 75
Margaret 31
Rebecca 52
Samuel 24
William 21
M'COCKRY Mary 20
Samuel A. 75
M'CONAUGHY John 9
M'CONNEL James 4
M'CORD Elizabeth 44
Lacy 8
Robert 8, 49, 51
Samuel 19
William 37
M'CORMIC Henry 51
Nancy 51

Steel 121
Thomas 62
MATUS Elizabeth 121
MAUNTZ Daniel 101
  Jacob 62
MAURER Lehna 102
MAXWELL Jacob 44
  John 17
  Margaret 122
  Sarah 69
  Susan H. 32
  William 32
MAY Barbara 81
  Christina 55
  Frederick 34, 42
  Jane 102
  Mrs. 34
MAYER Abraham 31, 39
  Catharine 39
  Christian 35, 37
  Ludwig 59
  Mary Ann 31, 96
  Rev. 68
MAYLONEY Maria 98
McALISTER Leacy 113
McANURLIN Thomas 117
McBRIDE Jane 122
  Nancy 113
  Tabitha 113
McCABE Betsy 116
McCAFFERTY John 106
McCAHAN Alexander 116
  Alexander 116
McCALEB J. 113
McCALISTER Margret 100
McCALMON Nancy 118
McCANDLESS Jane 120
  John 117
  Margaret 122
McCANDLISH Jane 114
  John 113, 114
  Maria 114
  William 114
McCANELL Eliza 121
  Joseph 121
McCANN Mary 109
McCANON Rosanna 113
McCARTNEY Andrew 102
  John 108
McCARTY Daniel 97
McCASLEM James 116
McCAULY Patrick 99
McCAVIT Peter 100
McCLAIR Miss 94
McCLAY Margaret 121
McCLEAN Eliza 121
McCLELLAND John 113
  William 113
McCOLLUM Jane 121
McCONNELL Issab. 121
  Sarah Ann 122
McCOOBRY Mary 120
McCORD Benjamin 92
  Margaret 105
  Robert 113
McCORMICK Eliza 114

George 105
Margaret Young 114
Maria 113
Samuel 113, 115
Thomas 113, 114
McCOY Issabella 119
  John 121
  Mores 96
McCREA Margaret 115
  William 115
McCREIGHT Alexander 117
McCUE A. E. 108
  Ann E. 110
McCULLOCH James 114
  John 114
  Tabitha 113
  Thomas 113
  William 115
McCULLOUGH Eliza 116
  Elizabeth 116
  J. W. 106
  John 113, 116
  Thomas 116
  William 116
McCUNE Alexander 118
  Eleanor 115
  George C. 121
  John 115, 116
  Joseph 113
  Mary Ann 115
  Robert 115, 119
  Thomas 113
  William 115
McCURDY Alexander 110
McDANNEL Daniel 115
McDONALD Anne 113
  Daniel 113
  Eliza 111
  Jane 98
  Nancy 111
  Thomas 111
McDONNAL John 103
McDONNEL Hetty 119
McDOWELL John 115
  Samuel 115
McELHENEY Samuel 116
McELHENNY James 116
McELWANE Jane 116
McFADDEN Catherine 102
McFARLAND Jane 118
McFARLANE Alexander 113
  Clemens 113
  Elizabeth 112
  James 113
McFARLENE James 116
McFATE John 103
McGLAUGHLIN Robert 116,
  119
McGUIRE Nancy 108
McGUOID Thomas 102
McHAMEE Eleanor 115
McHENRY --- 83
McHOE George 110
McILFRESH Charles 118
McILHENY Joseph 117
McINTIRE Benjamin 105

John 115
Margaret 115
McKEAN Alexander 118
  Eliza 105
McKEE Agnes 120
  Alexander 109
  Ann 110
  George 110
  James 113
  Jane 122
  Rachel Elizabeth 109
McKEEHAN Benjamin 115
  James 116
  John 113
  Margaret 114, 115
McKENYON Samuel 106
McKIBBEN Joseph 113
McKIMEY John 105
McKINLEY Daniel 58, 111
  Margaret 105
  Samuel 110
McKINNEY Dinah 119, 120
  Elizabeth 119
McKINNY Abram S. 119
McKINSTRY James 113
McKNIGHT Jane 112
McLANE Jean 117
McLAUGHLIN John 99
McLEAN William 120
McLENE John 118
McMAMMONY Susanna 117
McMANIME Katharine 118
McMANUS Mary 96
McMULLIN Hugh 54
McMURREY Mary 92
  Thomas 92
McNAIR Mary 112
McNEAL Daniel 95
  Eliza 116
McNEIL Samuel 113
McNICKLE Jane 112
McPHERSON Rebecca 92
  Robert 92
McSURDY Ellen 120
McWILLIAMS Esther 113
MEADE Richard W. 25
MEANES Molly 118
MEANS Griselda 121
  Jane 120, 121
  John 120
  Marshal 120
  Mary 120
MECLENE Jane 100
MEDER George 99
MEDTART Jacob 90
MEHAFFEY Rebecca 65
MEL Jacob 107
MELL Catharine 19
  John 101
  Sarah 5, 100
MELSHEIMER Rev. 74
MENICH John 32
MENIG Barbara 99
MENRICH charles 11
MERIDITH William 116
MERRIT Dorothy 11

REILLEY Abigail 75
REILLY James 75
REILY Rev. 18
REINBERGER Henry 99
REISINER George 2
REISINGER George 70,
  108
  Martin 98
RENAKER John 66
RENNIKER John 94
RESIDE John 121
RESSER Miss 94
REUBER Benjamin 104
REUSENBERGER Elisabeth
  100
REYNOLDS Ann 118
  Caleb 21, 81
  Catharine 15
  John 119
  Margaret 27, 119,
  120
  Mary 120, 121
  Rev. 78, 82
  Rev. C. 85
RHEA James 106
RHEEM Elizabeth 93
H. 61
  Susan 47
  Susanna 104
RHERER Susan 91
RHOADS Philip 1
RHODES Susan 46
RIBISON John 91
RICE Elijah 44
  Elizabeth 70
RICHARDS John 27
  Rev. 45
RICHARDSON Eliza 119
RICHERS Isabella 102
RICHESON Mr. 35
RICHIE Mary 112, 116
  Nancy 112
RICHTER Elis(z)abeth,
  78, 98
  George 97
RICHY William 115
RICKART Maria 82
RIDDLE Rev. 90
  Samuel 2
RIDGERS John 106
RIEBER Benjamin 67
RIFE Georgeia P. 115
RIFFLE Jesse 118
RIGGEL John 105
RIGGLEMAN -- 111
RILEY John 113
RINE Catharine 99
  David 64, 103
  Elis(z)abeth 85, 88,
  101
  John 17
  Margaret 17
RINGGOLD Hester Maria
  58
  Jacob 58
RINGWALT Col. 29

RIPPEY Lucinda 12
RIPTON Peter 113
RITCHEY David 71
  Mary 71, 118
  Susan 118
RITCHIE David 118
  Robert 9
RITCHWINE Catharine 63,
  103
RITNER Catharine 31
ROADS John 65
  Margaret 23
  Sarah 14
  Susan 93
ROAN Eliza 119
  Jacob 118
ROB Martin 86
ROBERTS Andrew 30, 113
  Charlotte 41, 91, 113
  John 41, 91
  Noble 118
  Robert 113
ROBERTSON Elliot 116
ROBINETTE Elizabeth 110
  James 110
ROBINSON Adolphius 117
  Robert 121
ROBISON John 104
RODDY Josiah 17, 37, 46
  Nancy 46
RODGERS Com. 10
  James 118
  Mary 118
  Mrs. 10
ROLLINGS Mary 101
ROMER Catharine 3
RONENBAUM Henry 10
ROSS Ann 83
  Jane 120
  John 108, 113
  Louisa 113
  Samuel 83
  William 53, 110
ROSSLER John 111
ROTHBAUST Sarah 14
ROUDEBAUGH Miss M. 54
ROUDROCK John 40
ROUSE George 39
ROWAN David 22, 45
  George 120
  Mrs. J'y 22
  Samuel 78
ROWLAND Mary 48
RUBY --- 97
  Samuel 98, 108
RUCH Catharine 98
  Elisabeth 104
RUDECILL John 54
RUDESILL Maria 101
RUDISELL Sarah 6
RUDISILE Maria 49
RUDISILL John 36
RUDY Daniel 49
  David 101
RUF Elizabeth 44
RUFF Daniel 32

RUGH(?) Elisabeth 90
RUNDECKER Polly 118
RUNK John 119
RUPERT Catharine 30, 31
RUPLEY Abraham 50, 86,
  95
  Catharine 74
  Elizabeth 10, 74
  Frederick 79
  Jacob 18
  John 10, 18, 74
  Margaret 79
RUPP Catharine 8
  Daniel 59
  David 8
  Elis(z)abeth 94, 98
  George 94, 110
  I. Daniel 109, 110
  J. D. 94
  J. Daniel 102
  Jacob 101
  Jonas 94
  Mary 95
RUPPLEY Robert 56
RUPPLY Robert 102
RUSSELL Joseph 71
  Mary 122
RUSTON Margaret 109
  William 109
RUTHERFORD Daniel 116
RITKUHNS Ann Margaretta
  95
RUTTER Mary Ann 105
RUTZ Dewalt 95
  Elizabeth 95
  George 95
RYAN Catharine 121
  Jane 112

SADERSON George 54
SADLER John 32, 97
SAILOR George 56
  John 27, 59
SALTER John W. 42
SALTZGEBER John 48, 101
SAMPLE Agnes 110
  Eliza 71
  Samuel 108, 123
SANDERSON Alexander 111
  George 91
  James 12
  Mary 5, 61
  Thomas 122
  William 13, 48
SANDS Samuel 108
SANNO Henrietta 29, 64
  Henriette 103
SANNON Frederick 64, 96
SAUDERS Margret 101
SAUL Lydia 70
SAUNDERS Hannah 68
SAVAGE Archibald 33
  Charles 27
  Elisa/Eliza 33, 66,
  103
SCANLAN James 27

James 116
John 26
John H. 22
Joseph 116
Matthew 73, 115
Rachel 113
Robert 117
Ruth 73
William 87, 99
THOMSON Ann 15
Charles 8
James 15
Jane 43
THOMTON Ann 106
THORN John V. E. 72
THORNBURGER George 46
THRUSH Barnabas 119
Jacob 117
John 121
Joseph 118
TILGHMAN William 57
TILLOTSON Captain 43
TIMMONS Mr. 68
TITLER John 15
Mary 92
TITZEL henry 70
TIZZARD James 61
Samuel 61
TOBIAS Catharine 13
Sarah 56, 102
TODD I. 39
John 40
Sarah 121
TOM 120
TOPLEY Alexander F.
64, 103
Elizabeth 25
TORBET James 98
TOWSEY Zalmon 80
TRAIT Elizabeth 119
Samuel 119
TRAUGH Catharine 40
John 40, 48
TREGO Moses 115
Rebecca 115
TRIMBLE Daniel 121
George 108
John 108, 109
Mary 78
Rebecca 110
Thomas 78, 106, 108,
111
William 108
TRISEBAUCH Mr. 94
TRITT Elizabeth 63
Jacob 63
William 91
William K. 40, 104
TROUGH Catharine 91
John 35, 91
Jonathan 103
Nancy 8
TRUXTON Thomas 81
TRYON Jacob G. 68
TURNBAUGH John 118
TURNER Eleanor 112

Elizabeth 85
Joseph 85
Mary 105
TUTTLE John P. 73
TYTLER Elizabeth 111
George 111

UDRIE Daniel 26
UHLER Adam 91
Jacob 26, 103
Sarah 113
ULERICH Nicholas 19
Sarah 19
ULRICH Sarah 101
UMBERGER --- 109
Catharine 109
UNDERWOOD Doan(?) 105
Herrman 99
John 114
URIE Catherine 106
Mary 88, 106
Sarah 106
Thomas 27, 88

VANASDLEN Jacob 44
VANCE Daniel 66
Mr. 33
Peter 66
William 66
VANDERBELT ( ) 119
John 25
Mary 119
William S. 59
VANNASDALL Christina 98

VARRENS Martha 98
VEASEY Mary 50
VEEY --- 107
VENASDLEN Isaac 23
VINTON Rev. 7, 74
Rev. R. S. 6, 72
Rev. S. R. 47
Robert 96
Virginia 25
Virginia, Charlestown
40
Virginia, Hampton 71
Virginia, Haywood 70
Virginia, Norfolk 72
Virginia, Woodstock 90

WADDLE John 121
WADSWORTH Alexander S.
10
Frederick M. 40
WAGGONER Catharine 40
John 25
WAGNER Michael 63
WAHL Charlotte 53, 102
George 104
WALER George 59
WALKER Azel 110
Barbara 10
Elizabeth 118
George 86
Isabella 69

James 111
John 18, 69, 75
Judge 6
Margaret 112
Margaret R. 75
Nancy 119
Sally 118
Samuel 121
William 57, 109, 110,
119
WALL Marg(a)ret 58, 102
WALLACE Agnes 115
James 3, 4, 116
John 92, 104, 105, 117
Mary E. 105
Mr. J. 16
WALLAGER Daniel 118
WALLIS Ann E. 60
Joseph J. 60
WALTER Catharine 7
Daniel 99
WALTERS Charles 72, 76
Charles S. 5, 98
WALTZER Christian 54
WAMPLER Joseph 53
Mary 53
WAMPOLD Adam 20
WANGER Michel 102
WARD Isaac 66
Jacob 52, 101
Maria 65, 103
WAREHEIM Eliza 23
Ellen 92
Philip 46
WARM Mary 100
WARNER Sarah 105
WARNS Mary 3, 100
WARREN Sarah 50
WARTZABACHER Margret 99
WARTZBACHER Margaretta
85
Washington City 16
Washington, D.C. 44
WASHINGTON William
Augustus 70
WASHMOOD Andrew 60
WATERBERRY Elizabeth
Ellenor 96
WATERHOUSE William 85
WATERS Jesse 97
WATKINSON Elizabeth 23
Henry 23, 93
WATSON --- 107
Alexander 18
Catharine 39
Elis(s)abeth 64, 103
Jehn 104
John 91, 104
Joseph 63
Michael 64, 103
Nancy 116
WATTERBERRY Elizabeth 72
WATTS David 7
Frederick 59
Sarah Ann 7
WATTSON Ann Elisabeth 98

Marriages and Deaths in the Newspapers of Lancaster County, Pennsylvania, 1821-1830

Marriages and Deaths in the Newspapers of Lancaster County, Pennsylvania, 1831-1840

Marriages and Deaths of Cumberland County, [Pennsylvania], 1821-1830

Maryland Calendar of Wills Volume 9: 1744-1749

Maryland Calendar of Wills Volume 10: 1748-1753

Maryland Calendar of Wills Volume 11: 1753-1760

Maryland Calendar of Wills Volume 12: 1759-1764

Maryland Calendar of Wills Volume 13: 1764-1767

Maryland Calendar of Wills Volume 14: 1767-1772

Maryland Calendar of Wills Volume 15: 1772-1774

Maryland Calendar of Wills Volume 16: 1774-1777

Maryland Eastern Shore Newspaper Abstracts, Volume 1: 1790-1805

Maryland Eastern Shore Newspaper Abstracts, Volume 2: 1806-1812

Maryland Eastern Shore Newspaper Abstracts, Volume 3: 1813-1818

Maryland Eastern Shore Newspaper Abstracts, Volume 4: 1819-1824

Maryland Eastern Shore Newspaper Abstracts, Volume 5: Northern Counties, 1825-1829
F. Edward Wright and Irma Harper

Maryland Eastern Shore Newspaper Abstracts, Volume 6: Southern Counties, 1825-1829

Maryland Eastern Shore Newspaper Abstracts, Volume 7: Northern Counties, 1830-1834
Irma Harper and F. Edward Wright

Maryland Eastern Shore Newspaper Abstracts, Volume 8: Southern Counties, 1830-1834

Maryland Militia in the Revolutionary War
S. Eugene Clements and F. Edward Wright

Newspaper Abstracts of Allegany and Washington Counties, Maryland, 1811-1815

Newspaper Abstracts of Cecil and Harford Counties, Maryland, 1822-1830

Newspaper Abstracts of Frederick County, Maryland, 1816-1819

Newspaper Abstracts of Frederick County, Maryland, 1811-1815

Sketches of Maryland Eastern Shoremen

Tax List of Chester County, Pennsylvania 1768

Tax List of York County, Pennsylvania 1779

Washington County Church Records of the 18th Century, 1768-1800

Western Maryland Newspaper Abstracts, Volume 1: 1786-1798

Western Maryland Newspaper Abstracts, Volume 2: 1799-1805

Western Maryland Newspaper Abstracts, Volume 3: 1806-1810

Wills of Chester County, Pennsylvania, 1766-1778

www.ingramcontent.com/pod-product-compliance
Lightning Source LLC
Chambersburg PA
CBHW060347090426
42734CB00011B/2066